Frameworks

William Nelles

Frameworks

Narrative Levels and Embedded Narrative

WIPF & STOCK · Eugene, Oregon

Wipf and Stock Publishers
199 W 8th Ave, Suite 3
Eugene, OR 97401

Frameworks
Narrative Levels and Embedded Narrative
By Nelles, William
Copyright © 1997 by Nelles, William All rights reserved.
Softcover ISBN-13: 978-1-7252-8565-1
Hardcover ISBN-13: 978-1-7252-8564-4
eBook ISBN-13: 978-1-7252-8566-8
Publication date 11/1/2020
Previously published by Peter Lang, 1997

This edition is a scanned facsimile of the original edition published in 1997.

For my family

ACKNOWLEDGMENTS

Many people have helped me with this book in many ways, but I owe special thanks to Harold F. Mosher, who started me on this project and guided me through it, and to Rosalie Hewitt, James Mellard, and Scott Vaszily, who read various sections of this book in various drafts and saved me from many — though not all — of my mistakes and misjudgments. Jacqueline Pavlovic always presented me with ideas for improvement rather than obstacles to overcome as she supervised the production of the book. Cheryl Zimmerman-Stern solved several computer problems, Sue Hum helped with the index, and Lisa Chase Bywaters supplied valuable advice on production matters as I prepared the final copy for the press. Dean Suzann Buckley, Associate Dean Lew Kamm, and my chair, Edwin Thompson, found ways to help me reconcile my teaching schedule with the demands of the final stages of my writing. My colleagues, especially in the English department and the library, were consistently helpful and patient, and several hundred students generously helped me work on these ideas in their classrooms over the past few years.

I am particularly indebted to James Miller, without whose constant (not to say relentless) support I would never have become a teacher, and above all to my family, who have always made everything possible.

Some of the material in chapters 1, 3, and 5 appeared in a different form in *Comparative Literature* 45.1 (1993), *Poetics Today* 11.2 (1990), *Studies in the Literary Imagination* 25.1 (1992), and *Style* 23.1 (1989). My thanks to the editors of those journals for their permission to republish that material.

CONTENTS

INTRODUCTION

There is thus a strict relativity, in criticism, not only of questions and
statements to frameworks but of frameworks to ends, that is, to the different kinds of knowledge about poetry we may happen, at one time or
another or for one or another reason, to want. And who is there with
authority sufficient to entitle him to inform critics what these may be?

— R. S. Crane, 1953

The structural device of the "story within a story," variously labeled "frame," "Chinese box," "Russian doll," "interpolated,"
"nested," "boxed," or "embedded" narrative, is so widely found
in the literature of all cultures and periods as to approach univer-
sality. Despite the form's ubiquity and durability, its history has
only begun to be sketched, and a good many studies will be
needed to complete the work begun in such surveys as Robert J.
Clements' and Joseph Gibaldi's overview of what they call "the
cornice tradition" of the novella and Katharine Gittes's examination of the framed narrative from the eighth-century *Panchatantra*,
"the earliest frame narrative of significance," (9) through the medieval period.[1] One of the problems in piecing together a comprehensive history, entirely apart from its sheer scope, is that no two
students of the genre appear to define it in quite the same way. In
a sense, then, a workable model for describing the device is prerequisite to a full outline of its history.[2] My interest in this book is
therefore in approaching the field through narrative theory rather

than literary history, pursuing a generally synchronic rather than diachronic approach (though a good deal of overlapping is inevitable and desirable). While the simple prevalence of the technique of embedding would itself justify considerable theoretical interest, an additional lure for narrative theory is offered by Gérard Genette's suggestion that the presence of narrative embedding may be one of the only formal criteria for differentiating fictional from factual narratives, and hence of potential value in the narratological Grail quest for definitions of such fundamental terms as "literature" and "narrative."[3] Despite these compelling scholarly attractions, however, the field remains largely unmapped by literary theory.

That is not to say that the device has not been discussed: indeed, the study of embedded narrative has become something of an academic boom industry in recent years. The SilverPlatter CD-ROM version of the *MLA International Bibliography*, to cite a convenient yardstick, yields 123 hits for "frame narrative" and another nine for "embedded narrative" for the period 1981–1995; twenty-two of these are dissertations, which suggests that the bull market may well continue as these writers advance in the profession. A great many of these discussions, of course, especially under "frame narrative," have little or nothing to do with the device of the story within a story: some critics use the model of framing to discuss narrative material set off or highlighted by verbal repetition, others to discuss conventions of spatial articulation (by analogy with the demarcation of space produced by a picture frame or a frame of film), others to describe the depiction of cultural or psychological thresholds or barriers in the sense popularized by the sociologist Erving Goffman.[4] The remarkable disparateness of the definitions and approaches applied to "framing" has led me to adopt instead the term "embedding," which brings considerably less critical baggage with it.

My own approach to the topic has been, by a predictable coincidence, through the same route taken by Gittes: the *Canterbury Tales*, doubtless the most familiar example of the genre for those of us trained in the United States. Having found little agreement among Chaucerians about how to analyze or even describe the structure of the poem, and being reluctant to reinvent the wheel, I began looking for a general model of embedded narrative that could be adapted to my purposes. But as I studied the numerous and remarkably diverse efforts of other toilers in the field of embedded narrative, it became apparent to me that there was no satisfactory wheel, and that all of us had arrived at more or less the same crux, attempting to describe specific works or solve particular problems without first settling on a general theoretical framework. Each critic defines the terms differently and then works out his or her own model, which never seems to be adopted for use by any subsequent critic. These ad hoc theories of narrative have, of course, produced a number of valuable individual critical studies — two notable book-length examples are Bernard Duyfhuizen's study of narratives of transmission in epistolary novels and Richard Shryock's discussion of the performative effects of embedded stories in modern French fiction — but no approach taken so far seems to have provided a generally-accepted foundation for the analysis or even for the definition and description of embedded narratives. Perhaps the only prudent definition of "embedded narrative" is Gerald Prince's circumspect "A narrative within a narrative" (*Dictionary*). While this does not seem to take us very far, no more detailed statement has gained any currency. Indeed, Shryock begins his own study by conceding, quite sensibly, that "it is impossible to define absolutely what an embedded narrative *could* be" (15 n. 1). But narrative theory has had a history of working back and forth from specific cases to general principles, and the time may be ripe to attempt a consolidation of the now-extensive work in print on embedded narrative by way of working out a comprehensive framework which can, in turn, be tested and modified through a new series of applied studies.

The wide range of conflicting definitions of terms used by different theorists of narrative makes it impossible to begin this discussion of embedded narrative at the apparently logical starting point, that at which one narrative is embedded within another. The fact is that the definition of narrative itself has never been settled. One approach to this problem is to consider that a new narrative begins when a new narrator takes over the narrating, an approach elaborated in chapter four, but that solution, it turns out, must be deferred because the definition of the narrator is even more subject to dispute than that of the narrative. Indeed, some theorists argue that there are narratives without narrators, and many others conflate the role of the narrator with that of the implied author or even with that of the historical author, two categories which are themselves in turn the subjects of a range of contradictory and inconsistent treatments. One is thus constrained to take several steps back before taking one forward, and to approach the definition of embedded narrative by the circuitous path of defining a series of other terms first. The logical, and at least from a certain theoretical point of view ontological, order in which these problems arise has dictated the organization of this work.

Chapter one therefore begins by distinguishing the various historical and implied authors and readers of narratives. Critical theory has usually ignored the point made by textual critics such as Jerome McGann that the historical author is often a group of people rather than a single person. An assortment of collaborators, editors, scribes, transcribers, and translators must also be placed under the heading of the historical author. This author must then be distinguished from the implied author of a text, that fictional construct inferred from the text who has consciously created and intended every meaning that the work holds. The historical authorship may in some sense be a fictional construct itself, as historians such as Hayden White have argued, but this construct is derived from texts other than the one subject to narrative analysis, and this latter text's meaning can never be limited to the historical author's intentions. The only definitive limitation of meaning other than the implied author's is the interpretation by the implied reader, another fictional construct derived from the text. It is of course the aspiration of most literary critics (a type of historical reader) to approximate the judgments of the implied reader, but such an approximation can never be exact.

The implied author and reader are frequently confused with the narrator and narratee, and the differentiation and definition of these categories is undertaken in chapter two. The simplest way to suggest the boundaries between these roles is by a formula describing their functions: the implied author means, the implied reader interprets; the narrator speaks, the narratee listens. The implied author never speaks; it is the creator of every word in the text, but these words are to be read as if uttered by the narrator. I call the narrator who is charged with the single (fictive) act of narrating the entirety of the text the general narrator, a concept which I trace back to Plato's model of narrative but which finds no exact counterpart in contemporary theory. This concept can be invoked to account for several problem cases in narrative such as nonnarrated narrative, epistolary novels with multiple editors, novels presented as monologues, and other cases which have thus far been seen as exceptions or aberrancies under prevailing notions of the narrator. The narratee has been frequently conflated with both the historical and implied readers, and this confusion is also analyzed and clarified through reference to canonical texts in which these levels are often supposed to converge.

Chapter three focuses on point of view, or focalization, a concept which has been subject to a similarly confusing gamut of contradictory definitions and interpretations. The model I offer is deliberately more narrowly defined than those of Mieke Bal and Seymour Chatman, in order that it may be correspondingly more precise in its terms, yet broader and more comprehensive than Gérard Genette's original formulation of the concept, which left several gaps and gray areas to be filled in.

Before finally proceeding to analyze embedded narrative it is necessary to define narrative itself. In chapter four a spectrum of contemporary definitions of narrative are examined, with special attention to the component of story. This survey leads to the conclusion that the valorization of story as an equal and parallel partner to discourse is largely derived from specific ideological emphases of the Russian Formalists who codified this binary model of narrative. The story in much women's writing and in

many nouveax romans and postmodernist texts is largely or entirely implicit. As the story may be only implicit in a work, its
derivation becomes a question of literary interpretation and critical ingenuity, making it much less susceptible to relatively objective analysis than discourse is and of debatable utility as a mark
of narrative. The discourse-centered model which follows from
these conclusions suggests a different mark of the narrated discourse, quite simply the point that it is narrated by a narrator to a
narratee. In such a model narrative analysis becomes a performative act by which a reader postulates a narrator and narratee for a
discourse. Thus any discourse is susceptible of being read as a
narrative, as though it were narrated.

This approach provides the theoretical basis for defining narrative embeddings in terms of shifts of narrator and of narrative
level, shifts marked by clear structural features in the text. Using
such readily discernible markers as the boundaries of embedding
has distinct advantages in practice as well as in theory. The
model offered in chapter five views these interstices or junctures
at which embedding occurs as places with exaggerated potential
for generating several kinds of dramatic, thematic, and formal significance. A set of classificatory categories is also provided for
the analysis and description of metalepses, violations of the
boundaries between embedded narratives.

R. S. Crane led up to the lines that have supplied the epi-
graph for this introduction (and title for this book) by forthrightly
noting the sometimes adversarial and dogmatic appearance of
"the verbal wars" (29) that characterize even the most pluralistic
criticism: "I can justify my choice only by arguing, and possibly
persuading others to agree with, that by means of the particular
framework I have selected certain important questions about poetry (in the common sense reference of the term) can be answered
which I could not even raise, much less answer intelligibly, in a
framework of the other sort" (27). Harold F. Mosher and I have
suggested elsewhere that the present stage of narrative theory
might be classified as a "silver age," following the long golden age
of theoretical invention and debate with "an era of consolidation,

application, testing, and polishing of these theoretical impulses"
(419). Such consolidation requires detailed comparative analyses
and fine sifting of the work that has come before, and I would like
to stipulate explicitly what I hope is implicitly clear throughout
this book: my disagreements with other writers are in no way intended to suggest any devaluation of their work but rather a recognition of its scope and importance. No exploration of such issues in contemporary narrative theory could help but make frequent reference to these theorists, and it is an unavoidable characteristic of close critical discussion that minor differences of opinion can sometimes be more illuminating than broad areas of
agreement.

1

HISTORICAL AND IMPLIED

AUTHORS AND READERS

In a sense all narrative is embedded, the narrative itself existing at the center of a series of real and fictional agents who present it and receive it.[1] A narrative is narrated by a narrator to a narratee, and the study of these relations is one proper focus of a narratological essay. But framing these elements are other relations among historical and implied authors and readers, and consideration of these relations is prerequisite to an examination of narrating. The failure by theorists of narrative to provide consistent definitions of these terms and to maintain distinctions among them has been a recurring source of confusion for theories of narrative and their applications. My sense of the meaning of these terms can be suggested briefly by postulating that each has its distinctive function: the historical author writes, the historical reader reads; the implied author means, the implied reader interprets; the narrator speaks, the narratee hears. This last pair of terms is to be understood as metaphorical: the narrator and narratee are constructed from the discourse of the text by inference and do not literally speak or hear, and indeed may be presented as silently thinking or writing and reading rather than speaking and hearing. In practice a certain degree of overlapping may seem to occur among these categories: the historical author may intend to mean something by a work and historical readers, especially if they are literary critics, will seek (and surely find) the work's meaning; many narrators also present themselves as having intent to mean. But these categories may be clearly defined and separated at the theoretical level. The historical author's physical acts, not the narrator's, produce the text; the implied author's implicit intentions, not those expressed by the historical author or narrator, are the definitive source of meaning in a work; and these intentions can only be entirely grasped by the implied reader, though the historical reader may speculate about them. A closer analysis will clarify this sketch.

The historical author, sometimes called the empirical author (Martínez-Bonati 87) is, minimally, the real flesh-and-blood person who writes a specific work or series of works. A historical author may, however, comprise more than one person. Historical authorship may — and usually does — include the roles played by editors and scribes. The historical author of Thomas Wolfe's three posthumously published novels includes not only Wolfe himself but also the editors who reconstructed them from his literary remains, chiefly Edward Aswell with the assistance of Maxwell Perkins and Elizabeth Nowell (McGann 79). We can in some cases accurately distinguish each person's contribution to this composite historical author. Such efforts, aimed at eliminating the editorial component, are routinely undertaken (by editors, of course) for writers in the canon. As the example of Wolfe demonstrates, however, this may not always be desirable. We could indeed retrieve his papers and read versions of his late novels written by a single historical author, but, as Jerome McGann has argued, "printing Wolfe's posthumous manuscripts in the form in which he left them would be to print an extended excerpt from the case history of a writer-at-work, and an eccentric one at that. It would not be printing a novel in any sense, however interesting the documents might be for other reasons" (79).

In other cases the identity of the historical author is much more problematic. The example of *Beowulf* is instructive. The anonymous author's identity will probably never be known. Further, and more crucially, we can not even recover his writing itself. Scholars can not even agree on the century of its composition or on the Old English dialect of its language: "The dates proposed, and fervently defended, range from the 7th to the 11th century" (Kiernan x). Modern editions of the poem propose a historical author made up of this unknown poet (time period unknown), the two unknown scribes who wrote in the early 11th century the unique manuscript in which it survives (and who made about 180 erasures and written corrections on their own MS), the work of two men (one of whom knew no Old English) who transcribed the poem in 1786–1787, and another who transcribed it in 1880–1882, and finally the modern editor, who makes on average about 300 emendations and interpolations, most of these based on the work of dozens of other scholars and editors (Kiernan 195, 246, 191; Chickering 245–46). The historical author is thus composed of at least seven flesh-and-blood people, among whom the initial creator is by far the least concrete. And this author exists only for those scholars who read the poem "in the original"; the identity of the historical author is complicated further if one reads the poem in a Modern English translation rather than in Old English.

The counterpart to the historical author is the historical reader, any flesh-and-blood person who has read the work or listened to a reading of it. Certain prominent historical readers, especially literary critics, have been extensively studied in their own right. Less well-known historical readers — usually college students — have been studied by reader-response critics such as David Bleich, Norman Holland, I. A. Richards, Louise Rosenblatt, and Walter Slatoff. Larger numbers of historical readers may also be studied in various groups, as in Ian Watt's consideration of the role played by the reading public in the rise of the British novel, Richard Altick's social history of nineteenth-century English readers, or the work of Hans Robert Jauss on readers' responses to medieval literature.

The term "implied author" was introduced by Wayne Booth to refer to the "second self" that an author creates when he or she writes, the image of the author that a reader infers from the written work itself, independently of extratextual information about the historical writer (70, 71).[2] This distinction can be compared to Erving Goffman's between the writer and the author of a work: "we learn about the *writer* from literary gossip, published and unpublished; we learn about the *author* from his books" (298). This more focused use of the two terms "writer" and "author" gives us a sensible and convenient shorthand for referring to the historical and implied authors in most cases. In cases calling for more rigorous delineation of the category of the historical author, the difference between the writer and historical author lies in the point that the writer is a single human being, while the historical author is usually made up of several different people. My own usage will follow this distinction. The active role the reader plays in forming this image of the implied author has led both Gérard Genette and Patrick O'Neill to suggest that the term "inferred author" would be more precise; Booth's term has, however, gained such currency that changing it would be difficult at this late date.

But as we shall see, the fact that a label is well-known or widely-used does not mean that its meaning has been settled. In fact Booth himself does not clearly define the implied author, especially in failing to distinguish the implied author of a work from its narrator. At some points he does seem to posit a distinction between the implied author and narrator: "'persona,' 'mask,' and 'narrator' . . . refer to the speaker in the work who is after all only one of the elements created by the implied author and who may be separated from him by large ironies. 'Narrator' is usually taken to mean the 'I' of a work, but the 'I' is seldom if ever identical with the implied image of the artist'" (73).

Booth's use of the masculine singular here is dictated by the immediate context — his illustration is Henry Fielding — and perhaps partly by the grammatical climate of 1961, but it should be stipulated that the implied author (or, for that matter, the narrator) may not ineluctably be a gendered agent. While we naturally conceive of all of the agents of narrative transmission as human beings, simply by virtue of their use of human language if nothing else, it may not be necessary or warranted to endow them in every case with the full range of human characteristics. To choose an intentionally trivial (i.e., noncontroversial) example, the typical historical author is either left- or right-handed, but it is difficult to conceive of a case in which we could say that an implied author was one or the other. That is not to say that readers do not usually ascribe gender (race, age, social class, sexual orientation) to implied authors — indeed, accounting for such ascriptions can be one of the more interesting subjects in the study of the implied author — but to emphasize the point that a work might be written in an androgynous or ambivalent style rather than in a distinctively masculine or feminine style.

Marie-Laure Ryan has made much the same point with respect to impersonal narrators: "in impersonal narrations, the formula 'either the narrator has p or does not have p' is no longer valid. It is not the case that the narrator of *Anna Karenina* is either a man or not a man" ("Pragmatics" 537). Roy Pascal's similar observation about the "omniscient" narrator of Jane Austen's novels raises the resultant terminological problem: "So truly is this narrator the 'spirit of the story,' that one cannot ascribe him/her a sex, and it is misleading to use either 'him' or 'her' for this function; I use 'him' throughout this study in the same way as one uses 'man' for 'mankind' (in Jane Austen's case it usefully makes a clearer distinction between the author and the narrator)" (45–46). Pascal's point about the drawbacks to the use of "him" and "her" is well-made, but few readers would now be so ready to consider the use of "man" for "mankind" (or even the use of "mankind" in the first place) so patently unobjectionable as it must have seemed to Pascal twenty years ago. Further, while his suggestion about using the "wrong" pronoun as a means of differentiating the historical and fictional agents is an interesting one, this model leaves out the intermediary agent of the implied author, which would seem to call for a third gender, especially in cases where the implied author and narrator are not so closely allied as in Austen.

Given these drawbacks, it seems to me that we may be better off referring to implied authors and impersonal narrators as "it" unless there seem to be relatively clear-cut reasons for attributing gender to them.

To return to Booth's example of Fielding, then, he begins promisingly by observing that *Jonathan Wild*, *Joseph Andrews* and *Tom Jones*, and *Amelia* are written by one historical author but can be considered as the products of three distinct implied authors: one "single-mindedly engrossed in his role as magistrate and reformer of public manners" (though the role of magistrate is really only the writer's: it is difficult to find an entirely consistent treatment of any of these categories in Booth); one with an "air of facetiousness combined with grand insouciance"; and one with an "air of sententious solemnity" (72). But he reveals that he is really talking about the narrators of these books, not the implied authors, when he argues that "these differences are most evident when the second self is given an overt, speaking role in the story" (71). He goes on to speak of "the author [historical? implied? or really a narrator?] who greets us on page one of *Amelia*" (72). The fact that this agent overtly "greets" its audience would indicate that it is not the implied author, who never directly speaks to its own implied audience. Later, in *Critical Understanding*, Booth still includes "dramatized authors" as one of five types of author, despite his acknowledgment that "Only the most inexperienced readers assume that the 'I' who purportedly narrates much fiction, the poet who speaks in all lyrics, or the 'author' who intrudes even into some modern drama has any simple or easily discovered relationship with the writer" (269). The most straightforward approach would be to treat such dramatized speakers strictly as narrators, and leave the implied author implicit rather than express. As Seymour Chatman has declared, "unlike the narrator, the implied author can *tell* us nothing" (*Story* 148).

I will define the implied author by postulating that it differs from the historical author in three ways.

(1) Each implied author is a critical construct, inferred from the text and with no existence outside that text, whereas every

historical author has a life outside the text which is, as Booth says, "immeasurably complex and largely unknown, even to those who are most intimate" (428). This life outside the text, however, may only be knowable through the medium of other texts; such documents as interviews with the writer and his or her intimates, for example, are themselves texts. In a certain sense this consideration may lead to the conclusion that the historical author is also a construct to some degree, as Hayden White has argued: "the presumed concreteness and accessibility of historical milieux, these contexts of the texts that literary scholars study, are themselves products of the fictive capability of the historians who have studied these contexts. The historical documents are not less opaque than the texts studied by the literary critic" (89). Later Booth will recognize this sort of objection by proposing that what I am calling the historical author has in theory three facets: "a postulated *flesh-and-blood person*," "the *postulated writer*, the figure made by a public with the help of more or less careful biographers," and the writer's "character" or "image" as perceived by the general public (*Critical* 268, 271). This circumspection being granted, the distinction between the historical and implied author is not entirely nor even primarily one of reality versus fictionality, but rather of the type of evidence admissible in the construction of them by the reader: the historical author may be created by recourse to any data while the implied author may be constructed only on the basis of the literary text being analyzed.[3] Jane Austen once told her nephew that Kitty married a clergyman near Pemberly and Mary married one of her uncle Philip's clerks (Honan 315), but the historical author's extratextual continuation of the story does not constitute evidence of the implied author's intentions in *Pride and Prejudice*.

(2) The implied author has consciously created and intended every implication, subtlety, ambiguity, and complexity that can be discovered in the text. Historical authors, on the other hand, may create meanings unconsciously, or while drunk, or may fail to successfully communicate their intended meanings. They may even be frankly baffled by their own works. When Howard Hawks was

making the film version of *The Big Sleep*, he wired Raymond
Chandler to find out who killed Owen Taylor, the Sternwood
chauffeur. "Chandler checked the text, thought about it, and
wired back: 'I don't know'" (MacShane 126). The implied author,
of course, fully intended to leave its readers — including Chandler
and Hawks — in the dark.

(3) A work may in certain unusual cases have more than one
implied author (a possible example is provided below), but its
function is always purely authorial.[4] It is responsible for every
word in the text, but is not a combination or collaboration of editors, scribes, translators, or transcribers, as may be the case with
historical authors. There can be much or little overlap between the
historical and implied authors in any of these regards. Neither
can ever appear in or speak in a text — only a narrator can narrate — but we can often infer facts about them both from a text.
The first component of the historical authorship of *Beowulf*, the
unknown poet who composed it, has no verifiable existence beyond the bare fact of the existence of the poem: in a case such as
this the writer's historical existence is itself inferred from the text
and there may be few profitable distinctions to be drawn between
his character and that of the implied author. As noted above, of
course, the text as it appears in a modern edition has a considerably more complex historical author, some of the components of
which can be analyzed quite closely. In other cases the difference
between historical and implied authors may be more pronounced.
Although this distinction is relatively new to literary theory, it has
been implicitly acknowledged by writers for much longer.

The adoption of male pseudonyms by women writers provides the clearest examples of this recognition. Writers such as
George Eliot were well aware that their works would be read differently if they were thought to have been written by men.[5] She,
along with other writers employing this strategy, was aware that
readers of the period would naively conflate the historical and
implied authors, and she therefore misled them as to the gender of
the historical author. In Eliot's case, the opposition between the
historical and implied authors turned out to be nearly complete.

As David Carroll observes, "when her pseudonym was lifted shortly after her first novel many readers felt they had been badly deceived: the clerical gentleman who stressed so impressively the demands of duty in his vivid picture of a Christian society turned out to be a female atheist living with another woman's husband" (2). This created a dilemma for moralistic critics who admired the works (and their implied author) but abhorred the behavior of the historical author and lacked the theoretical (or perhaps psychological) wherewithal to keep the two separate. As one especially shrewd reviewer observed, "George Eliot was already accepted as a great artist; her teaching had been dubbed clerical, and it was too late in the day to turn upon her and call her an atheist" (Carroll 225). Most commonly the separation of historical and implied author is a question of degree, of more or less similarity, but the attribution of gender to implied authors provides a convenient binary opposition that can serve as a clear index to the type of split that can be created between historical and implied authors.[6]

Jane Eyre, written by Charlotte Brontë but published under her masculine (or is it in effect androgynous or, as Genette has put it, "asexué," [*Seuils* 91]?) pseudonym, Currer Bell, is a particularly good example of the point that historical authors can differ from implied authors, and also illustrates two unusual situations: that in which a single work, according to a single historical reader, has multiple implied authors, and that in which two works, written by two historical authors, have one implied author as read by a single historical reader. While none of the novel's early reviewers used the term "implied author" (never having read Booth), they made their inferences about the author's gender from the text alone, having no recourse to accurate biographical information about the historical author. Thus, though they wish to attribute characteristics to the historical author, the fact that these are inferred entirely on the basis of the text entails their application to the implied author.

Some reviewers offered the gender of the narrator as evidence, taking literally the title of the first edition, *Jane Eyre: An Autobiog-*

raphy. The *Christian Remembrancer* review reasoned that "If the authoress has not been, like her heroine, an oppressed orphan, a starved and bullied charity-school girl, and a despised and slighted governess (and the intensity of feeling which she shows in speaking of the wrongs of this last class seems to prove that they have been her own), at all events we fear she is one to whom the world has not been kind" (Allott 89–90). As Brontë herself said of this approach, "he aims his shafts in the dark . . . the ill success of his hits makes me laugh rather than cry" (Allott 88), a success probably typical of efforts to conflate narrators and either implied or historical authors. The improbable plot quickly leaves any possibility of literal autobiography behind, of course, and the reviewer switches to other criteria later, including the portrait of Rochester, a piece of evidence seized upon by many critics on both sides of the popular debate over the writer's gender. Rochester is

> the characteristic production of a female pen. Not an Adonis, but a Hercules in mind and body, with a frame of adamant, a brow of thunder and a lightning eye, a look of love and voice of command, all-knowing and all-discerning, fierce in love and hatred, rough in manner, rude in courtship, with a shade of Byronic gloom and appetizing mystery — add to this that when loved he is past middle age, and when wedded he is blind and fire-scarred, and you have such an Acis as no male writer would have given his Galatea, and yet what c o mme n d s itself as a true embodiment of the visions of a female imagination. (Allott 90)

Certainly this description owes as much to the reviewer's imagination as to Brontë's, and reminds us of how dependent the image of an implied author can be on the variable cultural constructs that any given historical reader brings to the text. The seductive appeal of this omniscient, omnipotent, and commanding — if somewhat elderly — character may be due as much to the influence of the Old Testament as to *Jane Eyre* (the *Remembrancer* was a staunch organ of the High Church Party).

Those reviewers who argued that the author must be a man, of course, eschewed the identification of narrator and author and relied on other criteria. An unsigned review in *Era* analyzed the stylistic evidence: "It is no woman's writing. Although ladies have written histories, and travels, and warlike novels, to say nothing of books upon the different arts and sciences, no woman could have penned the 'Autobiography of Jane Eyre.' . . . it is the victory of mind over matter; the mastery of reason over feeling . . . . There is a vigor in all he says, a power which fixes the reader's attention . . ." (Allott 79). The reviewer's stylistic (and cultural) criteria for gender determination are, I assume, sufficiently familiar.

The most famous — or, as Barbara Timm Gates has it, "infamous" (12) — of the contemporary reviewers is Elizabeth Rigby, who critiqued the novel in the *Quarterly Review*. Rigby recognizes that Currer Bell is a pseudonym, but not that it conceals a female author:

> The question of authorship, therefore, can deserve a moment's curiosity only as far as "Jane Eyre" is concerned, and though we cannot pronounce that it appertains to a real Mr. Currer Bell and to no other, yet that it appertains to a man, and not, as many assert, to a woman, we are strongly inclined to affirm. Without entering into the question of whether the power of the writing be above her, or the vulgarity below her, there are, we believe, minutiae of circumstantial evidence which at once acquit the feminine hand. No woman — a lady friend, whom we are always happy to consult, assures us — makes mistakes in her own *métier* — no woman *trusses game* and garnishes dessert-dishes with the same hands, or talks of doing so in the same breath. Above all, no woman attires another in such fancy dresses as Jane's ladies assume — Miss Ingram coming down, irresistible, "in a *morning* robe of sky-blue crape, a gauze azure scarf twisted in her hair!!" No lady, we understand, when suddenly roused in the night, would think of hurrying on *"a frock."* They have garments more convenient for such occasions, and more becoming too. This evidence seems incontrovertible. (175–76)

The reviewer's attempts to pass off her own review's narrator, implied author, and writer as male ("a lady friend . . . assures us," "we understand," "they have garments") provide an ironic commentary on her analysis of the implied authorship of Brontë's novel, but they are as well a telling indicator of the pressures women writers felt to conceal their gender.[7] This seemingly bizarre situation, in which a pseudonymous woman novelist, trying to lead readers to believe she is a man, is reviewed by an anonymous woman reviewer, also trying to make readers believe she is a man, one of whose concerns in the review is to determine the true gender of the novelist, was probably not that unusual in practice. About two-thirds of the early reviewers of the Brontës, to pursue this example, remain anonymous to this day. Assuming that the ratio of men to women for the unattributed reviews is similar to that for the attributed reviews, something like a dozen other women would have been in the same position as Rigby with respect to the Brontës (and, one presumes, to other pseudonymous women writers).[8] In a further stroke of irony, Brontë at her end also fell for the gender subterfuge, convinced that the reviewer was really a man: "I read the *Quarterly* . . . the critic seems anxious to let it be understood that he is a person well acquainted with the habits of the upper classes . . . [but] I am afraid he is no gentleman" (Allott 105). One wonders how often women writers found themselves at cross-purposes with one another through such necessary subterfuges.

Rigby's review was a substantial one, and the *Quarterly* a formidable journal, so it is not surprising that subsequent reviewers felt obliged to defend Brontë against Rigby. In an interesting turn of the narratological screw, at least two reviewers found themselves speculating about the gender of both novelist and reviewer. George Henry Lewes attacks Rigby's analysis and sees through her male persona: "An eminent contemporary, indeed, has employed the sharp vivacity of a female pen to prove 'upon irresistible evidence' that *Jane Eyre* must be the work of a man. But all that 'irresistible evidence' is set aside by the simple fact that Currer Bell is a woman. . . . The fair and generous critic was misled by her own acuteness . . ." (Allott 162–63). Lewes was cheating about Brontë, by the way, having already discovered her identity by this time, which very nearly forces him to formulate the narrator/implied author/historical author distinction to explain his case (his "the simple fact" begs a most complex question here). Her anonymity was still intact, however, for James Lorimer, who addressed the same issue. Although arguing that Currer Bell was more likely to be a man, he felt that the reviewer was more likely to be a woman (Allott 113–16).

Another early reviewer, Edwin Percy Whipple, using a combination of stylistic and pseudo-sociological criteria for his analysis of the implied author, reached the remarkable conclusion that *Jane Eyre* was the product of multiple authors. This conclusion is the more remarkable because there is a single narrator (and historical author) throughout, a feature that would presumably make the detection of two distinct narrating voices (or authors) difficult.

> the said Currer divides the authorship, if we are not misinformed, with a brother and sister. The work bears the marks of more than one mind and sex.... The family mind is strikingly peculiar, giving a strong impression of unity, but it is still male and female. From the masculine tone of *Jane Eyre*, it might pass altogether as the composition of a man, were it not for some unconscious feminine peculiarities, which the strongest-minded woman that ever aspired after manhood cannot suppress. These peculiarities refer not only to the minutiae of the sick-chamber, but to various superficial refinements of feeling in regard to the external relations of the sex. It is true that the noblest and best representations of female character have been produced by men; but there are niceties of thought and emotion in a woman's mind which no man can delineate.... (Allott 98)

One can only remark that Brontë's supposed aspirations after manhood were, for Whipple at least, pretty successfully realized. He concludes, interestingly, with a bit of intertextual analysis, assigning to the implied author(s) of *Jane Eyre* the implied authorship of *Wuthering Heights*, actually written by Emily Brontë, another historical author altogether: "There are also scenes of passion, so hot, emphatic, and condensed in expression, and so sternly masculine in feeling, that we are almost sure we observe the mind of the author of *Wuthering Heights* at work in the text" (Allott 99). We may have approached something of a limit case here in the separation of the historical and implied authors.[9]

The definition of the implied reader could, one might suppose, be largely derived from the definition of the implied author. Indeed, despite the frequency with which the term is applied to works, its definition has been almost entirely a product of this sort of intuitive and informal derivation. The term has been treated so casually, in fact, that the presumed general consensus about what it must mean has concealed the point that no two writers seem to mean exactly the same thing by it. Booth himself does not use the term in the first edition of *The Rhetoric of Fiction* (for a discussion of the second edition's additions see below), and Wolfgang Iser, with whom most of us probably would identify the concept, and whose book of that title (in its English translation) has done the most to make the term well known, only uses it once, in his "Introduction" (xii), and never really defines it until his later *The Act of Reading*. W. Daniel Wilson, whose analysis of the topic in the writings of Iser and other German-language critics is the most thorough and reliable to date, establishes that Iser's concern in both books is almost invariably with either historical readers or with narratees (Wilson's "characterized readers") rather than with implied readers.[10] Other writers have considered the role of the implied reader at more length, but a clear definition of the concept has proven elusive.

Walker Gibson's "mock reader" is sometimes a narratee and sometimes an implied reader. His analysis of the mock reader of *The Great Gatsby* demonstrates how these roles shift. First he treats the mock reader strictly as Nick Carraway's narratee: "Here the mock reader must not only take in stride a series of 'jokes' formed by some odd juxtapositions . . . but must also be quick to share the attitudes and experiences of the speaker. For instance, the speaker by overt statement and the mock reader by inference have both attended a particular kind of college in a particular way . . ." (267–68). But then he treats the mock reader as an implied reader, responding to the implied author's covert message: "There is another speaker somewhere . . . and it is from this other speaker that the mock reader ultimately takes on some important attitudes. They speak right over Nick Carraway's head" (268).

Even Genette tends to see these three categories of historical reader, implied reader, and narratee as overlapping (to the extent that he eventually rejects the idea of the implied author and reader entirely). He does at some points clearly differentiate their three distinct functions: "Comme le narrateur, le narrataire est un des éléments de la situation narrative, et il se place nécessairement au même niveau diégétique; c'est-à-dire qu'il ne se confond pas plus a priori avec le lecteur (même virtuel) que le narrateur ne se confond nécessairement avec l'auteur" (*Figures III* 265; "Like the narrator, the narratee is one of the elements in the narrating situation, and he is necessarily located at the same diegetic level; that is, he does not merge a priori with the reader [even an implied reader] any more than the narrator necessarily merges with the author" [*Narrative* 259]). But he at once undercuts the distinction he has just made: "Le narrateur extradiégétique, au contraire, ne peut viser qu'un narrataire extradiégétique, qui se confond ici avec le lecteur virtuel, et auquel chaque lecteur réel peut s'identifier" (*Figures III* 266; "The extradiegetic narrator, on the other hand, can aim only at an extradiegetic narratee, who merges with the implied reader and with whom each real reader can identify" [*Narrative* 260]). Genette is correct to the extent that he means to present a possible rather than typical situation. At one limit of competence a particularly astute narratee might approach the status of implied reader, and of course one goal of the literary critic, a type of historical reader, is to approximate the implied reader. But even if this approach or approximation were exact, the theoretical distinctions among the three functions would persist. I would emphasize, however, that very few historical readers can identify exactly with any implied reader, for reasons which will become evident presently. I reserve discussion of the relation between the implied reader and the narratee for the next chapter.

Gerald Prince offers two categories of implied reader, the *lecteur virtuel* and the *lecteur idéal*. The *lecteur virtuel* is the reader imagined by the historical author as the eventual consumer of his work: "Tout auteur, s'il raconte pour quelqu'un d'autre que pour lui-même, développe son récit en fonction d'un certain genre de lecteur qu'il doue de qualités, de capacités, de goûts, selon son opinion des hommes en général (ou en particulier) et selon les obligations qu'il se trouve respecter" ("Narrataire" 180; "Every author, provided he is writing for someone other than himself, develops his narrative as a function of a certain type of reader whom he bestows with certain qualities, faculties, and inclinations according to his opinion of men in general [or in particular] and according to the obligations he feels should be respected" ["Narratee" 9]).[11] I would not include this imagined reader within my definition of the implied reader without some reservations, which are explained below. The *lecteur idéal* is itself subdivided into two categories, one imagined by the historical author and the other by a particular type of historical reader, the literary critic. "Pour un écrivain, le lecteur idéal serait sans doute celui qui comprendrait parfaitement et approuverait entièrement le moindre de ses mots, la plus subtile de ses intentions" ("Narrataire" 180; "For a writer, an ideal reader would be one who would understand perfectly and would approve entirely the least of his words, the most subtle of his intentions" ["Narratee" 9]). The implied reader under my model would exhibit such powers of understanding, but it would understand (and approve) not the intentions of the historical author, which may after all be unrealized in the text (or mercenary rather than artistic), but rather those of the implied author. Prince's second type of *lecteur idéal* is the closest of the above to my notion of the implied reader, though his definition is too narrow to be adopted as it stands: "celui capable de déchiffrer l'infinité des textes qui, d'après certains, se recouperaient dans un texte spécifique" ("Narrataire" 180; "one capable of interpreting the infinity of texts that, according to certain critics, can be found in one specific text" ["Narratee" 9]).

Michael Riffaterre's "superreader" is also similar to the implied reader, and he offers a procedure by which one might construct an example of this fictional reader: the synthesis of the best of what has been written by literary critics and other informants, including students (one can see some parallels here with the interests of reader-response critics such as Holland) on a given work, surveying as many responses as possible "to guard against physical interference with contact, such as the reader's fatigue or the evolving of the language since the time the poem was encoded" (215). The differences between Riffaterre's superreader and my implied reader would be (1) that the implied reader will always remain a tentative mental synthesis, insusceptible to a definitive reconstruction by any historical reader (although one might consider that this or that literary critic was closer or further from the ideal), while the superreader can be pretty closely approximated (at least by Riffaterre himself), and (2) that the implied reader could never have the "idiosyncrasy-oriented responses (positive or negative according to the reader's culture, era, esthetics, personality) and goal-oriented responses (those of the reader with nonliterary intent, who may be using the poem as a historical document, for purposes of linguistic analysis, etc.: such a reader will rationalize his responses to fit into his sphere of interest and its technical terminology) . . ." that Riffaterre would include as part of the superreader's response (214–15). The implied reader would function only to receive without addition or subtraction, without physical, psychological, or cultural "interference with contact," the complete intention of the implied author (which is not necessarily the same as that of the historical author) and to understand the full meaning of the text.

Recognizing that the definitions offered in the first edition of *The Rhetoric of Fiction* were sometimes ambiguous, and that these various terms had been used by later critics with a variety of meanings, Booth later supplemented his schema with Peter Rabinowitz's analysis of implied readers and produced a more comprehensive and self-consistent model to describe historical and implied authors and readers. Booth's revised model can be usefully compared to the one I have been sketching to further clarify my definitions and to indicate more precisely how the two systems differ, while also providing a framework for some final remarks on the models of Prince and Rabinowitz. The exposition of Booth's revised position appears in the "Afterword to the Second Edition" of *The Rhetoric of Fiction*. I reproduce his analysis on the following pages (omitting his category III, which treats narrators and narratees, a topic I reserve for the next chapter) and key my commentary to his outline for convenient reference.

Booth's category I.A corresponds to my historical author and reader, granting only the straightforward addition of collaborators, editors, scribes, translators, and transcribers (all of whom, including, as Booth thoughtfully notes, the historical reader, are

Authors (Whether Writing or Telling Orally)

I. THE FLESH-AND-BLOOD AUTHOR, WHO TELLS MANY STORIES, BEFORE AND AFTER A GIVEN TALE:

A. Who is immeasurably complex and largely unknown, even to those who are most intimate;

B. Who postulates (or implies), while composing any given tale, at least three kinds of listeners:

1. Flesh-and-blood people who want to listen (or read), who have the needed reading competencies, but who are themselves immeasurably complex and diverse in their responses;

2. Selected listeners, the special kind whom the tale both makes and relies on as it goes (*implied reader* [*sense one*]); who know some matters and are ignorant of others regardless of how much the flesh-and-blood persons know); whose values finally must — at least temporarily — accord with those of the tale told; and who yet know that the tale (much of it, some of it, all of it) is not real, is in some sense "only a story";

3. The relatively credulous listeners *within the tale* (the *implied reader* [*sense two*]), Rabinowitz's "narrative audience"), who accept it all as happening and who accept all of the narrator's values without questioning;

C. Who chooses (consciously or unconsciously) to create an "improved version, a second self (the *implied author* [No. II below])";

D. And who may, by creating an *unreliable narrator* (created as unreliable by the implied author), create additional *implied readers* (*sense three*) who mistakenly accept the distorted values of the fallible narrator.

Audiences (Whether Reading or Listening)

I. THE FLESH-AND-BLOOD RE-CREATOR OF MANY STORIES:

A. Who is immeasurably complex and largely unknown, either to authors or critics;

B. Who is, or is willing to become,

1. A working listener, exercising competencies, responding emotionally to "signs" that in themselves are seemingly inert;

2. The kind of reader selected, or implied, by a given tale: the *implied reader* (*sense one*), who knows some matters and is ignorant of others (even if, as working reader, the ignorance is faked) and whose values finally must accord with those of the tale told, yet who knows that much of the tale is in some sense "only a story";

3. A relatively credulous listener *within the tale* (the *implied reader* [*sense two*], Rabinowitz's "narrative audience"), who accepts it all as happening and accepts the narrators' values without questioning;

C. Who thus joins the implied author in creating an "improved version" of the self, both simpler than the breathing self but also complex in ways quite different from ordinary ways;

D. And who is capable, when required, of engaging in extremely complex ironic constructions, repudiating completely the professed values of certain unreliable narrators and thus refusing to become *implied reader* (*sense three*).

Authors (Whether Writing or Telling Orally)	*Audiences (Whether Reading or Listening)*
II. THE IMPLIED AUTHOR OF THIS TALE:	II. THE POSTULATED READER (IMPLIED READER [SENSE ONE] RABINOWITZ'S "AUTHORIAL AUDIENCE"):
A. Who has chosen, consciously or unconsciously (so any given reader will infer), every detail, every quality, that is found in the work or implied by its silences;	A. Who infers an author who "made it all up," choosing every detail and thus adding to the world one more "unnatural" object and one more "person";
B. Who knows that the story is not literally true (that Oliver Twist, Huckleberry Finn, Emma are invented), that some of the work's norms may not hold in "real" life, and that the implied reader (sense one) will also know all this;	B. Who knows that the story is not literally true, that Pierre and Natasha are invented, "fictional," while their war was real (or is "fictional" in some quite different sense);
C. But who, like that implied reader, *pretends* that it is all true, if read properly (correcting for irony, unreliable narration, other wheels within wheels, etc.), and that all norms hold in reality; thus creating	C. But who, like the implied author, willingly pretends that it is all true, if read properly, thus creating
III. THE TELLER OF THIS TALE [i.e., the narrator, a topic I will take up in the next chapter]	III. THE CREDULOUS LISTENER (IMPLIED READER [SENSE TWO], RABINOWITZ'S "NARRATIVE AUDIENCE"): [i.e., the narratee, which I will address in the next chapter]
IV. THE "CAREER-AUTHOR," WHO PERSISTS FROM WORK TO WORK, A COMPOSITE OF ALL THE IMPLIED AUTHORS OF ALL HIS OR HER WORKS.	IV. THE "CAREER-READER," WHOSE HABITS AND COMPETENCIES, PERSISTING FROM WORK TO WORK, BECOME A COMPOSITE OF ALL HIS OR HER READING EXPERIENCE, AND WHOSE VALUES INDETERMINATELY REFLECT OR ARE INFLUENCED BY THOSE OF ANY ONE WORK.
V. THE PUBLIC MYTH, A KIND OF SUPER-AUTHOR, OFTEN QUITE DIFFERENT FROM AND ONLY VAGUELY RELATED TO ANY OF THE OTHERS.	V. THE PUBLIC MYTH ABOUT "THE READING PUBLIC" (notions of "readers today" or "the Renaissance reader," always vague and full of contradictions but obviously having an effect on how authors conceive the task of getting themselves read and of how critics assume that works should be read).

"immeasurably complex and largely unknown") under the category I.A.Authors.[12] Booth's schema makes no allowance for consideration of these components of historical authorship, despite their obvious importance.

The two categories labeled I.B, however, introduce several complex problems. Booth presumes here to read the collective mind of every writer and reader who has ever lived or ever will live. I would accept part of I.B.1 under my historical author and reader to the extent that every writer's physical action of writing "implies" ("postulates" presumes the mind-reading ability I wish to deny here) at least one "working listener," the writer himself. It is frequently the case that authors write works not designed to be read by any audience other than themselves, and a model of narrative transmission ought to account for this. Many, though of course not all, diary and journal entries are likely to be written in this way, and there are no intrinsic reasons that would prevent someone from writing fiction in the same way (or from writing fictional diary entries). After all, work does not have to be published or even read to attain historical existence. Edward Taylor provides a concrete example with his *Preparatory Meditations*, evidently unread by anyone but himself until their discovery in 1937, more than two centuries after his death, and apparently never intended for any audience but himself. As Jane Eberwein explains,

> The *Preparatory Meditations* (1682–1725), Taylor's best poems, served as private reexaminations of his own conversion experience and as preparations for the bimonthly celebration of the Lord's Supper in the Westfield church. . . . It appears that Taylor· generally prepared a scholarly, tightly reasoned sermon on his chosen text, then wrote a poetic meditation on the same text to prepare himself spiritually and psychologically to deliver his sermon" (65).

It may indeed be the case that most writers do spend time considering one or more of Booth's audiences, but to allow that this is probable is not to make it a necessary or even an integral part of the definition of the category. Prince's *lecteur virtuel* and his first type of *lecteur idéal* would fall under the same objection;

both are supposed to exist only in the mind of the historical author, with no necessary realization either as flesh-and-blood readers or as what I call implied readers, readers whose characteristics would be those (and only those) called upon for interpretation of the text. It may be that some writers do create such audiences in their imaginations, but these are of critical interest only if they find embodiment as historical or implied readers. This does not mean that a writer's discussion of his ideas or intentions can not be relevant to critical discussion of his works. The point is that the author's critique of his own work is not necessarily to be privileged over that of other critics. As Paul Valéry remarks in "Littérature,"

> Quand l'ouvrage a paru, son interprétation par l'auteur n'a pas plus de valeur que toute autre par qui que ce soit.
>   Si je fait le portrait de Pierre, et si quelqu'un trouve que mon ouvrage ressemble à Jacques plus qu'à Pierre, je ne puis rien lui opposer—et son affirmation vaut la mienne.
>   Mon intention n'est que mon intention et l'oeuvre est l'oeuvre.
> *(Oeuvres* 557)

> Once a work is published its author's interpretation of it has no more validity than anyone else's. If I make Pierre's portrait and someone finds it more like Jacques than like Pierre, there's nothing to be said against this; his opinion is as good as mine. My intention was merely *my* intention and the work is — what it is. (*Collected* 14.109)

This principle would apply to any authorial intentions, not only to those regarding readers but also to the creation of meanings in a work. Such remarks by writers should be considered as coming from them as historical readers, to be evaluated against those of other historical readers and valued to the degree that they can help us approximate the judgments of the implied reader. Some authors are very good readers of their own works, while others are not.

   A parallel objection applies to the rest of I.B.Audiences. The fact that a given flesh-and-blood reader is not "responding emotionally to 'signs'" in a work, or does not (or is not willing to) become, for example, "ignorant" (I.B.2) or "credulous" (I.B.3), does not invalidate his or her classification as a historical reader. Bad historical readers are still historical readers despite their failure to conform to writers' hypothetical intentions; writers' unrealized fantasies are not literary artifacts unless they put them into writing, at which point they become critiques by historical writers (who are also readers), and are no longer simply intentions.

A further complication is created by Booth's failure to distinguish between readers "postulated" by the writer, readers "whom the tale both makes and relies on," and "flesh-and-blood" readers. He commits the error of not considering that these three agents are never quite identical. Whether the writer postulates anything or not, the text itself will automatically have an implied reader, the fictional construct who would be able to analyze and explain the significance of every component of that text. There may or may not be any historical readers for a given text (besides the writer, of course). But even the notion of the reader "whom the tale both makes and relies on as it goes," which might seem tolerably close to my implied reader, is confused here. The implied reader created by a tale is "ignorant" (I.B.2) of no matters: it understands every aspect of the tale completely. Booth fails to differentiate it from the narratee, who is the reader who properly possesses the attributes of being created by the tale and being knowledgeable of some matters and ignorant of others, as I.B.2 stipulates. But I.B.2 further stipulates that this reader know that part of the story is not real, a requirement which would seldom be met by narratees. I.B.3 compounds this confusion by referring to a listener within the tale. As cross-reference to Rabinowitz makes clear, Booth ought to say as well here "implied by the tale" to remain consistent. The distinction between Rabinowitz's authorial audience (placed by Booth as "implied reader sense one" in both I.B.2 and II) and narrative audience (placed by Booth as "implied reader sense two" in both I.B.3 and III — the room for confusion here is evident) is that one is an audience imagined by the writer (I classify this audience as historical under the analysis offered above) and the other an audience implied by the narrator (but that would make this reader a narratee under my system, not a historical or implied reader).[13]

Booth's heading I.C.Authors can be subsumed under my historical author only in the sense of recognizing that the historical author can unconsciously and consciously contribute to the creation of the implied author. But it is the essence of the definition of the implied author and reader that they are creations of the text itself, not necessarily dependent upon or determined by any authorial intentions to create such constructs. One variable outside the author's direct control is the reader. The writer "who chooses . . . to create" this construct can never succeed in limiting it to his or her own interpretation because every historical reader's reconstruction (from the text) of this implied author has the potential to be different from the writer's version. It can also be argued that the text itself escapes the author's control in some ways, that it can never reflect precisely the historical author's thought. Valéry offers this line of analysis:

> L "écrivain": Il en dit toujours plus et moins qu'il ne pense.
> Il enlève et ajoute à sa pensée.
> Ce qu'il écrit ne correspond à aucune pensée réelle.
> C'est plus riche et moins riche. Plus long et plus bref. Plus clair et plus obscur.
> C'est pourquoi celui qui veut reconstituer un auteur à partir de son oeuvre se construit nécessairement un personnage imaginaire.
> (*Oeuvres* 569)

> The "writer": He always says more and less than he thinks.
> He takes away from and adds to his thought.
> What he writes doesn't correspond to any real thought.
> It is more rich and less rich. More long and more brief. More clear and more obscure.
> That is why anyone who wants to reconstitute an author on the basis of his work necessarily constructs an imaginary character.

To take one fairly clear example of the way in which a work can elude authorial control, it must be frequently the case that a writer intends to write a very great book (with a brilliant implied author) but writes a poor one (with a rather pedestrian implied author). Booth's type I.D is, along with part of I.B.2 and all of I.B.3, as explained above, relevant only to narratees, and is not a component of either historical or implied authors as I define them.

Category II is, mercifully, less difficult to compare with my system. His category II.Implied Author corresponds to my implied author except for three points. (1) The implied author chooses nothing "unconsciously"; everything is consciously and fully intended. (2) Booth seems overly optimistic in asserting that "any given reader will infer" the implied author's intentions: no historical reader can ever do this with complete accuracy, every implied reader always does this, and narratees vary widely in this regard. (3) As explained above, Booth's implied reader (sense one) shares characteristics with my implied reader (knowledge of the fictional status of the text) and narratee (circumscribed knowledge). His category II.Postulated Reader corresponds to my implied reader, given the addition (implicit in his II.A.Implied Author) that the implied reader can accurately interpret the full signification of the choices made by the implied author.

Booth's categories IV and V do not seem to be fundamental. One could certainly construct a IV."Career-Author" by considering each separate implied author of a historical author's various works. Indeed, as demonstrated by the example given earlier, at least one critic of the Brontë novels constructed a composite implied author by considering the implied authors of works written by two different historical authors. But consideration of more than one implied author requires no new theoretical category. His category IV."Career-Reader" applies only to some historical readers and, assuming that it is really germane to the analysis of narrative, can be treated without the addition of a separate category of historical reader. Category V is also of marginal relevance and is, as Booth allows, "always vague and full of contradictions," "often quite different from and only vaguely related to" the other categories under discussion here. As with IV."Career-Reader," anyone wishing to study this narrative audience could do it under the rubric of the historical author and audience.

My definition of the agents in this narrative hierarchy may be completed by responding to the objections of two of the critics who question fundamentally the historical author/reader, implied author/reader, narrator/narratee line of analysis that I have offered: John Ross Baker and Gérard Genette.[14]

Baker claims that he "must speak of the 'implied author' as an invention and an evasion because despite Booth's protests to the contrary the distinction between 'real' and 'implied' author remains unearned and finally tends to evaporate" (203). On the next page, however, he decisively undercuts his position:

> in speaking of the "picture" the reader "constructs" Booth is doing nothing more than acknowledging (and providing a label for) the sort of linguistic convention we ordinarily employ when we use "Darwin" to refer to the complex of ideas about natural selection to be found in *The Origin of Species*. When we speak thus of "Darwin" we clearly are referring not simply to the man who lived at a certain time, but to the man as responsible for the ideas. (204)

It must be objected in the first place that acknowledging and providing labels for concepts is no mean activity, and that if such references are so unambiguous it is surprising that Baker feels the need to put quotes around Darwin's name: why would this be necessary unless the problem he denies is embodied in his denial? But his fundamental logical error lies in the unspoken assumption that Darwin's ideas are the things that are communicated by his text, when it is actually Darwin's words that the text contains. The inference of a set of ideas and a mental picture of the man responsible for them are additional steps that are highly problematic. A good many historical readers have found themselves in heated disagreement over the kind of man implied by the kinds of ideas implied by those words. To take only the most obvious example, is the implied author of *The Origin of Species* an atheist? The historical author was evidently not, but for generations of fundamentalist Christians the implied author most certainly is.

Genette, having begun from a somewhat equivocal position on this issue, as remarked above, has since become convinced that there are only two levels of analysis needed, and that the tripartite division is redundant. He does consider that the implied author may be separate from the real author in two cases, but then dismisses both.

The first case depends upon the competence of the reader: "Il va de soi qu'un lecteur incompétent ou stupide peut construire de l'auteur, à partir du texte, l'image la plus infidèle . . ." (*Nouveau* 97; "It goes without saying that an incompetent or stupid reader can, on the basis of the text, construct the most unfaithful image of the author . . ." [*Revisited* 141]). The fact that there are so many fallible readers in this fallen world would suffice in itself to make the concept of the implied author valuable (we would need a methodology for identifying the source of such misreadings), but it must also be insisted that Genette is exaggerating to make his point. It is frequently the case that two critics, neither of them incompetent or stupid, disagree about the meaning of a novel, thus creating two implied authors. Both can not logically be identical with the historical author (not that a fictional inference can ever be identical with a flesh-and-blood human being in the first place), but this does not forcibly result in the conclusion that one of the critics is stupid or incompetent; we can surely allow that some works are quite complex (indeed, such complexity has often been seen as an inherent characteristic of major works) and that their meaning may be legitimately disputed by rational people. While some critics have made strong cases for reading *The Merchant of Venice* or the *Prioress' Tale* as vehicles for anti-Semitic propaganda, others have made equally strong cases for reading them as exposés of prejudice and intolerance (in neither case, we should note, are the historical author's views available). Besides, even allowing for the case in which a critic has egregiously misread a work and postulated an implied author diametrically distant from the work's "true" norms (perhaps less rare an occurrence than it ought to be), wouldn't a carefully constructed model for the analysis of the implied author be precisely the solution to rather than the cause of the confusion?

Genette's second case depends upon the performance of the writer rather than that of the reader. The writer may create an implied author who differs from herself or himself by two means:

> La première hypothèse est celle de la *révélation involontaire* (au sens où la psychanalyse parle de lapsus "révélateurs") *d'une personnalité inconsciente*. Deux arguments sont ici invoqués: l'un est le témoignage de Proust, qui déclare comme chacun sait: "Un livre est le produit d'un *autre moi* . . . que celui que nos manifestons dans nos habitudes, dans la societé, dans nos vices . . . ." L'autre est la fameuse analyse "marxiste" . . . . selon laquelle Balzac aurait illustré sans le vouloir, dans la *Comédie humaine*, des opinions politiques et sociales contraires à celles qu'il professait dans la vie. (*Nouveau* 98)

> The first hypothesis is that of the *involuntary revelation* (in the sense in which psychoanalysis speaks of "tell-tale" slips) *of a subconscious personality*. Two arguments are invoked here: one is the testimony of Proust, who asserts, as we all know, "A book is the product of a different *self* . . . from the self we manifest in our habits, in our social life, in our vices. . . ." The other is the famous "Marxist" analysis . . . according to which Balzac in the *Comédie humaine* illustrated, without intending to, political and social opinions contrary to those he professed in his lifetime. (*Revisited* 142)

The quotes around "marxiste" and the use of the conditional suggest that Genette does not subscribe to this "famous" interpretation, but he responds nevertheless:

> l'image de l'auteur construite par le lecteur (compétent) est *plus fidèle* que l'idée que cet auteur se faisait de lui-même; Proust parle d'ailleurs ici d'un "moi profond" qui doit bien être *plus vrai* que le moi "superficiel" de la conscience. Ici, donc, *l'auteur impliqué est* l'authentique *auteur réel*. Pour faire scientifique, nous écrirons: AI = AR. (*Nouveau* 99)

> the image of the author constructed by the (competent) reader is *more faithful* than the idea that that author had of himself; Proust, moreover, is speaking here of a "deep self" that must indeed be *more true* than the "superficial" self of consciousness. Here, therefore, *the implied author is the* authentic *real author*. To play the scientist, we will write IA = RA. (*Revisited* 143)

Two flaws may be discerned in this argument. Genette's insistence upon the competence of the reader constitutes a veiled invocation of the category of the implied reader, which renders his dismissal of the implied author little more than sleight of hand, since the two categories are theoretically interdependent: the image that the implied reader constructs is, precisely, that of the implied author. Besides, the logical conclusion of this demonstration would not be "Exit AI," as he goes on to claim, but "Exit AR": it is the utility of the concept of the historical author he puts into question here and wishes to dismiss, not at all that of the implied author.[15]

There is one other way that the historical author can create a different implied author: "La deuxième hypothèse est celle de la simulation volontaire, par l'auteur réel et dans son oeuvre, d'une personnalité différente de sa personnalité réelle, ou l'idée . . . qu'il s'en fait" (Nouveau 99; "The second hypothesis is that of the deliberate simulation, by the real author and in his work, of a personality different from his real personality or from the idea he has of it" [Revisited 144]). The analysis that follows is, however, centered on the separation of the extradiegetic narrator and the implied author, which is entirely beside the point. The only relevant remark is the assertion that the implied author "n'a aucune raison — et j'ajouterai: aucun moyen — de se distinguer de l'auteur réel" (Nouveau 99; "has no reason — and, I will add, no way — to distinguish himself from the real author" [Revisited 144]).[16] The idea that it is the implied author who is concerned with creating this separation is somewhat confusing. Genette's position is more easily understood (and dismissed) by considering the variety of motives and means that historical authors have for separating themselves from their implied authors. The examples given above of Eliot and the Brontës may be reinvoked here.

This approach is also followed in parody, where the historical author creates an implied author who resembles not herself or himself but another historical author. Genette's analysis of this situation is that le lecteur d'un pastiche doit indentifier l'auteur modèle (en général, le pasticheur l'y aide), et donc percevoir dans le pastiche la double présence du pasticheur et du pastiché. Dans tous ces cas, donc, la duplicité de l'instance auctoriale est en principe clairement perçue par le lecteur, et le double "auteur impliqué" répond bien au double auteur réel. Ici encore, donc, AI = AR, exit AI. (*Nouveau* 101)

the reader of a pastiche must identify the author on whom it is modeled (in general, the pasticher helps with that) and must therefore perceive in the pastiche the double presence of the pasticher and the pastiched. So in all these cases the doubleness of the authorial agent is in principle clearly perceived by the reader, and the double "implied author" corresponds entirely to the double real author. So here, too, IA = RA, exit IA. (*Revisited* 146)

Genette's objection would seem to founder on the indisputable point that there is a single "auteur réel" doing the writing here, not two. The fact that a "lecteur optimal" (*Nouveau* 101; it is again suggestive that he finds himself constrained to rely on the concept of the implied reader in attacking that of the implied author) can perceive that this historical author is creating two implied authors leads to the conclusion that a historical author can indeed create an implied author different from himself or herself, which is precisely the point that Genette wishes to refute. The fact that one of these implied authors resembles that of some other historical author is irrelevant to the argument. There is also the possibility that an author may parody his or her own work, creating two implied authors which correspond to a single historical author. One might read such a parody, albeit unintentional, in some of Hemingway's late work such as *Across the River and Into the Trees*.

Genette discusses a related situation that he admits contradicts his new position:

celle de l'*apocryphe*, c'est-à-dire d'une imitation parfaite sans paratexte dénonciateur: le lecteur d'un apocryphe n'est évidemment pas censé y identifier la duplicité de son instance auctoriale; dans un parfait faux Rimbaud, il est censé percevoir un auteur et un seul, Rimbaud bien sûr. Le texte contient un auteur impliqué — parlons plus simplement: le texte implique un auteur — qui est Rimbaud; or l'auteur réel est (par exemple) Tartempion; donc, enfin, AI ≠ AR. (*Nouveau* 101) that of the *apocryphal* work, a perfect imitation without a tell-tale paratext. The reader of an apocryphal work is obviously not supposed to identify in it the doubleness of its authorial agent. In a perfect false-Rimbaud, he is supposed to perceive one author and one only — Rimbaud, of course. Let us speak more plainly: the text implies an author — who is Rimbaud; but the real author is (for example) John Doe. So here, at last, IA ≠ RA. (*Revisited* 146)

This exception also is an exception to Genette's rejection of the implied reader, one that he does not consider: the implied reader is, precisely, the reader who would realize that the implied author is not Rimbaud but merely intends to imitate him.[17]

The point can be pressed beyond these exceptions, however. Genette's fundamental objection to the implied author is that the implied author always (the above exception granted) resembles either the historical author or the narrator and is thus an unnecessary construction:

> AI me semble donc, *en général*, une instance fantôme . . . , constituée par deux distinctions qui s'ignorent réciproquement: 1) AI n'est pas le narrateur, 2) AI n'est pas l'auteur réel, sans voir que dans 1) il s'agit de l'auteur réel, et dans 2) du narrateur, et que nulle part il n'y a place pour une troisième instance qui ne serait *ni* le narrateur *ni* l'auteur réel. (*Nouveau* 100)

> So IA seems to me, *in general*, to be an imaginary . . . agent constituted by two distinctions that remain blind to each other: (1) IA is not the narrator, (2) IA is not the real author, and it is never seen that the first is a matter of the real author and the second is a matter of the narrator, with no room anywhere for a third agent that would be *neither* the narrator *nor* the real author. (*Revisited* 145)

But if one pursues Genette's quasi-mathematical notation, the resultant formula is not AI = nothing at all, but 1) AI = *auteur réel* (this equivalence is sufficiently undercut in my scheme by the fact that one is real and one fictional, but I suspend that objection here for the sake of discussion) or 2) AI = *narrateur* (again, undercut by the theoretical stipulation that the implied author never narrates). This analysis, rather than suggesting that the implied author is a "fantôme," merely suggests that it can play different roles in different narratives. It can be the case that implied authors are more or less close to historical authors and that narrators are more or less close to implied authors, though I would insist that these are not the only options available. It may be the case that this occurs frequently, though hardly as often as most critics assume. Certainly some writers appear to have thought of their own work that way. Henry James in his (extrafictional) prefaces always claims full authority for the meaning of and intention behind his works and makes it clear that he considers himself their narrator (though he seldom uses that term). As José Antonio Alvarez Amorós contends, "James had no notion whatsoever of anybody telling *The Golden Bowl* but his own empirical self. This is precisely the reason why James never spoke of an effaced narrator: because, within his mental framework, *there was no narrator to efface*" (51). Even here, of course, the enormous critical industry that has grown up around the analysis of the narrator and implied author in James suggests that the writer's own analysis (HA = IA = Nr) has failed to persuade all readers. For those critics who do agree with James (or approach another writer in the same way), perhaps a modified version of Genette's equation would provide a useful shorthand for noting such resemblances: a narrative in which the narrator claims to be both the historical author and, at least implicitly, the implied author, might be symbolized as "HA $\cong$ IA $\cong$ Nr," using the mathematical symbol for congruence rather than equality by way of stipulating that the resemblances are only partial.

John Barth's postmodernist epistolary novel *LETTERS* provides an example of such a narrative situation (as do many of Barth's works). One of the several narrators is "John Barth," a writer employed in the same English department as the historical author (50), who has written precisely the same previous literary works, and who outlines in the letters his current book project: "Its working title is *LETTERS*" (654): N $\cong$ HA. Another narrator, Ambrose Mensch (also a writer — the correspondences among agents become complicated), engages in some interpretative analysis of the meaning of the project-in-progress (which he has helped

"Barth" develop), suggesting, for example, that the character of Lady Amherst will function symbolically as "a fancied embodiment . . . of the Great Tradition" in literature (767): N ≅ IA. But the three levels, as defined in my system, also retain fundamental functional differences that persist even in narratives which seem to closely identify them in terms of personality. As postulated above, the historical author writes, the implied author means, the narrator speaks. The narrator "Barth," for example, corresponds back-and-forth with the other six intradiegetic narrators, while the historical author invented them and wrote all of the letters, and may well have had different notions about the book's meaning than those which have been attributed to the implied author by critics. In fact, Barth's success at conflating the three levels stems largely from his full recognition that the three levels are supposed to be distinct.

Genette also wishes to conflate the historical reader, implied reader, and narratee, but the premises he relies on do not hold true, at least not according to my definitions. "Contrairement à l'auteur impliqué, qui est, dans le tête du lecteur, l'idée d'un auteur réel, le lecteur impliqué, dans le tête de l'auteur réel, est l'idée d'un lecteur *possible*" (*Nouveau* 103; "Contrary to the implied author, who is the idea, in the reader's head, of a real author, the implied reader is the idea, in the real author's head, of a *possible* reader" [*Revisited* 149]). While a text may indeed function in part for a given historical reader as evidence about the nature of its writer, it functions exclusively for the implied reader as evidence about the intentions of the implied author, not the historical author. The implied reader exists not in the mind of the historical author but is itself a property of the text taken as a whole, inferable, like the implied author, by the historical reader (imperfectly) and the implied reader (perfectly). As Wilson has put it, "the implied reader is a function of no more and no less than the overall meaning (that is, the overall interpretation) of the text" and can never finally be "authoritative or prescriptive" (858). The same might be said of the implied author.[18]

But by way of clarifying and supplementing these theoretical distinctions, let me suggest that Jonathan Swift's *Gulliver's Travels* may serve as a concrete demonstration of the relatively abstract principles that Genette (and I) have been illustrating by hypothetical examples. I will focus here on one small episode, but would assert that a similar analysis could be applied to a good deal of Swift's work. Gulliver, the general narrator, reports a conversation he has with Redresal, Principal Secretary of Private Affairs for Lilliput, who explains for him the division of the kingdom into factions according to "the high and low Heels on their shoes, by which they distinguish themselves" (30). At the level of these narrators, the discussion is simply literal; the adherents of the two parties really do wear such heels and Redresal and Gulliver do no more or less than state the facts. Similarly, the strife between the kingdoms of Lilliput and Blefuscu derives from their long-standing dispute over which end of the egg to break before eating, the smaller or larger (31).

Even the earliest readers, of course, detected a satirical or ironical level behind this one that was attributable not to the narrators, but to the author. The Abbé Desfontaines, in the "Préface du Traducteur" of his 1727 translation of *Gulliver's Travels*, was perhaps the first to make this level explicit: "What the author says of Big-Endians, High-Heels, and Low-Heels in the Empire of Lilliput clearly refers to the unfortunate differences which divide England into Conformists and Nonconformists, into Tories and Whigs" (Williams 83). To the modern reader, the satire seems easy enough to interpret; the triviality of the grounds for dispute, heels and eggs, makes it clear how silly the participants on all sides are for concerning themselves with such unimportant distinctions, and thus suggests how silly the English were, and by extension how silly other people at other times have been, for fighting over equally trivial distinctions based on narrow sectarian and party principles. The insignificance of the basis of the disputes is underscored to a degree that would seem to admit of no ambiguity. When Gulliver learns that "his Majesty's Imperial Heels are

lower at least by a *Drurr* than any of his court," the valorization
of the inherently trivial implicit in the incongruous application of
"Imperial" to "Heels" is brought home emphatically in the subsequent parenthesis, "*Drurr* is a Measure of about the fourteenth
Part of an Inch" (30). This specification of the minuteness of the
distinction necessitates the interpretation that these controversies
are based upon inconsequential issues.

But this commonsense reading is presumably one that the historical author would reject. Swift himself was fiercely partisan on
these issues and is most unlikely to have intended to mean that
the disputes were just relatively minor matters of degree. As Gordon McKenzie summarizes the extrafictional evidence, "There is
not in any of his pamphlets the slightest indication of a willing-
ness to arbitrate, to grant certain points in order to gain others.
The Presbyterians are as dangerous as the Papists, and should be
kept in their place as firmly as any other sect" (120). The historical author's argument would have been for intolerance rather than
tolerance: "To Swift, the liberal in religion was even worse than
the liberal in politics, because there was more at stake: man's immortal soul" (124). His was a "battle against all sects other than
the Established Church" (125).

But this does not mean that the modern reader has misread
the passage. Heels and eggs are silly grounds for dispute, and no
reader is obliged to interpret the matter otherwise. The thrust of
the passage is clearly to mock the participants on both sides for
their short-sightedness and small-mindedness, here as throughout
Part I. The most logical way of interpreting the satire is to transfer
this mockery to the real-life analogues to these parties, and thus to
see other factional disputes over religion and politics as similarly
inappropriate. Our knowledge of the historical author's real an-
tipathy toward such liberal views does not force us to change this
reading of the implied author's meaning, but rather to remark that
the historical author chose a most inapt vehicle for his satire. The
implied author, of course, was right on target. Paradoxically, perhaps the uttermost misreading ever made of the passage is much

closer to what must have been the writer's own interpretation. Heels and eggs were apparently as deadly serious for the Abbé Desfontaines as they must have been for Swift: "This is an absurd spectacle in the eyes of a profane philosopher; but it excites compassion in a Christian philosopher attached to true religion and to unity which is only to be found in the Roman Church" (Williams 83). Such staunch support of the "Papists" was beyond doubt the single thing farthest from Swift's mind. But Desfontaines's reading, although directed 180° away, is based on precisely the same logic as Swift's own must have been, and makes the irony here truly double-edged: the premise that even minor political and religious differences are dangerous lends support equally to the argument for exclusive dominance by any of the parties in the dispute. As already noted, however, neither reading seems to take into account the radical disparity between the gravity of tenor and vehicle in their readings, a disparity which seems to aim the implied author's satire against intolerance rather than tolerance, and provides a relatively clear-cut example of a text in which the historical author ≠ implied author ≠ narrator (HA ≠ IA ≠ Nr).[19]

Having thus distinguished the historical author, the agent who writes, from the implied author, the agent who means, the next function to define is that of the narrator, the agent who speaks.

2

THE GENERAL NARRATOR

The concept of the narrator is even less clear, in terms of any real critical consensus, than the concepts of the historical and implied author and reader turned out to be. Again the difficulties can be approached by examining Booth's foundation stone. A look at the entry for "Narrator" in his index suggests how broadly he defines the term: "Narrator; *see also* Camera Eye; Center of consciousness; Central intelligence; Reflector." Under these headings, one finds further cross-references to other terms: "Point of view," "Inside views," "Commentary," and "Inconscience." Examination of the various discussions of narrators in his text bears out the suggestion in the index that he takes an extremely broad view of the term, using it indifferently to refer to implied authors, characters who never speak at all, and a variety of techniques used by narrators to reveal character's thoughts or to describe scenes.

In his fullest treatment of "Types of Narration," his chapter 6, he covers the entire range of possibilities. He suggests at one point that the implied author can be a narrator: "in Hemingway's 'The Killers,' for example, there is no narrator other than the implicit second self that Hemingway creates as he writes" (151).

Then, on the next page, he seems to retreat from this position: "When there is no such 'I,' as in 'The Killers,' the inexperienced reader may make the mistake of thinking that the story comes to him unmediated" (152). The suggestion seems to be that more experienced readers would not make this mistake, that they would recognize that the narrator plays an intermediary role between the implied author and the narrative. At this point Booth seems close to my own position, that only the narrator speaks in the text, that the contribution of the implied author must always be inferred from the speech of the narrator.

To consider briefly his example of "The Killers" — "tarte à la crème du récit 'objectif,'" as Genette observes (*Nouveau* 68; "the knee-jerk representative of 'objective' narrative" [*Revisited* 101]) — the distinction between the narrator and the implied author can be marked in two ways. One is to consider the idea, elsewhere supported by Booth himself, that the narrator (Booth's III.Teller) believes in the world of the fiction and addresses a narratee (his III.Listener) who shares that belief (430). Genette elaborates this point:

> Dans le récit le plus sobre, quelqu'un me parle, me raconte une histoire, m'invite à l'entendre comme il la raconte, et cette invite — confiance ou pression — constitue une indéniable attitude de narration, et donc de narrateur: même la première phrase de *The Killers*, . . . "The door of Henry's lunch-room opened . . . ," présuppose un narrataire capable entre autres d'accepter la familiarité fictive de "Henry," l'existence de sa salle à manger, l'unicité de sa porte, et ainsi, c o mme on dit fort bien, d'*entrer* dans la fiction. (*Nouveau* 68)

> In the most unobtrusive narrative, someone is speaking to me, is telling me a story, is inviting me to listen to it as he tells it, and this invitation — confiding or urging — constitutes an undeniable stance of narrating, and therefore of a narrator. Even the first sentence of "The Killers" . . . — "The door of Henry's lunch-room opened" — presupposes a narratee capable, among other things, of accepting the fictive familiarity of "Henry," the existence of the lunch-room, and the singleness of its door and thus, as it has so well been put, of *entering* into the fiction." (*Revisited* 101)

The implied author and reader are of course fully conscious of the fictionality of this world and know that the deeper interest of the story lies between the lines. But while this distinction is valid in the case of "The Killers," it would not be so for every narrative. Not every narrator believes in the authenticity of the characters and events making up the diegetic universe. The self-conscious narrator of John Fowles's *The French Lieutenant's Woman* is aware of the epigraphs and chapter numbers in the book, and frequently asserts that his characters are mere fictions and their actions determined by him. The narrator even underscores his control over the novel's events by tossing a coin to decide the order in which the two different endings of the book will occur.[1] Similar displays of pseudo-authority (the narrator is himself, of course, merely one more fictional character created by the author) may be found in the Victorian novels that provide Fowles with models for such narrating postures. The writer, author, and narrator may still be differentiated in such cases by other means, however, as explained in the preceding chapter.

A second distinction between the implied author and narrator in "The Killers" can be made on grounds that are primarily stylistic. The narrator is telling the story as objectively as possible, showing little sympathy for any of the characters, and offering few comments on or conclusions about the events.[2] The implied author, on the other hand, is concerned with making judgments on these characters and communicating something about, for example, its (or is it safe to attribute masculine gender to Hemingway's implied author and effaced narrators?) view of life.[3] A narrator who tells us that "Ole Andreson rolled over toward the wall" (Hemingway, *Complete* 221), makes an explicit observation about the physical position of the character; the implied author, at the same moment, makes an implicit observation about the moral or psychological position of the character. As Joseph M. Flora remarks in interpreting these observations, "The fighter continues to lie on his bed looking at the wall; he has come to a place of no exit" (102). The first part of Flora's commentary paraphrases the narrator's statement; the second part is Flora's interpretation of the implied author's meaning. The same ("career") implied author uses exactly the same symbol of the turn to the wall (and marks the significance of each statement by formatting it in both cases as an independent paragraph) in "Indian Camp" about another character: "The husband in the upper bunk rolled over against the wall" (Hemingway, *Complete* 68). Flora offers an interpretation of the implied author's meaning here as well: "The husband has been able to bear his own pain, but [his wife's] pain in addition is too much for him. His suicide suggests that he was dying in his wife's place" (31). The objective narrator, of course, only observes the action of rolling over, not discovering the suicide until later, and never comments on either the suicide or the frequently-remarked false optimism of the ending of the story.

But the fact that a narrator is being as objective as possible does not lead to the conclusion that its presence is so covert or effaced that it can be automatically dismissed. At the most fundamental level, of course, the mere use of language is a marker of human agency, and the fact that a narrator refrains from explicit commentary on or interpretation of its narrative can in itself imply a good deal. With the extremely objective narrators presented by such writers as Dashiell Hammett and Ernest Hemingway, "we feel we are encountering not so much an impersonal or direct transcript of life as a deliberately achieved simplicity and purity, a mind resisting ease and self-indulgence . . . . The pose of careful neutrality is a state of mind, not an absence of it" (Slatoff 105). As James McConkey has argued, it is rather the stereotypical or cliché-bound narrator of the slick or formula story who is truly impersonal and invisible, with only a generic identity (86–87). One might conclude, for example, that the objective narrator, far from passively and objectively recording the youthful Nick Adams' conclusion ("he felt quite sure that he would never die" [Hemingway, *Complete* 70]), in fact *im*passively accepts the implied author's much tougher message about the nature of life and suffering, a conclusion which demands the stoical stance the narrator has exhibited during (or learned from?) the narrative.

Besides conflating the narrator with the implied author, Booth also confuses it with nonnarrating characters. This is not to say that a character cannot be a narrator, but that only a character who speaks (even if only to itself, silently) is a narrator. Booth extends the definition to include reported (rather than quoted) thoughts or even gestures in addition to the speaking function, the telling of stories: "any sustained view, of whatever depth, temporarily turns the character whose mind is shown into a narrator" (164); "In a sense, every speech, every gesture, narrates; most works contain disguised narrators who are used to tell the audience what it needs to know, while seeming merely to act out their roles" (152). This trope about acting out roles is extended literally, so that even characters in plays are considered to be narrators:

> narrators who unconsciously betray themselves as brutal or insensitive or mean, or simply as moving toward tragic or comic error, may not require authorial reticence for their effect. In all great classical drama the speaker's mistakes and faults are corrected for the audience by what other characters do and say. When Othello approaches Desdemona in a jealous rage, we know that he is about to make a tragic mistake; Shakespeare has used Iago and Desdemona to tell us so. (305)

The inclusion of thought, and especially of gesture and action, as sufficient to render a character a narrator, makes Booth's concept too broad. There would seem to be nothing a character could do — including, as suggested by the Hemingway examples, giving up and failing entirely to act — that would not constitute a contribution to the narrative and hence make every character at all times a narrator, in which case the label would no longer make any useful distinction.

If Booth defines the narrator too broadly, other critics define its role too narrowly. The circumscription of this function is pressed to the limit by critics who argue for what Ann Banfield calls "narratorless" texts (36) and what Chatman terms "nonnarrated" or "unnarrated" texts (*Story* 34).[4] While Chatman has since changed his view about this category, his discussions of the theory were the most thorough, have been the most influential, and are still widely disseminated and cited (witness the anthology reprinting ten years later of an excerpt from the "Discourse: Non-narrated Stories" chapter of *Story and Discourse*). As often happens in such cases, his initial presentations had a good deal more impact than his subsequent rejection of them. A look at these critical analyses of how and where narrators are supposed not to function within other models will lead to a clearer picture of how they do function within my system and will also help clarify the definitions of the historical and implied authors that I have offered.

Chatman is well aware that the label "nonnarrated narrative" seems to defy logic. As he explains, "The seeming paradox is only terminological. It is merely short for 'a narrative that is not explicitly told' or 'that avoids the appearance of being told'" (*Story* 34). An obvious objection here is that theorists engaged in defining and labeling categories are in no position to dismiss confusions as "only terminological"; clear and consistent definitions of terms are precisely what is at stake. Chatman does at one later point recall his stipulation, reminding his readers that "I say 'nonnarrated': the reader may prefer 'minimally narrated'" (*Story* 147). But throughout his treatment of this category he neglects the distinction that he wishes the reader to maintain. This is partly an organizational problem caused by his designating a separate category, "covert narration," that would more logically cover the narrative "that is not explicitly told" or seems "minimally narrated." A covertly narrated story is to be differentiated from an unnarrated one by virtue of the point that "Unlike the 'nonnarrated' story, the covertly narrated one can express a character's speech or thoughts in indirect form" (*Story* 197). His concern with nonnarrated narrative as a category beyond covert narrative leads him to introduce labels such as "the absolutely 'nonnarrated' narrative" (*Story* 223). What could the quotes around "nonnarrated" mean in conjunction with "absolutely"? Chatman seems simultaneously to affirm and deny his category here.

This category of more or less absolute nonnarration owes its equivocal existence to two *dei ex machina*, which can be invoked to explain away what would otherwise seem to constitute pretty clear marks of narrators' involvement: "convention" and the "implied author." It is difficult to pin down precisely what Chatman means by "convention," as when he argues that tags used to assign speeches to characters should not be regarded as clear marks of a narrating voice: "The use of such tags, however, is not a strong indicator of narrative mediation, for the convention of 'he said' is not much more conspicuous than that of the use of separate paragraphs to indicate a change of speaker in dialogue" ("Structure" 237). The relative conspicuousness of these techniques is a moot point, but they are certainly not "conventions" in the same sense of the word. I can agree that the use of a paragraph break to show a change of speaker is a convention — there is no necessary logical connection between the typographical and rhetorical occurrences — but in what way is it merely a convention to write "John said" to show that John said something? The connection here is not simply arbitrary, but directly tied to the meaning of the words composing the narrator's discourse.[5] A third use of the term gives it another different meaning: "convention has it that we forget the act of transcription [in quoted dialogue] and assume that the expression is a pure act of mimesis" ("Structure" 238). Does he mean that some authorities have long believed that readers are unaware that they are reading, that they have the illusion that they are hearing someone speak? Or is this prescriptive? Are we supposed to have this illusion in order to read properly? It may be the case that some historical readers do fail to notice tags and do forget that they are reading narratives (are being narrated to). This seems quite unlikely to me, but even if it holds true for certain historical readers at certain times, the text will never forget that it is written and contains tags, and neither will the implied reader. The (extradiegetic) narratee is the agent who believes itself spoken to directly, but it is spoken to directly by the (extradiegetic) narrator, whose narration includes all of the tags, not the characters whose speech the narrator quotes. Only the (intradiegetic) character/narratee who exists at the same diegetic level as the (intradiegetic) character/narrator would be unaware of the tags, which are not part of the narrative embedded at that level.

In addition to the power of convention, Chatman also relies on the concept of the implied author to remove subtle traces of the narrator from "nonnarrated" texts. In "The Killers," to return to that touchstone text, "Whatever mediation appears is surely that of the 'implied author,' not that of a narrator" ("Structure" 218 n. 7). The traces of this mediation would presumably include not only all "he said" tags but also such hints as the use of definite articles — to say "the arc-light" rather than "an arc-light" suggests, at least to me, that the speaker is a degree more familiar with the area (Hemingway, *Complete* 219, 220).[6] Chatman appears here to ignore a point he does make later, that "unlike the narrator, the implied author can *tell* us nothing" (*Story* 148). He is correct in this latter remark, but draws a questionable conclusion from it: "Since a narrative never communicates the direct speech of the implied author, ethos can only apply to a narrator" (*Story* 227). Susan Lanser has objected on the grounds that this theoretical move "completely separates aesthetics from ideology, structural analysis from the cultural function of literature," and responds by entirely rejecting the notion of the implied author (*Narrative* 50 n. 52). But the moral nature or guiding beliefs of an implied author, by analogy with those of real people, are perhaps more readily determined by deeds than words. The fact that an implied author has constructed a certain type of narrative, told by a certain type of narrator and within which certain things happen to certain types of characters, gives the implied reader plenty of evidence for assigning ethical principles and norms to the implied author.

Chatman goes on to extend the function of the implied author to cover three roles properly assigned to the narrator: the presentation of characters' speech, of written documents, and of characters' consciousness. He argues that "In the transcription of speech, the implied author is presumed to be nothing more than a stenographer" ("Structure" 242). But the implied author has invented these utterances (and their utterers); it is their creator, not their recorder. The narrator is the agent who presents them to the narratee as having been actually said by another person. Similarly, Chatman holds that epistolary or journal novels "reduce the implied author to a mere collector of documents" ("Structure" 240). The same objection applies here: the implied author has invented all of these documents, not merely collected them; the role of assembler or editor is played by the narrator, who "believes" that the letters or journals were actually written by several different agents and who presents them as such to the fictional audience, the narratee, that also believes in their reality.

Chatman does later seem tacitly to recognize that his assignment of this role to the implied author may create some theoretical difficulties, but he resists assigning it to the narrator: "Of all the forms of literary narrative those that pretend to be constituted by found letters and diaries least presuppose a narrator. If we insist upon an agent beyond the implied author, he can only be a mere collector or collator" (*Story* 169). This is strictly an ad hoc reaction, however, motivated by his commitment to having a category of nonnarrated narrative. Rather than solving the problem, he disposes of it by sleight of hand. This "collector" can only exist in an undefined narratological limbo not accounted for by his theory, which does not allow for any levels other than the implied author and narrator. There is simply no third category of "collector or collator" into which such an agent could be articulated.

The same confusion of implied author and narrator is brought in to account for the presentation of consciousness: "The implied author has become mind-reader, in addition to stenographer" ("Structure" 249); "The convention of stream of consciousness has

it that there is no externally motivated organization of the character's thoughts, nor, of course, a narrator to make a selection among
them" (*Story* 194).   In the former example Chatman assigns the
narrator's function of verbal presentation to the implied author,
and in the latter example (aided again by the power of
"convention") assigns the implied author's function of selection to
the narrator. The implied author invents these thoughts and attributes them to the characters; it is the narrator who verbally presents them to the narratee as though it were reading the characters' minds. After all, the implied author knows that these characters are fictional, figments of the text, and have neither minds
nor thoughts to read.

The implied author's function is also assigned to the narrator
in the presentation of descriptions: "the very verbal detailing of
aspects of an object suggests that the narrator *intends* a description" (*Story* 221).   A narrator can, of course, have intentions,
among which can be the presentation of descriptions. But a narrator intends only if it explicitly says that it does or if an intention is
marked in some other way; it can be the case that a narrator describes an object "because it's there." Samuel Beckett's characters
frequently review the contents of their rooms as part of a ritual or
out of boredom. They often list them in a random, interrupted, or
incomplete way, since their primary intent is not the presentation
of an ordered description. Malone, for example, speaks primarily
to await, or perhaps defer, the stasis of death, and intends his
descriptions as means to that end: " . . . I shall speak of the things
that remain in my possession, that is a thing I have always
wanted to do. It will be a kind of inventory. In any case that is a
thing I must leave to the very last moment, so as to be sure of not
having made a mistake" (*Malone Dies* 3). It is the implied author
rather than the narrator who is automatically charged with having
an intent behind the details and arrangement of the narrative —
and it might be argued that this intent is not description either, but
rather some statement about the nature of consciousness or perception.

A narrator, however, does not necessarily have to intend the full range of meaning of what is narrated or even to consider that it has a meaning at all. This is frequently the case with narrators who are children. The twelve-year-old narrator of William Faulkner's "A Justice," for example, having presented to his narratee a tale told to him by another character, admits that "to me the story did not seem to have got anywhere, to have point or end" (*These* 206). Here we have an unreliable narrator in Booth's sense: an inconscient narrator who does not express or even understand the implied author's intentions. The implied reader, of course, does see the point of the implied author's story. At times Chatman eliminates almost entirely this intending function of the implied author: "There are hundreds of reasons for telling a story, but these reasons are the narrator's, not the implied author's, who is without personality or even presence, hence without motivation other than the purely theoretical one of constructing the narrative itself" (*Story* 158). But even though the implied author may be a purely theoretical entity, the construction of narratives is not a purely theoretical undertaking, and a good deal may be inferred about the personalities and motives of implied authors from the texts we attribute to them. The implied author is the agent who always has reasons for creating a certain story — the narrator may or may not indicate that it has intentions.

Even when a narrator specifically states that it does have an intention in telling its story, it may be quite different from that of the implied author and diverge considerably from the intent perceived by the implied reader. In Jorge Luis Borges's "El jardín de senderos qui bifurcan" ("The Garden of Forking Paths") the narrator makes his intention explicit:

En la página 242 de la *Historia de la Guerra Europea* de Liddell Hart, se lee que una ofensiva de trece divisiones británicas (apoyadas por mil cuatrocientas piezas de artillería) contra la línea Serre-Montauban había sido planeada para el veinticuatro de julio de 1916 y debió postergarse hasta la mañana del día ventinueve. Las lluvias torrenciales (anota el capitán Liddell Hart) provocaron esa demora — nada significativa, por cierto. La siguiente declaración, dictada,

> releída y firmada por el doctor Yu Tsun, antiguo catedrático de inglés
> en la *Hochschule* de Tsingtao, arroja una insospechada luz sobre el
> caso. Faltan las dos páginas iniciales. (*Obras* 472)

> On page 242 of Liddell Hart's *History of the First World War*, one
> reads that an offensive by thirteen British divisions (supported by
> fourteen hundred artillery pieces) against the Serre-Montauban line,
> planned for 24 July 1916, had to be postponed until the morning of the
> 29th. The torrential rains (notes Captain Liddell Hart) caused this de-
> lay — certainly nothing of special significance. The following deposi-
> tion, dictated, read over, and signed by Dr. Yu Tsun, former teacher of
> English at the Tsingtao *Hochschule*, casts an unexpected light upon this
> event. The first two pages are missing. (my translation)

The narrator's expressed intention, to annotate a passage in a
book of military history, diverges considerably from the intent of
the implied author, which is more likely closer to the intention expressed by the writer in his "Prologue," that of creating a certain
effect in the reader: "El jardín de senderos que se bifurcan," Borges explains, "es policial; sus lectores asistirán a la ejecución y a
todos los preliminares de un crimen, cuyo propósito no ignoran
pero que no comprenderán, me parece, hasta el último párrafo"
(*Obras* 429; "'The Garden of Forking Paths' is a detective story; its
readers will be present for the execution, and all the preliminaries,
of a crime whose purpose will not be unknown to them, but which
they will not understand, it seems to me, until the last paragraph").[7] The writer and author, who are writing fiction, are thus
also working in an entirely different genre than the narrator, who
is writing history, a situation exemplified in more traditional fiction by such genres as the epistolary novel, in which the narrators
write letters while the writer and author produce a novel. The response Borges describes, by the way, would be that of the historical reader, not the narratee (who believes that it is reading a
scholarly annotation to a history book) or the implied reader (who
always already knows the contents of the final paragraph).

   Similar to Chatman's "nonnarrated narrative" is Banfield's
"narratorless" model, which rests on some of the same conflation
of the functions of the implied author and narrator:

Once the concept of a narrator is sufficiently abstract to account for all cases where it does not explicitly appear, even the traditional division between drama and narrative is blurred. Todorov is led to posit a narrator in *Les liaisons dangereuses* . . . , a classic example of a text which Plato would call "pure imitation." And to account for texts like Swift's "A Modest Proposal." which has a narrating "I" whose "moral appreciation" cannot be said to coincide with the text's moral, a second "effaced" narrator would have to be proposed. The same would apply when the narrator becomes the third person of the free indirect style, like the "reporter" in Norman Mailer's *The Armies of the Night*. Our prospect is for narrators behind narrators to distinguish texts whose narrators are reliable from more complicated ironic ones. At this point, it becomes difficult to see the difference between a narrator and the real author — a difference which has been the point of departure for all recent discussions of the narrator. (36)

The last phrase effectively points up the source of this confusion: the difference she has trouble seeing is that between the narrator and the implied author; the "real author" is not at all relevant at this point. Her choice of problematic examples further suggests some confusion about these categories, since all represent pretty straightforward cases. The agent behind Swift's narrator, if he is indeed unreliable, is the implied author, not another narrator. In fact, certain details of the text suggest that the narrator is rather ironic than unreliable. In this reading, the use of italics in the first edition between "Therefore let no Man talk to me of other Expedients" (519) and "Therefore I repeat, let no Man talk to me of these and the like Expedients, till he hath a least some Glimpse of Hope, that there will ever be some hearty and sincere Attempt to put them in Practice" (520) functions to mark with a shift in tone the interpolated practical and humanitarian proposals the narrator only pretends to find unacceptable, and the narrator's moral sense does coincide with the implied author's meaning.[8] Banfield's suggestion that the shift to the third person in Mailer's novel marks a significant complication ignores what has become a critical commonplace, that all narrators refer to themselves in the first person (usually singular but occasionally, as in Faulkner's "A Rose for Emily" or John Barth's *Sabbatical*, plural) and to their characters in the third (or, as in Michel Butor's *La Modification*, the second) person.[9] There are no extra narrators created by "third-person" narration — there is still one, and only one, extradiegetic narrator, whether "Mailer" narrates his own story or has an anonymous narrator do it.

The first part of her complaint brings up another issue which is fundamental to the narratorless model. She invokes Plato to uphold a division between imitation, or mimesis, and narration. According to her argument, direct quotation of speech (or, as in *Les liaisons dangereuses*, transcription of writing) is pure mimesis, not mediated by a narrator. But this analysis is based on a combination of faulty logic and a questionable reading of Plato. Her logical slip is apparent in the passage just quoted. She speaks of the "traditional division between drama and narrative" being blurred, yet offers an example of a novel to illustrate the point. It is the performed drama that Plato would call "pure imitation," and *Les liaisons dangereuses* is simply not a drama at all, but a written narrative, which would not seem to call for any blurring of divisions. If Tzvetan Todorov had proposed a narrator at a live performance of, say, *Oedipus Rex* (the perusal of a written text of the play would be another matter), Banfield's argument would raise the perfectly valid question of whether the concept of a narrator or "monstrator" of some type is necessary for the analysis of plays (or, especially, films), an issue that has been, and continues to be, widely disputed.[10] But Plato would never have called a written narrative "pure imitation"; under his system the drama alone is pure imitation — the narrative is always narrated.

The passages in book 3 of *The Republic* in which Plato explains his position make the distinction clear and establish that he considers even the directly quoted speech of characters to be narrated by the narrator: "'Now, it is narration, is it not, both when he presents the several speeches and the matter between the speeches?' 'Of course.'" (227); "'In such case then, it appears, he and the other poets effect their narration through imitation.' 'Certainly.'" (229). He goes on to allow specifically for poets to narrate either exclusively through direct quotation or through a mixture of quotation and direct presentation in the narrator's own voice, for "poets to narrate as imitators or in part as imitators and in part not" (231). The case of poets narrating entirely "as imitators" would be illustrated by *Les liaisons dangereuses* or *La chute*. The other limit case is also considered: "if the poet should conceal himself nowhere, then his entire poetizing and narration would have been accomplished without imitation" (229). An example of such a text would be Samuel Beckett's *Le dépeupleur*, in which no characters speak at all within the general narrator's discourse. The poet who uses the mixed mode and speaks most often in his own voice seems privileged stylistically by Plato: the ideal narrative "will be one that partakes of both, of imitation and simple narration, but there will be a small portion of imitation in a long discourse" (239, 241). That the entirety of every narrative discourse is narrated is never in question.

My definition will follow in stipulating that all narrative is entirely narrated by a narrator from beginning to end. As Käte Hamburger has put it, narrative "does not exist independently of the act of narration but rather . . . it only is by virtue of its being narrated" (136). Barbara Herrnstein Smith's observation may provide the best formulation of the position I am occupying: "the act of narration is itself understood to be fictive and the entire verbal structure of the work is understood to be not a tale told but the representation of a telling" (*Margins* 196). The agent charged with this single fictive act of narrating, in its entirety, I will call the *general narrator* of a work. While I follow the Platonic model in this regard, my model differs slightly with respect to characters' speeches that are presented by the general narrator. Plato called the conveying of such speeches mimesis, but this label can be applied with equal validity under my model to the fictive act of the general narrator himself. Genette has recognized the problem raised here, that "la fiction *consiste* en cette simulation qu'Aristote appelait *mimésis*" (*Nouveau* 11; "fiction *consists* of that simulation that Aristotle called *mimésis* [*Revisited* 15]). He has therefore suggested a division within the category to differentiate the narrator's speeches from those of other characters: "Dans un récit, il n'y a que *rhésis* et *diégésis* — on dit ailleurs, et fort clairement, texte de personnages et texte de narrateur" (*Nouveau* 29; "In a narrative, there are only *rhésis* and *diégésis* — or, as has been said elsewhere, and very clearly, the characters' discourse and the narrator's discourse" [*Revisited* 43]). He also calls *rhésis* "citation," and I will view all quoted dialogue in this way, not as direct speech spoken by characters but as spoken by the general narrator in the persona of a character. Such quotation may be viewed as a rhetorical figure akin to *dialogismus*, considering the general narrator to be "speaking in another man's person" (Lanham 34).

I have used the metaphor of speaking to refer to the narratorial act which represents the telling of a story and have concentrated on the narrator's citation of characters' direct discourse to explain my position that every part of the narrative text, even quoted dialogue, is narrated by the general narrator. The metaphor is not intended, however, to privilege the representation of a novel written in "spoken" dialogue over a "written" epistolary or journal novel; my theory treats transcription as a form of citation, in the same way that it treats dialogue. Other critics, however, have seen the spoken and written situations as qualitatively different; this view would seem to be behind Banfield's assertion that *Les liaisons dangereuses* is a narratorless text. The role of the general narrator is not always clear in such situations, and I will take Choderlos de Laclos' work, which seems to have become the standard test case for the genre, as an example to explain how the epistolary novel will be accommodated under this model.

Banfield's reference to Todorov's postulation of a narrator behind the letters is to his study of this novel in *Littérature et signification*, and it will be useful to first examine Todorov's own description of the historical reader's response in assigning a narratee and narrator to the epistolary novel: "la conscience de lire un roman et non un document nous engage à jouer le rôle de ce lecteur imaginaire; et en même temps apparaît le narrateur, celui qui nous rapporte le récit, puisque le récit lui-même est imaginaire" (89; "our awareness that we are reading a novel and not a document commits us to playing the role of the imaginary reader; and at the same time the narrator appears, who relates the narrative to us, since the story itself is imaginary"). I would modify his position here to the extent that the narrator and narratee may, and usually do, believe that the text represents reality and not fiction: the implied author and reader, agents that Todorov makes no allowance for in this scheme, are the agents who are always aware of the fictional status of the text. But he is correct in noting the key point that the gathered letters have a different audience than the separate letters, which are addressed to separate readers. The significant gap in Todorov's reading, however, lies in not considering the roles of the redactor and editor as presented in the text in relation to the role of the narrator, a difficulty that most analyses of the novel's structure tend to evade.

The primary difficulty to be resolved is the problematic status of the two prefatory sections, the "Avertissement de l'Editeur" ("Publisher's Note") and the "Préface du Rédacteur" ("Editor's Preface"). Are these parts of the narrative, and thus themselves narrated by the general narrator, or are they genuinely prefatory to the narrative, provided by the historical author and not intended to be part of the fiction?[11] To adopt the terminology proposed by Genette, do they belong to the text or to the paratext? The editor himself claims the latter; indeed, he suggests that the reader might skip over his preface and "passer tout de suite à l'Ouvrage même" (6; "turn straight to the work itself" [4]). In this case the novel consists only of the letters themselves and is entirely narrated by an effaced general narrator, who can be shown distinct from the individual correspondents in the text by recourse to Genette's model of narrative levels and Prince's theory of the narratee (the model of the narratee, as shall become evident, is particularly useful as a tool for keeping track of narrative levels in epistolary texts). Each correspondent writes his or her letters as part of the narrative itself, or intradiegetically; each letter is addressed to an-

other character in the fiction, an intradiegetic narratee. None of
these letters is aimed at a reader of *Les liaisons dangereuses*, since
these correspondents (as writers and as readers) "believe" that
they are real people, not characters in a novel.

This single agent, for presentation to whom the general narrator narrates these letters, I will call the *general narratee*. Prince has
made a similar distinction under a different terminology: "le narrataire à qui sont destinées toutes les narrations de tous les nar-
rateurs, est le narrataire principal. Au contraire, le narrataire à
qui une partie seulement des événements est racontée, le narrataire
qui ignore certains faits plus ou moins importants, est un narrataire secondaire" ("the narratee to whom are directed all the
narratives of all the narrators is the principal narratee. On the
other hand, a narratee to whom only some part of the events is
recounted, a narratee who is ignorant of certain more or less important facts, is a secondary narratee"). Accordingly, for the example under consideration, "dans *les Liaisons dangereuses* . . .
Valmont et Mme de Merteuil, aussi importants semblent-ils, sont
des narrataires secondaires. Le narrataire principal . . . est le destinataire ultime de toutes les lettres que s'écrivent les personnages
et de tous les commentaires qui s'y rapportent" ("Introduction"
190; "Valmont and Madame de Merteuil, as important as they
appear to be, are secondary narratees. The principal narratee . . .
is the ultimate addressee of all the letters written by the characters
and all the comments that they relate in them"). Prince's focus in
this essay is of course on the narratee, but he would presumably
agree that a complementary "narrateur principal," who assembles
all of the individual narrations, is logically entailed by his model.
I offer my own terminology rather than adopt his here partly because of the problem that he appears to anticipate in his own insistence on the importance, despite their labels, of the secondary
narratees: "principal" and "secondary" are already value-laden
terms (perhaps more in English than in French), unlike the relatively neutral "general." We might recall in this context the disputes over references to "primary" and "secondary" narratives in

the early versions of Genette's model that eventually led him to drop the terms.

It should be stipulated that the general narratee may be more or less fully described or dramatized in a work. Perhaps the limit case for the development of the narratee would be Butor's *La modification*, in which the narratee is quite fully described and is in fact the protagonist of the novel. In the third volume of Laurence Sterne's *Tristram Shandy*, the narratee is something of a chameleon, shifting gender from chapter to chapter (chapter 5 is addressed to "Madam" and chapter 7 to "Sir") or even from one sentence to the next (171). In chapter ten the previously singular narratee becomes the collective "your reverences" or "Sirs" (180). Evidently the general narrator is to be conceived here as addressing a (fictional) cross-section of society, "both male and female, of what age, complexion, and condition soever" (225), aiming his remarks at now one hearer or reader (he presents the narratee alternately as "hearing" [215] and as "readers" [225]), now another, now one subgroup or another.

To return to the example of *Les liaisons dangereuses*, then, the general narrator can thus be defined in part here by its audience, the general narratee. Although it nowhere speaks in its own voice, its act of narration can be clearly differentiated from the acts of the characters by considering that it presents the letters as a whole, not to the characters they were written to, but to another audience entirely. As I have suggested above, this would constitute one of the limit cases foreseen by Plato, that in which the text is narrated entirely through imitation.

But *Les liaisons dangereuses* may be read in other ways, and my remarks to this point about the commentaries that frame the letters constitute something of an oversimplification. The complexity here lies in the fact that there are two distinguishable agents responsible for these sections. The editor's insistence that the letters which make up the text have been selected and transcribed from the correspondence of historical authors implies that his preface is itself a fiction and part of the narrative, since the letters and their supposed writers are in fact fictional. In this reading the editor is the general narrator of the preface and also of the rest of the novel. Further support for this interpretation is offered by the publisher in his "Avertissement," where he argues that the letters (and therefore the preface attesting to their reality) are a work of fiction: "Nous croyons devoir prévenir le Public que, malgré le titre de cet Ouvrage et ce qu'en dit le Rédacteur dans sa Préface, nous ne garantissons pas l'authenticité de ce Recueil, et que nous avons même de fortes raisons de penser que ce n'est qu'un Roman" (3; "The Public is notified that despite the title of this work and what is said by the editor in his preface, we do not guarantee the authenticity of the collection and we have good reason to believe it is only a Novel" [1]). The point that the publisher's remarks precede the editor's gives them extra weight; once the idea has been presented that the work is a fiction, the reader can not go on naively, but is influenced to consider the work in that way. As Philip Stewart has remarked, "The [editor] appears soberly realistic and moralistic, but, coming second, has in effect already been undercut by the irony of the 'Avertissement'" (222–23). The question then reverts in turn to the status of the publisher's remarks. Are they really written by the historical author solely for the historical reader, as a genuine (extrafictional or paratextual) disclaimer, or do they also form part of the fiction?[12] Todorov's own position would seem to be that the historical author is the sole agent responsible for this part of the text. Throughout the rest of the text it may seem as though "l'auteur ne prend jamais la parole . . . . Mais dans son Avertissement de l'Editeur, Laclos détruit déjà cette illusion" (*Littérature* 89; "the author never speaks . . . . But in his Publisher's Note, Laclos has already destroyed that illusion"). The point here would, however, seem to be moot; each historical reader must decide the issue individually as best he or she can (the implied reader alone can be secure here in its analysis).

Let us say, to pursue the example to the limit case, that the publisher's warning is also part of the narrative. This would im-

ply that the novel is in part the ironical story of its own writing, a
self-reflexive examination of its own genre.[13] Given this line of
analysis, we can say that the narrating begins at the opening
"Publisher's Note" and continues through the "Publisher's
[End]Note" which closes the text. We now have two logical
branches to follow: is the publisher to be trusted or not? I refer
here not to narrative reliability in Booth's sense, implying that the
narrator "speaks for or acts in accordance with the norms of the
work (which is to say, the implied author's norms)" (158), but
only to mean "telling the truth." Is he really a separate agent from
the editor, or is this part of a complicated game in which he assumes different roles?[14] If we postulate a duplicitous publisher,
who is himself responsible for the presentation of (is perhaps the
author of) the editor's remarks and the letters, then he is the general narrator. The publisher's satirical remarks about the morality
of contemporary French society, presented ironically under a ve-
neer of naïveté, would seem to suggest this reading: he argues that
the work must be fictional because

> En effet, plusieurs des personnages qu'il met en scène ont de si mau-
> vaises moeurs, qu'il est impossible de supposer qu'ils aient vécu dans
> notre siècle: dans ce siècle de philosophie, où les lumières, répandues de
> toutes partes, ont rendu, c o mme chacun sait, tous les h o mme s s i
> honnêtes et toutes les femmes si modestes et si réservées. ([3])

> Indeed, several of the characters he describes have such abominable
> morals that it is impossible to suppose they could have lived in our
> own century — that century of philosophy in which enlightenment,
> spreading on all sides, has rendered (as everyone knows) all men so
> worthy and all women so modest and reserved. (1)

If we take the publisher to be sincere, again in the interest of
pursuing the limit case, the situation becomes somewhat more
complex. The general narrator in this case never speaks in its own
voice: every word in the text is attributed to the publisher, the editor, or one of the several correspondents. But the general narrator
and his function persist nonetheless. He is the agent who is telling
the story of *Les liaisons dangereuses*, a story which is "about" the

prefatory materials as well as the letters. In Genette's terms (though not applied here as Genette might apply them, as I explain below) he is an extraheterodiegetic narrator: he narrates, from outside the fiction, or diegesis, to the general narratee (an extraheterodiegetic audience itself not represented in the fiction) the fictional work that includes the prefatory materials as part of the story. The publisher becomes an intrahomodiegetic character: he speaks, from inside the fiction, to an audience also inside the fiction, who are reading a different novel from the one addressed to the general narratee; the novel they read does not include the prefatory note by the publisher. For them the publisher is not undertaking to write part of a narrative, but a genuine preface to the narrative consisting of the editor's note and the letters.

To read *Les liaisons dangereuses* in this last way is to take the thorniest possible path, but limit cases such as this are the surest way to discover the limitations of a theory. The theory of narrative proposed by Franz Stanzel, for example, has been shown by Dorrit Cohn to fail to account for texts that purport to be edited or compiled in this manner. She argues that "diegetic outsiders of this type have no legitimate place in Stanzel's uni-diegetic typology.... Editors and frame-narrators ... narrate from a level twice-removed from the diegesis, before they yield the narration to extra- or intradiegetic narrators. Their indirect presentation of the diegesis therefore cannot be placed on a continuum with direct narratorial mediation of any kind" (165–66). Stanzel responds, quite rightly, by pointing out that "many of these frame-narrators and editors present themselves as contemporaries of the characters whose story they are narrating in that they allege to have heard about the event or have received the manuscript from precisely these characters." The reading of *Les liaisons dangereuses* that assigns the publisher's role strictly to the historical author and makes the editor the general narrator would create this situation, and Stanzel's system can indeed account for this case. The two readings offered above that include the publisher's note in the fiction, however, can not be described with Stanzel's model, as he goes on to admit: "Editors and frame-narrators, on the other hand, who have no personal contact with the characters of their stories cannot be placed" anywhere within his model (269 n. 39).

Genette's theory can describe one of the two readings that include the publisher's remarks in the fiction, that in which the publisher is unreliable and is himself the general narrator. But the scenario that posits a reliable publisher creates some difficulty. Unfortunately, Genette's discussion of this novel appears en passant and does not make his analysis entirely clear:

> Mais toute narration extradiégétique n'est pas nécessairement assumée comme oeuvre littéraire et son protagoniste un narrateur-auteur en position de s'adresser . . . à un publique qualifié c o mme tel. Un roman en forme de journal intime . . . ne vise en principe aucun public, sinon aucun lecteur, et il en va de même du roman par lettres, qu'il comporte un seul épistolier, c o mme *Pamela, Werther* ou *Obermann*, . . . ou plusieurs, c o mme *la Nouvelle Heloïse* ou *les Liaisons dangereuses*: . . . Richardson, Goethe, Senancour, Rousseau ou Laclos se présentent ici c o mme simples "éditeurs," mais les auteurs fictifs de ces journaux intimes ou de ces "lettres recueilliés et publiées par . . ." ne se considérent évidemment pas . . . comme des "auteurs." (*Figures III* 240)

> But not every extradiegetic narrating is necessarily taken up as a literary work with its protagonist an author-narrator in a position to address himself . . . to a public termed such. A novel in the form of a diary . . . does not in principle aim at any public or any reader, and it is the same with an epistolary novel, whether it include a single letter writer (like *Pamela, Werther*, or *Obermann* . . .) or several (like *La Nouvelle Héloïse* or *Les Liaisons Dangereuses*). . . . Richardson, Goethe, Senancour, Rousseau, and Laclos present themselves here simply as "editors," but the fictive authors of these diaries or "letters collected and published by . . ." . . . obviously did not look on themselves as "authors." (*Narrative* 230)

Obviously, Genette does not pretend to be offering a rigorous analysis of the narrating of *Les liaisons dangereuses* at this point (nor, for that matter, do I). But the hints he gives may profitably be followed for the clarification they lend to my analysis. He seems to consider the publisher to be the extradiegetic narrator, and assigns him the narrating of the letters. If we assume that he is also assigned the narrating of the editor's remarks (that he is also the editor), then this reading would follow the first of my readings that include the publisher as a narrator. But if the publisher is reliable (if he is not the editor), a complication arises. The publisher and the editor are both extradiegetic narrators, narrating at the same level to the same narratee. Genette's model does not allow for this possibility. Each of these two extradiegetic narrators recounts a narrative that takes place at the same diegetic level, a *récit premier*, or first narrative: "l'instance narrative d'un récit premier est donc par definition extradiégétique" (*Figures III* 239; "The narrating instance of a first narrative is therefore extradiegetic by definition" [*Narrative* 229]). Because of their narrative level, neither of these could logically be inserted within the other as a récit second: "l'instance narrative d'un récit second (métadiégétique) est par definition diégétique" (*Figures III* 239; "the narrating instance of a second [metadiegetic] narrative is diegetic by definition" [*Narrative* 229]). There are thus two *récits premiers* in the novel. But the situation I have postulated here is that the entire text forms one narrative whole, one *récit premier*, which includes both prefatory sections. The same problem arises in considering *Les liaisons dangereuses* under the model of the "inserted text" proposed by Lanser (*Narrative* 134). Her analysis of the novel's structure ignores the role of the publisher entirely, conflating him with the editor and making no allowance for a text with two introductory sections at the same narrative level (135–36). Thus neither Genette nor Lanser can account for both the publisher and the editor.

This paradox can be resolved by recourse to the concept of the general narrator who is responsible for the narrating of the complete work, though it nowhere speaks in its own voice. It is not necessary, however, to reject Genette's model as a result of this analysis. Indeed, Genette has foreseen the possibility that the extradiegetic narrator of a text may be entirely effaced, although he did not consider that *Les liaisons dangereuses* exemplifies this situation. His remarks about *La chute*, another novel in which the extradiegetic level is present only implicitly, may be applied here:

> ... un narrateur ne peut être perçu comme intradiégétique que s'il est posé comme tel par un récit où il figure .... Mais il est vrai que ce récit-cadre peut fort bien, au moins en littérature moderne, être soumis à une ellipse complète: c'est par exemple le cas de *la Chute*, où le monologue de Clamence en présence de son auditeur muet ne peut être qu'implicitement "enchâssé" dans un récit-cadre sous-entendu, mais clairement impliqué par tous ceux des énoncés de ce monologue qui se rapportent, non à l'histoire qu'il raconte, mais aux circonstances de cette narration. Faute de recours à cet enchâssement implicite, *la Chute* échapperait au mode narratif .... (*Nouveau* 59)

> A narrator can be perceived as intradiegetic only if he is presented as such by a narrative in which he appears .... But it is true that that frame narrative, at least in modern literature, can very well be resolved into a complete ellipsis. An example is *La Chute*, where Clamence's monologue in the presence of his silent listener can be "embedded" only implicitly in a frame narrative that is understood — that is clearly implied by all the statements in the monologue that relate not to the story it tells but to the circumstances of the narrating. Without its recourse to this implicit embedding, *La Chute* would escape the narrative mode .... (*Revisited* 89)

Genette's dismissal of the narrative complexity of premodern literature, although uncharacteristic for him, is common among theorists, and has often led to similar assumptions. *Les liaisons dangereuses* is, after all, an eighteenth century novel. To adapt Genette's model to the line of analysis that posits an effaced general narrator, the narrative levels must simply be shifted one degree. The general narrator is the extraheterodiegetic narrator of the *récit premier*; the publisher and the editor are thus intrahomodiegetic (homodiegetic because they play roles in the fictional account of the novel's production) narrators of separate *récits seconds*; the writer of a letter is the metadiegetic narrator of a *récit troisième* (to extend Genette's terminology) that is embedded in the editor's narrative act.

We have seen that the "Avertissement" in *Les liaisons dangereuses* can be read as the work of the historical author alone, considering it to be external to the narrative proper and thus not narrated (nor intended to contribute to the meaning of the narrative by the implied author). A few other textual elements may be considered in the same light, and the definition of what the general narrator does may be clarified by a brief consideration of what it does not do. Hazard Adams has pointed out that titles are not always narrated, especially if the general narrator does not present itself as the author or editor of the narrative: "The reason that the titles in Cary's trilogies loom so large is that the novels are all narrated by characters in the trilogies, and there is no other narrator or authoritive voice" (17). Such titles are to be attributed only to the historical and implied authors and not to the narrator. It can also be the case that the narrator presents itself as the author of the text it is narrating and does know the title; in this case the title itself is narrated. The same considerations may apply to epigraphs, chapter numbers and divisions, and explanatory footnotes.

Book dedication provides an interesting marginal case. The presumption is usually that here the historical author alone speaks. As Goffman explains,

> here there is a sense in which the writer exploits the authorial channel to convey — nay, to broadcast — a personal message in a voice different from the one he will immediately take up [as narrator]. A Durkheimian twist. As if the self-demanding labor of doing the book gave the writer the privilege and obligation to show that he has a separate, private life and is committed to it, while at the same time those who make up his life have a right to be so recognized. (298 n. 68)

Though this is the unmarked case, Genette supplies an example of a dedication which, while of course written by the historical authors, can apply literally only to the implied author and narrator: "les deux auteurs réels, Marie et Frédéric Petitjean de la Rosière, poussaient la dissimulation d'identité jusqu'à dédier leur premier livre (*Une femme supérieure*, 1907) 'à *mes* chers parents,' ce qui introduit la fiction pseudonymique la où en principe elle n'a point place" (*Nouveau* 102 n. 2; "the two real authors . . . carried the dissimulation of their identity so far as to dedicate their first book . . . 'to *my* dear parents,' which injects the pseudonymous fiction where, in principle, it does not belong" [*Revisited* 147 n. 21]).

A different type of textual component may also be at least partially excepted from the provenance of the narrator: the appearance in a text of factual errors or inconsistencies.[15] When Jules Verne has his Professor Aronnax explain that, for a floating block of ice, "la partie immergée de cette banquise est à la partie émergeante comme quatre est à un" (171; "the submerged part of this ice field is to the exposed part as four is to one"), the narrator is responsible for making the statement but not necessarily for making the error in physics. As Barbara Herrnstein Smith observes, we realize in such cases "that we are confronted by art, not nature, so that we are never really deluded by the fictive construction and thus receive no *false* information from it" (*Margins* 13). This is not quite the same as saying, with Sir Philip Sidney, that "for the poet, he nothing affirms" (168); it is the narrator who speaks in the Verne example, not the poet, and he does indeed affirm. But in the diegetic world his statement is true, even though false in the real world. The point that the narrator is not necessarily wrong has its corollary in the point that the narratee who is deluded by the fictive construction here also receives no false information; indeed, Captain Nemo authoritatively confirms that the narrator's statement is relatively accurate within the terms of that diegetic universe: "A peu près, monsieur le professeur. Pour un pied que les icebergs ont au-dessus de la mer, ils en ont trois au-dessous" (171; "Very nearly, Professor. For one foot of iceberg above the sea there are three below it").

Lubomír Dolozel has analyzed this interesting problem:

> Once the narrative world is at least partly constructed, are not the narrator's sentences subject to truth-valuation as well? Not necessarily if logical consistency is made a necessary prerequisite of the narrator's authentication authority. Contradictions in facts are explained as the *author's* errors. The case of the narrative technique which tol-

> erates, or even requires, contradictions falls outside the binary model
> and will be considered later. (14 n. 10)

His last sentence suggests the way in which we should interpret
his use of the term "author": the errors belong solely to the historical author, the writer, unless they are read as part of the implied
author's meaning, intended to be ascribed to the narrator. Patrick
McCarthy has argued, for example, that the numerous factual errors found in the mathematical descriptions in the "Ithaca" section of Joyce's *Ulysses* are part of the implied (and, in his opinion,
historical) author's meaning, undercutting the unreliable narrator's
attempts to "reduce the characters to purely rational terms"
(613). It may even be the case that a historical author's error can
become part of the implied author's meaning, as in the accidental
substitution of "soiled fish of the sea" for Herman Melville's intended "coiled fish of the sea," the result of a misprint in Consta-
ble's edition of *White-Jacket* (Nichol 338–39). F. O. Matthiessen,
unaware that he was relying on a corrupt version, produced a
reading that suggests that the implied author of the misprinted
edition created the superior version: "hardly anyone but Melville
could have created the shudder that results from calling this
frightening vagueness some '*soiled* fish of the sea.' The *discordia
concors*, the unexpected linking of the medium of cleanliness with
filth, could only have sprung from an imagination that had appre-
hended the terrors of the deep, of the immaterial deep as well as
the physical" (392).

One curious example remains to be considered under the
topic of the narrator. In Augustin Gomez-Arcos' *L'agneau carnivore*, one of the characters, who has spoken only French in this
text written entirely in French, receives a letter written in French
she is able to read only by good fortune: "Heureusement que j'ai
appris un peu de français dans mon enfance" (241; "Fortunately I
had learned a little French in my childhood"). The implicit convention here is that all of the French in the text, except for this letter, represents Spanish. The novel is indeed set in Spain and written by a Spanish author, but is not a translation; Gomez-Arcos,

forced to leave Franco's Spain for political reasons, lives in France and writes only in French. Is the narrator narrating in French? Evidently. But the dialogues it narrates must be in Spanish; most of the characters do not know French. We must postulate here a narrator engaging in simultaneous translation as it narrates. This example would fit somewhere between "explicit attribution" and "homogenizing convention" on Meir Sternberg's spectrum of intratextual translation possibilities ("Polylingualism" 232). We are never directly told that the French of the text represents Spanish, as in explicit attribution, but neither is this substitution entirely unremarked. Adding a category to Sternberg's model would be necessary to account for this case: we may as well label it "implicit attribution."[16]

Having sketched out the borderlines separating the historical author and reader, implied author and reader, and general narrator and narratee, a logical next step might be to continue the movement toward the interior of the narrative text by considering those narrators whose discourses are embedded within that of the general narrator. But the path leading to that discussion leads first through an analysis of the durable problem of point of view in narrative and then to a definition of narrative itself.

3

FOCALIZATION

As Gérard Genette has remarked, "l'étude des focalisations a fait couler beaucoup d'encre, et sans doute un peu trop" (*Nouveau* 44; "My study of focalizations has caused much ink to flow — no doubt, a little too much" [*Revisited* 65]). Comprehensive treatments of the concept have been undertaken by Genette himself (1972, 1983), Mieke Bal (1977, 1981), Shlomith Rimmon-Kenan (1983), Raquel Gutiérrez (1986), Seymour Chatman (1986), and Patrick O'Neill (1994). The work of Bal and Genette in particular has also led to several more specifically focused articles that propose theoretical refinements (Bronzwaer, 1981; Vitoux, 1982; Jost, 1983; Briosi, 1986; Edmiston, 1989; Ronen, 1990) or apply the theory to specific texts (Erickson, 1985; Viswanathan, 1985; Aronne-Amestoy, 1986; Ifri, 1987; Flint, 1993). Given the number and the distinction of these writers, it would be presumptuous to spill yet more ink on the subject without good reason. But it seems to me that most of these critics have misanalyzed certain key aspects of Genette's original conception of focalization and that as a result their discussions are based on, and sometimes compromised by, a set of false premises about it. Obviously, such general misreading can only be the result of a degree of ambiguity or inconsistency, of "miswriting," in Genette's own presentation, and I can not guarantee my own reading immunity from this contagion. However, the concept is important enough for the analysis of narrative that even an improved misreading may be useful.

The concept stems from Genette's interest in separating two elements of what used to be called point of view: the difference, as he put it, "entre la question *qui voit?* et la question *qui parle?"* (*Figures III* 203; "between . . . the question *who sees?* and the question *who speaks?"* [*Narrative* 186]).[1] His interest was in describing two aspects of narrating, not two agents, but his implicit postulation of an agent who sees, together with the unfortunate choice of a visual metaphor, has been the source of most of the misspilled ink. Seymour Chatman has summarized the sort of critical confusion that Genette's metaphor has caused for even the most meticulous readers:

> Genette has always seemed to mean more by *focalisation* than the mere power of sight. He obviously refers to the whole spectrum of perception: hearing, tasting, smelling, and so on. What is not so clear is the extent to which he means it to refer to other mental activity, like cognition, and to functions other than mental. For Rimmon-Kenan, the term's "purely visual sense has to be broadened to include cognitive, emotive and ideological orientation" (1983: 71). Neither Genette nor Bal, to my knowledge, have accepted that extension. ("Characters" 192)

Chatman goes on to emphasize that "in Genette's theory and in Bal's and Rimmon-Kenan's modification of it there is an insistence that *somebody* always 'sees' the story" (193).

While he is certainly correct in remarking Bal's insistence on the visual nature of focalization, a point to which I will return, it would be a mistake to attribute any such emphasis to Genette. His first uses of the term, in the "'Stendhal'" essay in *Figures II* (185, 191), do not suggest any very specific meaning, but the detailed discussion of focalization in the "Discours du récit" makes it clear that the concept is tied to the sense of sight only metaphorically (*Figures III* 203–24; *Narrative* 185–210). Genette has since recognized that the metaphor of seeing was a poor choice: "Je ne reviens pas sur la distinction . . . entre les deux questions 'Qui voit?' (question de mode) et 'Qui parle?' (question de voix) — si ce n'est pour regretter une formulation purement visuelle, et donc trop étroit" (*Nouveau* 43; "My only regret is that I used a purely visual, and hence overly narrow, formulation" [*Revisited* 64]). Focalization literally addresses matters of cognition alone, one of the applications that Chatman would deny Genette's model. The only question to be addressed in the determination of focalization is how much the narrator tells the narratee about the story in relation to the characters' knowledge about the story. Three logical possibilities exist for this relation between the narrator's report and the characters' knowledge: in the first case,

> *Narrateur > Personnage* (où le narrateur en sait plus que le personnage, ou plus précisément en dit plus que n'en sait aucun des personnages); dans le second, *Narrateur = Personnage* (le narrateur ne dit que ce que sait tel personnage) . . . ; dans le troisième, *Narrateur < Personnage* (le narrateur en dit moins que n'en sait le personnage). (*Figures III* 206)

> *Narrator > Character* (where the narrator knows more than the character, or more exactly *says* more than any of the characters knows. In the second [case], *Narrator = Character* (the narrator says only what a given character knows) . . . . In the third [case], *Narrator < Character* (the narrator says less than the character knows) . . . . (*Narrative* 189; translation modified)

Genette's major addition to this summary has been to create a terminology for the three situations: "Nous rebaptiserons donc le premier type . . . récit *non-focalisé*, ou à *focalisation zéro*. Le second sera le récit à *focalisation interne* . . . . Notre troisième type sera le récit à *focalisation externe*" (*Figures III* 206–07; "So we will rechristen the first type . . . as *nonfocalized* narrative, or narrative with *zero focalization*. The second type will be narrative with *internal focalization* . . . . Our third type will be the narrative with *external focalization*" [*Narrative* 189–90]).

So far, so good. The three categories of focalization are roughly (though only roughly) coordinate with the traditional categories of omniscient, selective omniscient, and objective narration. The question is exclusively one of the relation between narrator, character, and narratee: does the narrator provide the narratee with information unknown to any of the characters, or only what is known by the characters, or does the narrator refrain from, or present itself as incapable of, all mind reading? There is no necessary visual component: the character in question could be blind, as in this example of nonfocalized narrative (the narrator tells more than the character knows) in D. H. Lawrence's "The Blind Man": "He did not know that the lamps on the upper corridor were unlighted" (355). In fact, as the following passage from *Ulysses* indicates, it makes no difference even if the character shifts back and forth from seeing to unseeing: "Shut your eyes and see. Stephen closed his eyes to hear his boots crush crackling wrack and shells. You are walking through it howsomever. I am, a stride at a time" (31). This passage is in internal focalization, and certainly there is no shift of focalization when Stephen closes his eyes (although the movement between what Dorrit Cohn has termed "quoted monologue" and "psycho-narration" does suggest that different degrees of internal focalization might be distinguished here). Further, there is no place for any agent called the focalizer who would be different from the narrator or the character. The only other agents we might invoke here would be the author and perhaps the writer, as the agents responsible for the decision to create a certain type of narrator and narrating situation. Despite his occasional lapses into the visual metaphor, Genette has consistently maintained this analysis:

> . . . ce n'était jamais qu'une reformulation, dont le principal avantage était de rapprocher et de mettre en système des notions classiques telles que "récit à narrateur omniscient" ou "vision par-derrière" (focalisation zéro), "récit à point de vue, à réflecteur, à omniscience sélective, à restriction de champ," "vision avec" (focalisation interne), ou "technique objective, behaviouriste," "vision du dehors" (focalisation externe). (*Nouveau* 44)

It was never anything but a reformulation, whose main advantage was to draw together and systematize such standard ideas as "narrative with an omniscient narrator" or "vision from behind" (zero focalization); "narrative with point of view, reflector, selective omniscience, restriction of field" or "vision with" (internal focalization); or "objective, behaviorist technique" or "vision from without" (external focalization). (*Revisited* 65-66)

It must be allowed that certain of Genette's remarks on this point, as with his use of the visual metaphor, seem inconsistent and have contributed materially to misunderstandings of his theory. In fact, he has occasionally used terms that I would argue have no place in his model. For example, his stipulations that "*focalisé* ne peut s'appliquer qu'au récit lui-même, et *focalisateur*, s'il s'appliquait à quelqu'un, ce ne pourrait être qu'à celui qui *focalise le récit*, c'est à dire le narrateur" (*Nouveau* 48; "*focalized* can be applied only to the narrative itself, and if *focalizer* applied to anyone, it could only be the person who *focalizes the narrative* — that is, the narrator" [*Revisited* 73]) must, I would suggest, be understood as an inauspicious resort to a purely hypothetical concessive argument. His model would be best understood by reading him here as meaning "if there were such things as the focalized or the focalizer (but there are certainly not), even then they would not be new categories requiring any new agents, but simply ways of (loosely) thinking about the narrative or the narrator." Focalization is a *relation* between the narrator's report and the characters' thoughts. The narrator either has no access to them, has (and is limited to) access to them, or has (but is not limited to) access to them. It is crucial to imagine this relation without resorting to the postulation of a "relator" and "relatee," which are not, after all, logically inevitable categories.

Taking this summary, then, to be an accurate representation (or viable interpretation) of Genette's original model, I would advocate a series of modifications aimed at clarifying several of these terms and functions. While I agree entirely that we need no new labels or agents here for the role of the narrator, Genette's position that "il n'y a pas de personnage focalisant ou focalisé"

(*Nouveau* 48; "there is no focalizing or focalized character" [*Revisited* 73]), while theoretically consistent, will invite further misreading unless modified. I think that critics have been led into applying these labels to characters simply because there is no specific term for the character involved in any given relationship of focalization (surely not "focalizee"?). Chatman has proposed the use of the term "filter" to designate this character: "The narrator can elect to tell a part or the whole of a story neutrally or 'from' or 'through' one or another character's consciousness. This function should I think be called 'filter.' A character who serves as a filter may be central (the protagonist) or not (the 'witness')" ("Characters" 196).

Claude-Edmonde Magny, here as elsewhere seemingly a generation ahead of other theorists, was in 1948 already speaking of the events of a narrative as being "filtered" (63), and of the narrative as passing through a "filter" (64). Chatman chose this term entirely independently, of course, but the coincidence underscores the aptness of the coinage. The word "filter" is especially attractive here because of its relative freedom from visual connotations and the confusions that have so persistently accompanied such connotations. Gene Moore suggests that the Magny/Chatman coinage "filter" might profitably be extended to provide a series of convenient substitutes, with the added advantage that "filterer," the obvious analogy to the misleading "focalizer," is awkward to say in English and perhaps less likely to draw in unwary critics. Chatman has argued persuasively that "focalization" has come to be such a problematic term that it should be abandoned entirely. While I continue to employ "focalization" in the following discussion, reflecting the consensus under the status quo, I do see compelling advantages to the Magny/Chatman/Moore terminology, and would readily agree to replace "focalization" and "focalized" with "filtration" and "filtered."

Chatman has also pointed out the "uneasy dissymmetry" posed by the terms "zero focalization" and "non-focalization." As he sensibly remarks, "the opposite of 'non-focalized' would seem to be 'focalized'" ("Characters" 201), and the use of a quantity, "zero," seems to imply the confusing notion that one somehow has a lesser amount of focalization in this case. I will follow Susan Lanser's lead here in suggesting that "zero focalization" be renamed "free focalization."[2] This avoids the misleading implications of absence and quantity carried by Genette's coinage and has, for me at least, the more appropriate connotations of an extended range of narratorial options, of a narrator not tied to or limited by the knowledge of characters. I would also specify here what seems to be implicit in Genette, that free focalization is not merely another label for omniscient narration. The narrator says more than the characters know, but is by no means necessarily all-knowing. This stipulation will prove crucial for the analysis of focalization in homodiegetic narratives.

An important modification of Genette's theory is called for by the relatively common example of the relation by homodiegetic narrators of what they experienced and thought and the concomitant limitation of such narrators, under the conventions of realistic fiction, to what they could plausibly know. This constituted something of a gray area in Genette's original formulation of his model, which never specifically analyzed focalization in terms of the differences between homodiegetic and heterodiegetic narrating. He has since corrected this lacuna and proposed the useful term *prefocalization* to designate this automatic limitation of the homodiegetic narrator (*Nouveau* 52; *Revisited* 78). William Edmiston has presented a thorough analysis of this problem, arriving at a version of the theory which not only eliminates the category of external focalization in heterodiegetic narratives but also eliminates free focalization (except as a case of infraction) in homodiegetic narratives. The former argument depends, however, on controversial redefinitions of "internal" and "external," and is therefore not really a discussion of Genette's original model, while the latter rests on an incautious identification of zero (or free) focalization with omniscience. Edmiston's analysis is based on his claim that free focalization "means that the narrator is unlimited spatially

and unrestricted in his psychological access to the characters." If
this were valid, of course, one would have to agree that (at least in
realistic fiction) no homodiegetic narrator "can be omniscient or
omnipresent" (730). But Edmiston then acknowledges that "the
[homodiegetic] narrator knows more than the character [although]
his knowledge is not boundless" (731), and this relation is all that
is called for in free focalization. The narrator need only *say* more
than the character knows, a stipulation entirely within the scope
of homodiegetic narrators and, as I will argue, within the scope of
autodiegetic narrators as well.

A suggestion for further refinement to the theory at this point
would be to retain the original tripartite division of focalization
and to distinguish three parallel subcategories of prefocalization.
The distinction between the narrating self and the experiencing self
in these cases has been often noted but seldom analyzed in depth.
I can not pretend to definitively sort out that difficult problem
here, but one step toward a more rigorous approach to it might be
to consider it in terms of focalization. Does the narrating self tell
more than, the same amount as, or less than the experiencing self
knew? In other words, one could apply Genette's master formula,
in a somewhat different manner, to this subcategory, arriving at
divisions which might be called, but for the risk of confusion, free,
internal, and external prefocalization. The classic example of the
first type is of course *David Copperfield*, in which the adult narrator often emphasizes that his present knowledge exceeds that of
the child filter: "my later understanding comes, I am sensible, to
my aid here" (18). The second type may be exemplified by the
epistolary novel in those cases when the letter is being written
(virtually) simultaneously with the thoughts occurring in the
writer's mind, with little opportunity for hindsight, as in Fanny
Burney's *Evelina*: "This house seems to be the house of joy; every
face wears a smile, and a laugh is at every body's service" (23).
The third type would accommodate works like · Dashiell
Hammett's *Red Harvest*, in which the anonymous homodiegetic
narrator consistently refrains from telling us what he knew, merely

reporting his actions much in the manner of a heterodiegetic narrator in a narrative with external focalization: "I let her [and the historical reader and narratee as well, I would add] get whatever she could out of a grin" (4).

The second of these cases, which I find myself provisionally designating internal prefocalization, suggests a response to one of Chatman's objections to the theory of focalization. He proposes that

> The use of "focalization" or any other single term to refer to the quite different functions performed by characters and by narrators violates the distinction between story and discourse. . . . A character can literally see (perceive, conceive, etc.) . . . . A narrator can only "see" it imaginatively, or in memory if he/she is homodiegetic, that is, participated in the events of the story "back then" when they occurred. ("Characters" 194)

My example of the epistolary novel may be inadequate to answer this objection — I would argue that such a novel might be most usefully thought of as being narrated in its entirety by an undramatized general narrator whose narrative act includes all of the individual narrations presented in letter form — but in many of Samuel Beckett's novels this complication would not arise. "For it is evening, even night, one of the darkest I can remember, I have a short memory. My little finger glides before my pencil across the page and gives warning, falling over the edge, that the end of the line is near" (*Malone* 32). The distinction between the character and narrator here would have to be a very subtle (or arbitrary) one and may serve little purpose. The narrator's seeing and conceiving seem to be identical with the character's, and there is surely no "back then" involved. Any argument that these agents are separate seems to flout the text's claims. Indeed, the character's main activity seems to be, precisely, the narrating of the story.

Such refinements can help us in characterizing certain general types of narrating and also in the close analysis of particular local narrative effects, but no level of refinement is likely to help us adapt the model for a thoroughly rigorous analysis or classification of entire narratives. In fact it is difficult to find entirely pure examples of any of the three types of focalization. Genette has explicitly recognized this in regard to the category of zero (free) focalization: "La formule juste serait donc plutôt: *focalisation zéro = focalisation variable, et parfois zéro.* Ici comme ailleurs, le choix est purement opératoire" (*Nouveau* 49; "Instead, therefore, the right formula would be: *zero focalization = variable, and sometimes zero, focalization.* Here as elsewhere, the choice is purely operational" [*Revisited* 73–74]).

This disclaimer is presumably meant to be applied to the other two categories as well, and it is probably the case that almost every narrative could be read as an example of variable focalization. It is difficult to find internally focalized narratives in which nothing at all is narrated that would not be perceptible to some observer other than the filter, and hence arguably the product of external focalization at those points, and equally difficult to find pure examples of external focalization maintained throughout entire narratives. As Sandro Briosi has argued, "Entre la focalisation interne et la focalisation externe il n'y a pas de changement de niveau, mais plutôt un passage, toujours graduel et jamais discret, de l'une à l'autre manière de la vision de l'auteur" (514; "Between internal and external focalization there is not a shift of level, but rather a crossing, always gradual and never unobtrusive, from one mode to another of the author's vision"). I will offer here what strike me as relatively clear examples of each; while conceding in advance that other readers might find grounds for disagreement, I hope that the principles are clear enough that each reader can provide his or her own more appropriate examples where necessary.

Pure internal focalization could be obtained in the narrative of a dream, provided that there are no framing passages that could be interpreted as the result of zero or external focalization. Every element of the dream would thus be imperceptible to anyone but the dreamer and therefore filtered strictly through him or her; the narrator would tell us only what the dreamer, and no one else, thinks and perceives. In practice, such narratives are rare, but John Barth's "Night-Sea Journey" specifically offers this as one possible reading: "Is the journey my invention? Do the night, the sea, exist at all, I ask myself, apart from my experience of them? Do I myself exist, or is this a dream?" (*Lost* 3). The purely externally focalized narrative is also hard to find. The canonical example, Hemingway's "The Killers," contains some diction that seems to partake of internal focalization and at least one sentence that would be hard to justify other than as a "lapse" into internal focalization: "Nick stood up. He had never had a towel in his mouth before" (*Complete* 220). One alternative would be to posit an external focalization that assumes the narrator's otherwise unacknowledged objective observation of every instant of Nick's prior existence. Such a narrator could indeed provide the observation, without access to Nick's thought, that he had never had a towel in his mouth before. But such a line of argument, although possible, seems rather overwrought in this context. Lanser offers two other sentences for which even such tortuous reasoning would seem to fail: "It sounded silly when he said it," which must represent Nick's immediate mental response to his own previous remark, and instance of internal focalization entirely unavailable to an objective observer, and "He was trying to swagger it off," which evidently represents a level of analysis unavailable to Nick himself, and hence the product of the narrator's free focalization.[3]

A better example of strict external focalization would be another Hemingway story, "Hills like White Elephants" (though again some might consider phrases like "she saw the river through the trees" [213] as marking internal focalization), and Dashiell Hammett's *The Glass Key* is a remarkable example of this technique extended for the length of a novel. Claude-Edmonde Magny discussed this technique in Hammett's work most perceptively, and noted that its use carries certain drawbacks: "this simplicity is occasionally obtained only at the expense of clarity. The very rigor with which Hammett limits himself to a behaviorist psychol-

ogy leads him to complicate his narration and forces him into
strange circumlocutions" (41). Her analysis provides, I think, the
most plausible explanation of lapses in point of view such as that
in "The Killers": the stylistic detours required to eliminate the narratological inconsistencies may seem too high a price to pay to
many writers, and an elaborate explanation of the external signs
by which one could deduce that Nick's experience was a novel one
would have disrupted Hemingway's narrative. For a range of reasons, then, and conceding the occasional rigorously executed *tour
de force*, it is best to consider that focalization is always variable
over the course of a narrative and that classification as one of Genette's three types is to be viewed as denoting that focalization
which is predominant.

The most thoroughgoing and influential revision of Genette's
model has been that proposed by Bal, which ultimately adds little
to the study of focalization as I have defined it but implies a good
deal for other areas of analysis. The literalization of the visual
metaphor and the proliferation of indistinct terminology have been
particularly troublesome in Bal's applications of her theory, which
always specifically posit someone who sees, quite literally, the
events narrated. She does not, however, limit the concept to the
sense of sight. For Bal focalization means point of view in the
broadest imaginable interpretation. Every event, state, or description in a text that could possibly be thought of as being perceived
in any way is considered to be the product of a focalization. The
range of perceptions is not limited to those available to human
beings, but includes mind reading and predicting future events
and, in short, everything that might appear in any text. Any perceived entity is a *focalisé*, "focalized," and may be either perceptible or imperceptible to a hypothetical spectator (*Narratologie* 38;
"Narrating" 250). These entities are focalized by a *focalisateur*,
"focalizer," to a *focalisataire*, "spectator" (*Narratologie* 40;
"Narrating" 245). These are agents occupying a theoretical middle ground between the narrator and the actor, or character. As
Bal outlines these three levels,

l'acteur, utilisant l'action comme matériau, en fait l'histoire; le focalisateur, qui sélectionne les actions et choisit l'angle sous lequel il les
présente, en fait le récit, tandis que le narrateur met le récit en parole: il
en fait le texte narratif. Théoriquement, chaque instance s'adresse à un
destinataire situé sur le même plan: l'acteur s'adresse à un autre acteur,
le focalisateur à un "spectateur," l'objet indirect de la focalisation, et
le narrateur s'adresse à un lecteur hypothétique. (*Narratologie* 32–33)

the actor, using the acting as his material, creates the story; the focalizer, who selects the actions and chooses the angle from which to present them, with those actions creates the narrative; while the narrator
puts the narrative into words: with the narrative he creates the narrative text. Theoretically, each agent addresses a receiver located on the
same plane: the actor addresses another actor, the focalizer addresses
a "spectator" — the indirect object of the focalizing — and the narrator addresses a hypothetical reader. ("Narrating" 244–45)

The most fundamental problem caused by the role of the focalizer in this paradigm would result from the assigning of the *selection* of events and techniques, and the *presentation* of events by
means of techniques, to the same agent. In more traditional narra-
tologies, the events of the narrative are selected or invented by the
implied author and presented by the narrator: no third agent is
required as an intermediary and there are no shared or overlapping functions. Bal's three levels are not parallel, but intersect in
confusing ways. It is not clear how the character uses actions to
make the story or how this would relate to the focalizer's act of
selecting actions to make the narrative. The characters themselves
are selected just as surely as their actions, and have no independent or prior existence to this act of selection. The narrator itself is
also selected, just as the characters and actions are, and constructed by the same verbal means. Nor is it clear how the focalizer "presents" anything; the words on the page are presented by
the narrator, and everything else is inferred from that single
(fictive) act of presentation.

Bal has remarked that the functions of her focalizer seem to
intersect with those of the implied author, and has suggested that
the concept of the implied author may as a result be unnecessary:
"Tout ce qu'on a traditionnellement considéré comme *intrusions*

d'auteur, les traces du *implied author*, peut être analysé en traces du narrateur et traces du focalisateur" (*Narratologie* 38; "Everything that has traditionally been looked on as author's intrusions, the traces of the implied author, can be analyzed as traces of the narrator and of the focalizer" ["Narrating" 250]). The example is, however, not really to the point. "Authorial intrusions" are always made by the narrator, of course, the only agent who speaks (these intrusions are always verbal), never by the implied author, who, as the label suggests, is only implicit in the narrative. The implied author is not the agent charged with speaking (or intruding), but rather the agent charged with meaning, especially when the real meaning of a text is perceived to lie outside the dramatized narrator's intentions (or intrusions), as in the case of an unreliable narrator.

But leaving aside more specific objections to this analysis, the general point to be made is that there is no advantage to eliminating the implied author in order to give its functions to the newly created focalizer.[4] Bal's objections to the implied author model, that it "is not a hypothesis but an axiom" and that it is often confused with the narrator, do not seem persuasive ("Laughing" 208–9). The confusion is not an inherent or even especially complex problem (most often merely the result of carelessness, as in Bal's own misuse of the term remarked above) and in any event is hardly as confusing as the focalizer model. And whether we call our concepts axioms or hypotheses is immaterial (the *OED* defines both as "propositions"): all of these categories, including the most fundamental of all, the narrator, could be labeled axioms.[5] The object is to ground the theory on the most strategically viable premises, not to somehow arrive at objectively verifiable transcendent truths about narrative. The functions of the focalizer are already carried out by the implied author and the narrator, and it makes more sense to refine existing categories about which there has been a long history of discussion and potential for broad agreement than to create a new category to assume those same functions.

Perhaps the best way to illustrate the theoretical redundancy of this agent who focalizes is to give a specific example of the application of the model to a text. Take the following sentence from Colette's *La chatte*: "Elle le regarda boire et se troubla brusquement à cause de la bouche qui pressait les bords du verre" (9; "She watched him drink and felt a sudden pang of desire at the sight of his mouth pressing against the rim of the glass" ["Cat" 72]). This would seem to be an example of internal focalization: the narrator is able to tell the narratee what goes on in Camille's mind. Bal's analysis is as follows: "Le verbe 'regarda' dans la première phrase dénote un changement de niveau de focalisation. Alain, puis sa bouche, sont l'objet du focalisateur Camille. Alain est focalisé au deuxième degré, par le focalisateur focalisé" (*Narratologie* 41; "The verb 'watched' in the first sentence denotes a change in the level of focalization. Alain, then his mouth, are the object of the focalizer Camille. Alain is focalized in the second degree, by the focalizer who is focalized" ["Narrating" 252]). Pierre Vitoux, following Bal's model, offers a slightly more refined view of this same passage, in which he indicates whether a focalization is attributed to a specific dramatized focalizer or not (*deleguée* or *non deleguée*) and whether it is internal or external. The sentence may thus be expressed in the schematic form, "Fs nd → Fo ext sur Camille (puis) → Fo int sur Camille qui du même coup devient Fs d à partir de Camille sur Alain en Fo ext" (361). The most nearly mathematical formulation of this same sentence would be "Fs nd → Fo ext sur X (puis) → Fo int sur X qui peut prendre la form de Fs d à partir de X en Fo sur Y" (367). A prosier paraphrase of these equations might be something like "a non-dramatized focalizer focalizes externally on Camille, (then) focalizes internally on Camille, who at once becomes a focalizer in turn, focalizing externally on Alain."

Two objections must be offered here, leaving aside the obvious one that this jargon is incomprehensible. After all, if the technique could really demonstrate its value, if the jargon were in fact necessary, we could probably learn to use it. Rather, I would object that these descriptions do not more precisely focus the text but in fact distort it, and that the categories are used inconsistently. Note for example the interesting parenthetical insertion: "puis." This indication that we first see Camille (from an external point of view) and then later see Alain (from Camille's point of view) is a product of Vitoux's application of this methodology, not an element of the text. Or is it to some degree a product of the methodology itself? Bal also provided a "then" when she explained the sentence, asserting that Camille first looks at Alain and then at his mouth, a sequence that is similarly absent from the text. It seems significant that these two readers, although they distort the text by the same means, do not distort it at the same point, a suggestion that even the type of problem generally predictable from this methodology, a predisposition to read the text as if it were a sequence of camera shots in a film, will also lend itself to idiosyncratic variation within that type of problem. I would argue that this tendency to restructure narratives as screenplays is a technique of misreading fostered by this model of focalization.

Further, these focalizations are not consistently parallel. Bal and Vitoux are mixing apples and oranges.[6] The narrator (do we gain anything by calling it a focalizer?) tells us what its filter, Camille, feels, an example of internal focalization, but does not describe her appearance (the focalization is never external) or give the slightest clue that it *sees* anything at all. Camille, on the other hand, tells us nothing at all, not even that she sees anything, for the simple reason that she is not a narrator and has no direct relationship with the narratee. The first focalization is a question of metaphorical point of view, a question of narrating, the second a matter of literal point of view, a question of camera angles, and the failure of this model to distinguish the two constitutes its most serious flaw.

A criticism of this approach worth remarking is one inadvertently provided by Bal herself, when she analyzed the same sentence some years earlier without benefit of a theory of focalization. In 1974 she had written

> Ici on pourrait être tenté de dire que le narrateur s'est identifié à Camille parce qu'il décrit ses sentiments. Pourtant, la distance est assurée avec soin. Le verbe "regarder," à l'encontre de "voir," n'exclut pas la perception par autrui de cette action. "Se troubler" est également un verbe à deux faces: il contient un aspect intérieur, le sentiment éprouvé, et un aspect extérieur, la manifestacion de ce sentiment. (*Complexité* 16)

> Here one might be tempted to say that the narrator identifies with Camille because he describes her feelings. Yet the distance is carefully maintained. The verb "watched," as opposed to "saw," does not rule out the perception by others of this action. "Became flustered" is equally a verb with two sides: it contains an interior aspect, the emotion felt, and an external aspect, the manifestation of that emotion.

The greater flexibility and precision of the earlier reading is evident, as is the extent to which the model of focalization has flattened out and oversimplified the text. While I would still maintain that the passage is in internal focalization with Camille as a filter, Bal makes a good case for seeing it as delicately poised between internal and external focalization: do we really get the thoughts of Camille from a reading of her mind or from a reading of her appearance?[7] My only two reservations would be that, first, we are not given any suggestion that this interpretation has been made on the basis of external perception by some outside character; the text only gives us the information, not the means by which it was obtained, and after all there is no candidate on the scene to fill the role of this Jamesian sensitive observer. Second — and Bal's point about the ambiguity of the verbs is well-taken here — the notion of focalization or point of view is a metaphor: we do not really "see" anything any more than we really "hear" anything or "read" Camille's mind. To press the point, Camille has no thoughts or mind to read: there is no Camille. This is only a text, and the metaphor of point of view must not get in our way by being taken literally.

An even clearer example of the sort of misreading invited by
Bal's theory of focalization, and one which carries consequences
for our consideration of narrative embedding, appears in her
analysis of *Wuthering Heights*, which she relies upon to illustrate
the "complex embedding of multiple focalization" ("Notes" 46).
The passage she examines is "He evidently wished no repetition
of my intrusion" (17). The line is written by Lockwood in his diary and refers to Heathcliff. Bal's analysis is as follows, with NS
indicating narrative situation, N narrator, and F1–3 three levels of
focalization: "Lockwood relates that Lockwood sees ('evidently')
that Heathcliff sees ('wished'): NS — N1F1 [F2 [F3]], or N1F1
= Lockwood writing in his diary, F2 = Lockwood interpreting the
expression on Heathcliff's face, and F3 = Heathcliff wishing inside
himself that Lockwood would not repeat his visit" ("Notes" 46).
A glance at the immediate context seems to call Bal's reading into
question: "I found him very intelligent on the topics we touched;
and, before I went home, I was encouraged so far as to volunteer
another visit to-morrow. He evidently wished no repetition of my
intrusion. I shall go, notwithstanding" (17). The manner in which
Lockwood determines Heathcliff's wishes, as well as the accuracy
of that determination, is simply not given in the text. Heathcliff
may have made some remark, or no remark at all, or allowed an
expression to cross his face, or shown no reaction at all. Any of
these possibilities, or perhaps some other entirely, could have suf-
ficed for Lockwood to draw his inference. What is evident is that
Lockwood lays no claim to having seen anything, that no expression of any kind is attributed to Heathcliff (Bal's F2), and that we
are not given the least access to anything that Heathcliff may wish
inside himself (F3). It may be inferred that Lockwood does see
some type of reaction but it may also be inferred that Lockwood's
own inference is unfounded.

In fact, the supposedly obtuse Lockwood has, only two pages
earlier, explicitly recognized (and warned the reader) that his interpretations of Heathcliff's behavior are suspect: "I know, by in-
stinct, his reserve springs from an aversion to showy displays of

feeling — to manifestations of mutual kindliness. He'll love and hate, equally under cover, and esteem it a species of impertinence to be loved or hated again — No, I'm running on too fast — I bestow my own attributes over-liberally on him" (15). The implicit content can only be accurately determined by the implied reader and it may be the case that the correct determination is that this content is left ambiguous by the implied author in order to render Lockwood's reliability suspect. Focalizations 2 and 3 are Bal's imaginative creations, not Brontë's, triggered more by her theoretical bias than by anything in the text. Focalization 1, "Lockwood writing in his diary," is of course simply a narrating circumstance with no component of perceptual focalization attached. As I would describe this scene, the passage exhibits the simplest kind of internal prefocalization (the narrator tells us what he thought), not "complex embedding of multiple focalization." The analyses that Bal develops with her theory usually turn out to be a matter of one reader's idiosyncratic imaginings rather than a strictly textual property. As Genette points out, "A la différence du cinéaste, le romancier n'est pas obligé de mettre sa caméra quelque part: il n'a pas de caméra" (*Nouveau* 49; "Unlike the director of a movie, the novelist is not compelled to put his camera somewhere; he has no camera" [*Revisited* 73]).[8]

But even though Bal's methodology does not prove useful for the analysis of focalization, one can extrapolate at least two other applications for her approach.[9] Not all imaginary visualizations of literary scenes would be idiosyncratic, and the development of a theory for the study of such frequently-shared reader responses might be fruitful. The work of V. A. Kolve on the iconography of medieval narrative, for example, aims at discovering what sorts of conventional visual images might have been triggered for a medieval audience by certain story elements, and one can imagine a wide range of analogous studies of more modern readers' responses. To take an obvious example, there must be a significant proportion of readers, perhaps a majority, who visualize Sam Spade of Dashiell Hammett's *The Maltese Falcon* as Humphrey

Bogart, mentally seeing him under the influence of John Huston's otherwise scrupulously faithful film version even though Bogart does not at all match the description of the "blond satan" "six feet tall" in the book (295, 296). But clearly this is a different approach from Bal's own, and in fact would not be a study of focalization or even of perceptual point of view at all (the literal viewpoint of the characters is not at issue), but rather a study of readers' psychological responses.

The term "iconology" seems to have become accepted as the blanket designation for the study of visual images, and W. J. T. Mitchell has coined the narrower label "iconology of the text," to refer to "such matters as the representation of objects, the description of scenes, the construction of figures, likenesses, and allegorical images, and the shaping of texts into determinate formal patterns. An iconology of the text must also consider the problem of reader response, the claim that some readers visualize and that some texts encourage or discourage mental imaging" (*Picture* 112). It might be objected that narrative theory has already made considerable progress in the matters listed in the first sentence, which sounds like a plan to put old wine in new bottles, but his second suggestion, if applied to the study of culturally-determined visual images shared by large groups of readers rather than studies of individual psychology, seems to offer a useful term ("textual iconology"?) to refer to the study of the visual images created by verbal texts. Such overdetermined images arguably contribute not just to the response of a typical historical reader, but also to that of the implied reader, inviting the analysis of their textual structures and functions.[10]

The second application of Bal's model would develop out of the efforts that have been made to apply focalization to the description of films, usefully summarized by Harris Ross (5–16). Treatments of this problem have thus far resulted in a range of interpretations comparable to that found among literary theorists, some of which have theoretical implications in turn for the study of written narrative. Particularly interesting is François Jost's suggestion that Bal's terminology be changed to prevent just the sort of confusion among the different metaphorical connotations of focalization that Bal invites by having the term designate all possible (and impossible) modes of perception. As Jost remarks, it would make more sense to reserve the term "focalization" for Genette's original purpose, "pour désigner ce qui *sait* un personnage . . . . Pour caractériser la relation entre ce que la caméra montre et ce que le héros est censé voir, je propose de parler d'*ocularisation*" (196; "to designate what a character *knows* . . . . To designate the relation between what the camera shows and what the character is supposed to see, I propose to speak of *ocularization*"). I would suggest that Bal's efforts to determine what characters might see or what angles they would be seen from might be subsumed under the same label. Despite her emphasis on the visual, one can also imagine a study of the places from which noises are generated or heard in a text. Jost again comes to our aid: "ce domaine du 'point de vue' sonore mériterait une étude autonome qu'il me faut remettre à plus tard. Par symétrie avec le concept d'*ocularisation*, je proposerai le terme d'*auricularisation*" (210 n. 10; "the field of aural 'point of view' merits a separate study which I will have to put off until later. For symmetry with the concept of *ocularization*, I would propose the term *auricularization*").

The terms "ocularization" and "auricularization" (or less unwieldy alternative coinages) might prove useful for discussion of those rare cases in which the precise details of a character's physical line of sight or hearing ability are in fact specified in a written text and call for close analysis.[11] Alain Robbe-Grillet's *La jalousie*, for example, frequently presents descriptions closely linked to such details: "La silhouette de A . . . , découpée en lamelles horizontales par la jalousie, derrière la fenêtre de sa chambre, a maintenant disparu" (41; "A . . . 's silhouette, outlined in horizontal strips against the blind of her bedroom window, has now disappeared" [*Jealousy* 55]); "Ensuite son bruit diminue peu à peu, à mesure qu'il s'éloigne vers l'est" (153; "Then the sound

gradually fades away, as the truck drives east" [107]). By extension, it might be supposed, we could coin the parallel terms
"gustativization," "olfactivization," and "tactilivization" to cover
cases centering on details of a character's ability to taste, smell, or
touch. Barring a narratological inquiry into the handful of films in
1959–1960 which "introduced Aromarama and Smell-o-Vision,
systems designed to let theater audiences smell what they saw on
screen" (Cook 532), however, it is difficult to imagine texts that
call for such tools (would Proust's episode of the madeleine constitute an exception here?).[12]

The fundamental difference between the two genres might
make it seem at first that Jost's revisions would be more useful for
analyzing film than literature. For written narrative the speaking
function, narrating by a narrator, is the sine qua non while ocularization, point of view in the literal sense, is usually of negligible
importance. In fact, however, the cinema already has such a
wealth of vocabulary to address such problems that additional
nomenclature in that area seems unnecessary, while fiction does
have a lack of specific terminology for such discussion. Some
writers, especially modernists writing under the influence of the
cinema, made efforts to approximate ocularization in their works,
as suggested by André Gide's note in "The Journal of *The Counterfeiters*": "Admit that a character who is exiting can only be seen
from the rear" (384), and Robbe-Grillet and other New Novelists
often put restrictions on a character's line of sight to impose an
ocularization. But such effects are seldom important elements in
fiction, and authors seldom completely realize their attempts, in
Conrad's phrase, "by the power of the written word . . . to make
you *see*!" (147), a desire which goes back at least to Horace's "ut
pictura poesis" (480). When Robert Pinget has his narrator explicitly "make a decision here . . . to describe lunch as if I were
watching myself" (18), the shift turns out to have little specifically
visual orientation: "So there he is at last, the old fogey. At least
we might have chairs in this alcove" (19). And even in such a
limit case as Alain Robbe-Grillet's *L'Immortelle*, an avowed at-

tempt at a *ciné-roman,* or "cine-novel," a comparison of the scenes described with the photographs accompanying them suggests how very much must be left to the reader's imagination in the most meticulously-described setting. Scene 3, for example, fails to specify that the man is facing left or even to describe his clothing, elements ineluctably specified in the photograph of the scene (*L'Immortelle* 15–16; *Immortal* 12–13). Gide's observation about his own characters that "I do not worry if the lenses of my glasses fail to show them completely 'in focus'; whereas I perceive the least inflections of their voices with the greatest sharpness" (410), might be generally applied to all written narrative. As Ralph Cohen concluded his analysis of the related issue of theories of "word-painting" in poetry, "there is no need to create a theory of visual poetry when we admit that much of the poem is not subject to it" (245).

In films, on the other hand, every scene must necessarily be photographed from some specific physical location and thus depend upon some sort of specific ocularization (though not necessarily attributed to any character, of course) while, as Brian Henderson has observed, narration per se seldom occurs except in the voice-over of classical cinema, and then only for those parts of a film, especially at the beginning, which require narrative summary (15). Without voice-over there is not, strictly speaking, narrating, and thus no relation between what the narrator says and what the character knows, and thus no focalization (the resultant paradox of narrative without a narrator raises, as I have suggested, a number of interesting problems in defining terms). Two objections might be raised here. First, as Sarah Kozloff has pointed out, voice-over, and with it the opportunity for focalization, occurs much more frequently than most of us would have guessed, and Henderson's point that it usually occurs at the beginning of a film, while well-taken, does not undercut its significance. Indeed, the beginnings of narratives are often the most fruitful sites for narrative analysis. Second, Henderson neglects to consider the important functions of intradiegetic narrators, characters who speak from within the diegesis.

Alfred Hitchcock's *Dial M for Murder* presents an example particularly relevant for the study of this subtype of focalization in cinematic narrative. Near the end of the film the Inspector not only describes Tony's actions to the other characters from his window vantage point, but he then enters into the relation of internal focalization with Tony as filter when he offers psychonarration of Tony's thoughts and even quotes interior monologue: "Of course, it's Swan's key!" It might, of course, be argued that the inspector could not "really" know Tony's thoughts. My response would be that the narrator may only need to *say* what the character knows, not necessarily to *know* it, for there to be internal focalization. Interestingly, however, viewers I have questioned are invariably convinced that the inspector's reporting is accurate, though they are not sure why they are convinced of this. Seymour Chatman has suggested to me in conversation that it may be a function of the virtual infallibility of the British police in other Hitchcock films.

The preceding analysis, then, is meant to provide a clearer description of Genette's model of focalization than has thus far been available. The presumption of such a claim is evident, and I would not wish to be understood as insisting that my own version is somehow the "true" one or even that Genette himself would agree with any or all of the interpretations and modifications I have proposed. I would only claim a strategic, pragmatic validity for this version of the theory: it retains as much as possible of Genette's original model; it incorporates wherever possible valuable revisions that have been suggested by Bal, Chatman, Jost, Lanser, and others; and it suggests changes in terminology that seem to me at least to be clearly defined and internally consistent. Such a model obviously makes no claim to be definitive other than as a relatively stable foundation for further discussion and revision.

4

STORIES WITHOUT STORIES:

NARRATIVE AS A TEXT-TYPE

Before proceeding to a discussion of embedded narrative, it will be necessary to settle on a definition of narrative itself. Up to this point I have been relying on the assumption that all of the examples cited have been narratives, but in fact definitions of narrative vary considerably from one theory to another. A typical dictionary definition of "narrative" (from *Merriam-Webster's Collegiate*, tenth edition, as it happens) is "something that is narrated: STORY," of which I can accept the first half but not the second, because of the specialized meaning that the latter term has come to have for narrative theory. My position will be that every narrated discourse is a narrative, defining narrative as that class of discourses which are narrated by narrators to narratees. This (only apparently) tautological definition may seem merely facile, but a survey of other definitions of "narrative" and especially of "story" will help justify my approach. Two major lines of analysis have been proposed for the conceptualization of the ideas of narrative and story.

The first of these two schools, both in terms of chronology and popularity, considers that a narrative is made up of two major components. The distinction between the two is that between form and content. As Aristotle maintains, "it is possible for the poet on different occasions to narrate the story . . . or to have the imitators performing and acting out the entire story" (6). In the latter case the content is in dramatic form as a tragedy or comedy; in the former the content assumes non-dramatic form as an epic. It is the presence of both elements, a content and a form, a story and a mode of presentation, that produces narrative. In the 1920s the Russian Formalists codified the applications of this binary model for narratology under the terms "fabula," or "story," and "sjuzet," or "plot."[1] Boris Tomashevsky outlined the distinction in a 1925 essay: "Plot is distinct from story. Both include the same events, but in the plot the events *are arranged* and connected according to the orderly sequence in which they were presented in the work" (67).

French and then American structuralists have since elaborated upon these concepts and have provided terms for them in their own languages. The difference in order of events has continued to be seen as fundamental despite changes in terminology. As Tzvetan Todorov explains,

> Le rapport le plus facile à observer est celui de l'*ordre*: celui du temps racontant (du discours) ne peût jamais être parfaitement parallèle à celui du temps raconté (de la fiction); il y a nécessairement des interversions dans l'"avant" et l'"après." Ces interversions sont dués à la différence de nature entre les deux temporalités: celle du discours est unidimensionelle, celle de la fiction, plurielle. (*Qu'est-ce que* 53)

> The easiest relation to observe is that of *order*: the order of narrating time (the order of discourse) can never be perfectly parallel to the order of time narrated (of fiction); there are necessarily interversions in the "before" and the "after." These interversions are due to the difference in nature between the two temporalities: that of the discourse is one-dimensional, that of fiction, plural. (*Introduction* 30)

Seymour Chatman, whose important *Story and Discourse* has perhaps functioned more than any other book (and title) to fix the

English labels for these two components, has further analyzed the components of story:

> Structuralist theory argues that each narrative has two parts: a story (*histoire*), the content or chain of events (actions, happenings), plus what may be called the existents (characters, items of setting); and a discourse (*discours*), that is, the expression, the means by which the content is communicated. In simple terms, the story is the *what* in a narrative that is depicted, discourse the *how*. (*Story* 19)

According to this view the same story may be expressed by a variety of discourses to make up different narratives. One can tell the story of Romeo and Juliet, for example, as a play, a ballet, a film, a symphony, or a pantomime. All of these would be narratives. The live performances, the images passing on the screen, the sounds recorded on discs or tapes are discourses just as much as a novelization of Shakespeare's play *Romeo and Juliet* would be; the story, as expressed in a chronologically-ordered paraphrase or summary of the plot, might be exactly the same for each discourse.

The definition of each of these elements must be specified. Chatman's idea of discourse is rather broader than the prevailing sense of the term and leads him occasionally to such claims as "flashbacks are just as possible in ballet or mime or opera as they are in a film or novel" ("What" 118). The genre of opera, which has a discursive element and written text, certainly seems to present opportunities for narratological analysis.[2] And although ballet and mime have not thus far proven fertile ground for narrative analysis, even these nonverbal genres may be short of the boundary line limiting the scope of narratology. Jay Caplan and Mieke Bal have gone a step further in seeking to apply narrative theory to works of art with no necessary temporal dimension in their "performance" or consumption, Caplan in his study of Diderot's tableaux and Bal in her study of paintings and sketches as narratives (*Reading*). The most important application of narrative theory to a largely nonverbal medium has, of course, been the study of narrative film. Narratological studies of this genre by Chatman, David Alan Black, David Bordwell, Linda Dittmar, Brian Henderson, Sarah Kozloff, and Kristin Thompson have already produced interesting results. A still newer development has been the study of narrative in music, which has produced a "recent flurry of narratological activity among musical critics and analysts" (Kramer 141–42). Discussion of how cinematic or musical narrative fits into the model I am developing would require extensive separate treatment, though I will point out particular analogies and applications from time to time. For the purposes of this study, however, and without ruling out the possibility of wider application, I will generally limit my examples and discussion to discourse in what the *OED* gives as "the prevailing sense" of the term: "A spoken or written treatment of a subject in which it is handled or discussed at length . . . ." Given this restriction to verbal discourse, we might provisionally say that a narrative is any spoken or written text that tells a story, though the *OED*'s interesting phrase "at length" must be at least briefly considered here.

To my knowledge, no theorist of narrative has attempted to prescriptively specify a minimum length for admission to the genre. John Gerlach, in his discussion of "the very short story," offers as his boundary case the example of "Taboo," by Enrique Anderson Imbert, which weighs in at a trim 32 words (31 in Spanish):[3]

> His guardian angel whispered to Fabian, behind his shoulder:
> "Careful, Fabian! It is decreed that you will die the minute you pronounce the word *doyen*."
> "Doyen?" asks Fabian, intrigued.
> And he dies. (qtd. in Gerlach 76)

Gerlach argues plausibly that "Taboo" "feels, to some extent, like a story," and in fact it would meet the formal criteria set forth in most discussions. As will become evident from the examples to be considered, however, narrative theorists frequently base their definitions on even briefer, and often artificial, texts (Genette's selection of Proust would constitute a major exception to this tendency). Philip Sturgess has suggested that the extreme brevity of these examples may well compromise the value of the analyses they support: "The idea of narrativity seems to depend for its definition, perhaps in some not easily perceivable way, on the idea of self-extension and hence of length. It is by virtue of its length that any narrative demonstrates its own narrativity, and it is with the fact of length that any adequate grammar of narrative should come to terms" (8). I agree with Sturgess that many of the points made with these relatively abstract examples, especially in cases purporting to exclude certain texts from the realm of narrative, lose their force when applied to real texts. A initial survey of these illustrations, however, will be useful to prepare for the subsequent analysis of more extended examples and also to lay the foundation for my own admission in the next chapter of instances of *embedded* narrative as brief as a single word.

The term "story" remains to be defined. The most extended attempt to define the meaning of story in the binary model, to determine what it is about a discourse that enables it to tell a story, has been Gerald Prince's. Although he later modified his views on this subject, as remarked below, his earlier study nevertheless raises most of the important issues involved in other discussions of story. He claimed that "everybody distinguishes stories from non-stories, that is, everybody has certain intuitions — or has internalized certain rules — about what constitutes a story and what does not" (*Grammar* 9). Like sentences in a transformational grammar, stories have an underlying deep structure that readers perceive at some sub- or preconscious level. But Prince's reliance on intuition as a tool for deriving this grammar produced a model that was not at all self-consistent. The methodological problem he posed himself may well have been insoluble.

On the one hand, his expressed goal was the "rigorous analysis" of what makes up stories, the "explicit definition of these units meeting certain formal standards and allowing us to determine them as easily and unambiguously as possible" (*Grammar* 16). On the other hand, his analysis was based entirely on examples that he claimed "would intuitively be recognized as stories" (*Grammar* 19). I have shown several of the examples he offers to colleagues and students and have found little correlation between his intuitions and theirs; none of my test subjects (admittedly a small statistical sample) managed to guess with any consistency which examples were stories and which were not, despite Prince's frequent assurances that some were "clearly" or "obviously" recognizable as such (*Grammar* 20, 21). It may well be that my colleagues were not as discerning as Prince, but I would maintain that any criterion as limiting as direct access to Prince's intuitions presents an insuperable pragmatic obstacle. Beyond this procedural difficulty, however, there are contradictions within his methodology that are equally telling. His logical framework weakens when he then extends the principles drawn from his intuitions about some examples to deny the validity of intuitions about other examples. He presents an example that "would certainly be recognized as a story" (*Grammar* 30; indeed, this is one of the few examples that my test subjects can identify "correctly"), but then argues despite this that it is "not a minimal story" on the basis of rules he had derived from previously presented examples, which had in their turn been given status as evidence solely on the basis of apparently identical intuitive recognition.

Although Prince's inconsistent methodology undercuts his results, it is still useful to consider the definition of story that results in order to compare it to those of other theorists: "A minimal story consists of three conjoined events. The first and third events are stative, the second is active. Furthermore, the third event is the inverse of the first. Finally, the three events are conjoined by three conjunctive features in such a way that (a) the first event precedes the second in time and the second precedes the third, and (b) the second event causes the third" (*Grammar* 31). An example of such a story would be, "He was rich, then he lost a lot of money, then, as a result, he was poor" (*Grammar* 29).

Todorov's definition is slightly less strict in that the final state does not have to be the inverse of the first:

> L'intrigue minimale complète consiste dans le passage d'un équilibre à un autre. Un récit idéal commence par une situation stable qu'une force quelconque vient perturber. Il en résulte un état de déséquilibre; par l'action d'une force dirigée en sens inverse, l'équilibre est rétabli; le second équilibre est semblable au premier mais les deux ne sont jamais identiques. (*Poétique de la prose* 121)

The minimal complete plot consists in the passage from one equilibrium to another. An "ideal" narrative begins with a stable situation which is disturbed by some power or force. There results a state of disequilibrium; by the action of a force directed in the opposite direction, the equilibrium is re-established; the second equilibrium is similar to the first, but the two are never identical. (*Poetics* 111)

An example might be, "He made some money, then he spent some, then, as a result, he had less."

Other definitions of story are still less restrictive — Todorov's implication that his definition applies only to "complete" and "ideal" narratives previews the slippery slope we shall descend — and one can create a sort of continuum of definitions that become progressively less constraining. William Labov and Joshua Waletzky, relying on empirical evidence gathered from stories told by their test subjects, move the definition a degree further in concluding that "any sequence of clauses which contains at least one temporal junction is a narrative" (28). A minimal story might thus be, "He made some money, then he spent some." Shlomith Rimmon-Kenan offers a similar analysis: "temporal succession is sufficient as a *minimal* requirement for a group of events to form a story" (18). This would "mean that any two events, arranged in chronological order would constitute a story" (19). Both of these definitions allow that the causal link or force prescribed by Prince and Todorov may be left implicit, to be inferred by the reader. This constitutes a clear break with the Russian Formalists, who argued that "a story requires not only indications of time, but also indications of cause" (Tomashevsky 66). Roland Barthes explains the reasoning behind this shift: "le ressort de l'activité narrative est la confusion même de la consécution et de la conséquence, ce qui vient *après* étant lu dans le récit comme *causé par*; le récit serait, dans ce cas, une application systématique de l'erreur logique dénoncée par la scolastique sous la formule *post hoc, ergo propter hoc*" ("Introduction" 10; "the mainspring of narrative is precisely the confusion of consecution and consequence, what comes *after* being read in narrative as what is *caused by*; in which case narrative would be a systematic application of the logical fallacy denounced by Scholasticism in the formula *post hoc, ergo propter hoc*"

["Introduction" 94]). Mieke Bal's definition is a degree less strict still in requiring only one event, although she adds the stipulation, perhaps implicit in many of these other definitions, that an event can not take place without other elements:

> La combinasion *nécessaire* d'un événement avec un ou plusieurs acteurs, un lieu et une durée constitue l'*unité minimale* de l'histoire. Une combinasion est *nécessaire*, lorsque l'un de ses éléments ne peut pas se réaliser sans les autres. Un événement n'est pas possible sans acteur — même si celui-ci relève d'une catégorie abstraite, comme *le temps, Dieu, le sort* — et doit se dérouler quelque part. Il occupe toujours du temps. (*Narratologie* 5)

> The *necessary* combination of one event with one or more actors, a place, and a period of time constitutes the *minimal unit* of a story. A combination is *necessary*, since no one of the elements can be produced without the others. An event is not possible without an actor — even if it belongs to an abstract category, like *the weather, God*, or *fate* — and must take place somewhere. It always occupies some time.

An example of such a story might be, "He spent money there all day."

Michel Mathieu-Colas has focused on the one element that is common to all of the above definitions and that Bal has spelled out: "Il occupe toujours du temps." Mathieu-Colas argues that the key element that suffices to make a discourse narrative is temporal succession: "Si le texte semble s'ordonner comme une sorte de récit c'est dans le mesure précise où *le contenu représenté se deploie dans le temps*. Hors de ces conditions, je doute qu'un discours puisse se voir attribuer le moindre caractère narratif" (107; "If a text seems to be organized in a narrative manner it is precisely to the degree that *the represented content is spread out over time*. Failing that condition, I doubt that any discourse should be attributed the least degree of narrativity"). Such a definition would encompass a wider range of texts than has been traditionally studied as narrative, and might allow for studies such as Anne Henault's application of narratological analysis to a philosophical text (145–70).

Mathieu-Colas himself discusses as an example of narrative a passage from Immanuel Kant's *Critique of Pure Reason* on the analysis of mathematical propositions: "For first I take the number 7, and, for the conception of 5 calling in the aid of the fingers of my hand as objects of intuition, I add the units, which I before took together to make up the number 5, gradually now by means of the material image of my hand, to the number 7, and by this process, I at length see the number 12 arise" (10). Mathieu-Colas considers that the presence of temporal markers here is what makes the text narrative. An interesting problem presents itself when one compares the French translation of Kant he relies on with the English translation I have just quoted. The expression "I add" appears in the French version as the more distinctly temporal expression "j'ajoute alors une à une," "then I add, one by one" (for the German "nach und nach") (41), which Mathieu-Colas underscores as one of the crucial elements that allows him to classify the passage as narrative (107). The absence of that particular marker does not, however, change the sense of the passage to the extent that it renders the English version non-narrative. The event "I add" is readily understood to be subsequent to "I first take" and would be read so even without the prior marker "first." The fact that the word "add" occurs after the word "take" in the discourse implies that the actions designated would also take place in that order, in the absence of any explicit indications of temporal succession. The unidimensional temporality of discourse remarked by Todorov will necessarily create sequence and therefore imply temporal precedence and antecedence. Even a single event, for example, "He spent money," would suggest the passage of time, since in the reader's experience this type of event does entail some duration. Further, as Patrick O'Neill has noted, a single event typically implies multiple states: "'The king died,' for example, is a single event, but it clearly refers to two separate *states* of events, in the first of which the king was still alive and in the second of which he is no longer so" (18).

Gérard Genette has narrowed the definition further, arguing that the presence of a single verb suffices:

> Puisque tout récit — fut-il aussi étendu et aussi complexe que la *Recherche du temps perdu* — est une production linguistique assumant la rélation d'un ou plusieurs événement(s), il est peut-être légitime de le

traiter comme le développement, aussi monstrueux qu'on voudra, donné
à une forme *verbale*, au sens grammatical du terme: l'expansion d'un
verbe. *Je marche, Pierre est venu*, sont pour moi des formes minimales
de récit, et inversement l'*Odyssée* ou la *Recherche* ne font d'une certaine
manière qu'amplifier (au sens rhétorique) des énoncés tels
qu'*Ulysse rentre à Ithaque* ou *Marcel devient écrivain*. (*Figures III* 75)

> Since any narrative, even one as extensive and complex as the *Recherche du temps perdu*, is a linguistic production undertaking to tell of
> one or several events, it is perhaps legitimate to treat it as the development
> — monstrous, if you will — given to a *verbal* form, in the grammatical
> sense of the term: the expansion of a verb. *I walk, Pierre has
> come* are for me minimal forms of narrative, and inversely the *Odyssey*
> or the *Recherche* is only, in a certain way, an amplification (in the rhetorical
> sense) of statements such as *Ulysses comes home to Ithaca* or
> *Marcel becomes a writer*. (*Narrative* 30)

The minimal narrative version of our illustration is thus "He
spent." Evelyne Birge-Vitz has extended this analysis to include
examples in which this verb is not even expressed: "Indeed, the
definition of . . . 'récit' would be, simply, 'an utterance containing
at least one verb (or implied verb)'" (661). At this point it becomes
rather difficult to imagine the next step in reducing the requirements
for classification as a story. The bare presence of an
actor (not necessarily human, as Bal has emphasized), with the
relations surrounding it remaining largely implicit, would seem to
suffice. Attempts have been made to tell stories in just this way,
a point to which we shall return.

Chatman has tried to draw the line at such cases by stipulating
that "Stories only exist where both events and existents occur.
There cannot be events without existents. And though it is
true that a text can have existents without events (a portrait, a
descriptive essay), no one would think of calling it a narrative"
(*Story* 113). Chatman here slides from prescriptions about stories
to prescriptions about discourses (texts), and, as will become
clear below, I, for one, would be willing to call many descriptions
narratives. But this distinction between event and existent is not
easily maintained. Is "John was angry" an event or an existent?
Which is "John became angry easily"? Would "John quickly became
angry" (an existent, a characteristic of his personality) and

"John quickly became angry" (an event, a particular instance of this trait) belong to different groups? As Genette has noted, "la description ne se distingue pas assez nettement de la narration" (*Figures II* 60; "description . . . does not distinguish itself sufficiently clearly from narration" [*Figures of Literary Discourse* 137]). The distinction has been disputed on other grounds by Rimmon-Kenan:

> Unlike Chatman, . . . I do not insist on an opposition between state and event (or stasis and process), because it seems to me that an account of an event may be broken down into an infinite number of intermediary states. That is why a narrative text . . . need not include any sentence denoting a dynamic event; a succession of states would imply a succession of events, as it does in "He was rich, then he was poor, then he was rich again." Just as any single event may be decomposed into a series of mini-events and intermediary states, so — conversely — a vast number of events may be subsumed under a single event-label (e.g. "The Fall of the Roman Empire"). (15)

Assuming that happiness, for example, is a state, we might extend her argument to allow that the series "happy, unhappy, happy" would by itself imply a succession of events something like "someone was happy, then someone was unhappy, then someone was happy again," and indeed constitute a story, since, as noted above, she allows that the causal link between these events may also remain implicit. As I have suggested above, one can readily find examples of just such texts, and in fact the story told by the series "happy, unhappy, happy" seems easy to interpret when compared to that told by a series such as Samuel Beckett's "Imagination morte imaginez" (*Imagination* 9; "Imagination dead imagine").

Some adherents to the story-plus-discourse definition of narrative have been led to argue that such discourses tell no story at all, and thus should not be considered narratives. There can be no story, the argument goes, because the reader can not produce an organized summary or paraphrase of the events presented in (or inferred from) the discourse. According to Claude Bremond, "Tout récit consiste en un discours intégrant une succession d'événements d'interêt humain dans l'unité d'une même action.

Où il n'y a pas succession, il n'y a pas récit . . ." (62; "Every narrative consists of a discourse integrating a succession of events of
human interest into the unity of a single action. Where there is no
succession, there is no narrative . . . ").[4] The requirement that a
narrative discourse must be reconstructible as a coherent story
was at one time also supported by Prince, who argued that there
are authors who

> write storyless novels and who achieve this goal by making it impossi-
> ble for the reader to establish any chronology of events. In Alain
> Robbe-Grillet's *La Jalousie*, for instance, the crushing of the centipede
> which, in a novel telling a story, would provide a good point of refer-
> ence around which to situate the other events in time, is made to occur
> before the trip taken by Frank and A., during their trip, and after it.
> (*Grammar* 23)

It should be pointed out that Prince himself has since come to
consider that a clear chronology of events is not an essential component of story and that *La jalousie* is a narrative ("Narratology").
I would argue further that the failure of the narrator to be clear
about this chronology is itself part of a fascinating story, a story
not after all about the death of a centipede but about the psychological deterioration of the narrator, who is himself unable to determine exactly what is going on (are his wife and neighbor having
an affair?). The significant fact is not the exact moment of the
insect's death but the obsessive frequency with which the scene
passes through the narrator's mind. It is the act of narration itself
that constitutes a story whose main event is its own narrating.[5]
The reluctance of proponents of the story/discourse dichotomy to
consider narratives in this light has excluded novels by authors
such as Robbe-Grillet and Beckett from the field of narrative and
has created obstacles for the discussion of other types of writing
as well.[6]

As feminist critics have pointed out, novels written by
women, perhaps even in the premodernist period, tend to fall into
this category as well. Susan Lanser has argued that "these theories of plot assume that textual actions are based on the
(intentional) deeds of protagonists; they assume a power, a pos-

sibility, that may be inconsistent with what women have experienced both historically and textually, and perhaps inconsistent even with women's desires" ("Feminist" 356). Josephine Donovan has characterized the feminine story as "static, and in a mode of waiting. It is not progressive, or oriented toward events happening sequentially or climactically, as in the traditional masculine story plot" (218–19). In such stories "telling becomes the single predicated act" (Lanser, "Feminist" 357). Lanser proposes therefore that a more appropriate theory of story would "incorporate the plot that may be generated by the relationship between narrator and narratee" (357). The only definition of story that would apply to all narratives would thus have to include the minimal story "this narrator addresses this discourse to this narratee." The resulting position is similar to that suggested by my remarks above on *La jalousie*, and it is not surprising that the Russian Formalist definition of narrative based on a model developed in the 1920s — belonging, as Genette remarks, "à la préhistoire de la narratologie" (*Nouveau* 11; "to the prehistory of narratology" [*Revisited* 14]) — should fail to account for texts written since the 1950s (the *nouveau roman*) or for a critical approach that became influential in the 1960s (feminism). Gertrude Stein presciently announced this shift away from traditional notions of story as early as 1935:

> It is a much more impressive thing to any one to see any one standing, that is not in action than acting or doing anything doing anything being a successive thing, standing not being a successive thing but being something existing. That is the difference between narrative as it has been and narrative as it is now. And this has come to be a natural thing in a perfectly natural way that the narrative of to-day is not a narrative of succession as all the writing for a good many hundreds of years has been. (19–20)

Rather than exclude much contemporary fiction and women's fiction (including Stein's, of course) from being classified as narratives, I would suggest that the classification be reworked to include them. It seems evident that the binary model privileges the story of successive events inordinately. After all, the discourse, which is a physical object directly accessible to analysis, is not really an equal partner with any type of the story, a concept that does not even seem readily susceptible to definition, as the range of remarks above suggests, and that is derived from the discourse itself. These derivations will of course vary from reader to reader, and feminist critics have noted that gender can play a role here as well. Emily Toth claims that "women writing about *The Awakening* generally saw the suicide as a positive decision — Edna's taking control of her life. Men generally saw the suicide as a failure on Edna's part" (1005). Two quite different stories might thus be generated from the same discourse, one summarizing the story by "Edna tries to break away from convention and fails" and the other offering "Edna tries to break away from convention and succeeds" as a summary. The derivation of a story from a discourse becomes in this way a matter of literary interpretation rather than of (even relatively) objective description. The logically necessary succession in narrative is not that of events, but of words. As Philip Sturgess has argued, "what is 'sequentialized' in any narrative is often not so in respect of this story being told. Every narrative consists of 'sequences' whose elements are not necessarily chronological-causal in their interlinking. They are sequential, rather, in terms of the discursive or narratological aims of the work" (22). These considerations will lead to my definition of narrative, but it will be useful first to examine a second line of analysis that also rejects the story/discourse dichotomy.

Genette has modified the binary model by postulating a third category and creating a tripartite model consisting of "*histoire* (l'ensemble des événements racontés), *récit* (le discours, oral ou écrit, qui les raconte) et *narration* (l'acte réel ou fictif qui produit ce discours, c'est-à-dire le fait même de raconter)" (*Nouveau* 10; "*story* [the totality of the narrated events], *narrative* [the discourse, oral or written, that narrates them], and *narrating* [the real or fictive act that produces that discourse — in other words, the very fact of recounting]" [*Revisited* 13]).[7] Bal has proposed a similar model, differing from Genette in her definition of the third level. She believes that this level should be called "le texte narratif" ("the narrative text") a concept that designates the text "dans laquel une instance *raconte* un *récit*" ("within which an authority *relates* a *narrative*"). This "authority" is the agent of Genette's *narration*: "*Raconter* un récit est produire des phrases qui signifient ce récit. . . . Cette activité d'énonciation est la *narration*" (Bal, *Narratologie* 4; "To *relate* a narrative is to produce sentences that signify that narrative. . . . That activity of enunciation is *narration*"). The difference here is due to Bal's desire to render the three terms more exactly parallel. She prefers to view the three levels as three distinct products rather than as two products and a process, as Genette does. The choice of metaphor here does not seem consequential for my analysis. Rather than seeing these elements as equally important or coordinate, as in the binary model, Genette privileges narration as the source of both story and narrative in fiction: "l'ordre véritable serait plutôt quelque chose comme

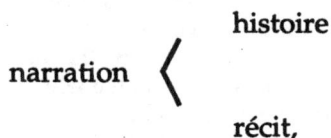

$$\text{narration} \left\{ \begin{array}{l} \text{histoire} \\[1em] \text{récit,} \end{array} \right.$$

l'acte narratif instaurant (inventant) *à la fois* l'histoire et son récit" (*Nouveau* 11; ". . . with the narrative act initiating (inventing) *both* the story and its narrative, which are then completely indissociable" [*Revisited* 15]). Bal sees this relation somewhat differently: "Un RÉCIT est le signifié d'un texte narratif. Un *récit* signifie à son tour une *histoire*" (*Narratologie* 4; "A *narrative* is the signified of a narrative text. A *narrative* signifies in turn a *story*"). As her concern with parallelism in definitions suggests, she regards these elements as equal in importance for narratological analysis: "La narratologie est la science qui cherche à formuler la théorie des relations entre texte narratif, récit et histoire. Elle ne s'occupera ni du texte narratif, ni de l'histoire pris isolément" (*Narratologie* 5; "Narratology is the science which seeks to formulate the theory of the relations among the narrative text, narrative, and story. It is not concerned with the narrative text nor the story taken in isolation"). Applying here the analysis developed above, I would argue that Bal's valorization of story leaves her model open to the

same objections as the binary model. Her system is further compromised by her introduction of the concept of focalization at the
level of *récit* (*Narratologie* 32–33), a problem I have discussed in
the preceding chapter. I will therefore follow Genette's model
from this point.

His privileging of narration leads him to regard the analysis of
story as peripheral to narratological theory:

> les analyses de contenu, grammaires, logiques et sémiotiques narra-
> tives, n'ont guère jusqu'ici revendiqué le terme de narratologie, qui
> reste ainsi la propriété (provisoire?) des seuls analystes du mode
> narratif. Cette restriction me paraît s omme toute légitime, puisque la
> seule spécificité du narratif réside dans son mode, et non dans son
> contenu, qui peut aussi bien s'accommoder d'une "représentation"
> dramatique, graphique ou autre. (*Nouveau* 12)

> analyses of narrative contents, grammars, logics, and semiotics have
> hardly, so far, laid claim to the term *narratology*, which thus remains
> (provisionally?) the property solely of the analysts of narrative
> mode. This restriction seems to me on the whole legitimate, since the
> sole specificity of narrative lies in its mode and not its content, which
> can equally well accommodate itself to a "representation" that is dra-
> matic, graphic, or other. (*Revisited* 16)

My interest is also in the analysis of narrative in this more restricted sense, concentrating on narration. I will thus exclude
story as an integral component of narrative, partly on the strength
of Genette's analysis and, more importantly, because of the evident difficulty of defining story itself, as the attempts at such
definition surveyed above suggest. After all, it is of questionable
value to define a term (narrative) by recourse to an undefinable
term (story). As I have argued, the only definition of "story" that
would cover all cases would have to include the minimal implied
story "narrator narrates to narratee"; but since these three elements are already explicitly required by the category of
"narration" this would be a redundant stipulation. The only remaining elements of the definition of narrative would thus be discourse and narration. As argued in the preceding chapter, however, the narration may be entirely implicit, as in *Les liaisons dangereuses*.

Given that narration is in some cases only implicitly present, it is not surprising that Rimmon-Kenan has suggested that Genette's valorization of narration may be as vulnerable a position as other theorists' emphasis on story. As she points out, the component of text — the words on the page (or sounds in the air) — is the only indispensable element of the three and the only one that readers (and narratologists) have direct access to. Story and narration are both inferred from text. As the inferred *cause* of the text, narration would seem to be built in to every text in a way that story, effectively a possible but not inevitable *result*, is not, but certainly the point that text logically generates the other two components might justify our revising Genette's diagram accordingly:

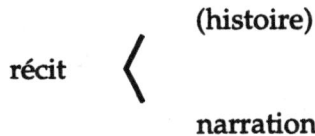

$$\text{récit} \left\{ \begin{array}{l} \text{(histoire)} \\[1em] \text{narration} \end{array} \right.$$

It should be emphasized that I am concerned here with a definition that will cover all limit cases; obviously, most narratives are explicitly narrated and have clearly discernible stories.[8] But there are many cases of texts which are obviously narratives, at least in the generic sense of being novels or short stories, that have no clear story or are not explicitly narrated. What is it about such discourses that enables us to assign them narrators, and hence classify them as narrative texts? There seems to be no objectively verifiable criterion. I would conclude that discourses are not inherently narratives nor inherently not narratives. As Prince now concedes, "Depending on circumstances, a simple statement like 'Mary ate the jam' can function as a narrative. . . . a text constitutes a narrative if and only if it is processed as such a representation" ("Narratology" 163). A propos of Prince's apparently fanciful culinary example, one ought to consider Susan J. Leonardi's analysis of the narrative structure of recipes: "Like a story, a recipe needs a recommendation, a context, a point, a reason to be. A recipe is, then, an embedded discourse . . ." (340).

What makes a given discourse a narrative is not some objectively discernible element it contains but the application of a certain approach to its analysis. As A. J. Greimas has concluded, "on s'est aperçu que [narratological analysis] pouvait être utilisée et rendait indifféremment compte de toutes sortes de discours: tout discours est donc 'narratif.' La narrativité se trouve des lors vidée de son contenu conceptuel" (18; "it can be seen that [narratological analysis] can be used indiscriminately to account for all types of discourse: all discourse is thus 'narrative.' Narrativity from that point on turns out to be emptied of its conceptual content").

Narrativity, if I may so call it, is the product of a tropological operation by which the metaphor of narration is applied to a series of words on a page. To read a text by means of the trope of narration is to read out of it a narrator and its voice, and a narratee and its ear. A narrative text is any text that is read as if narrated by a narrator to a narratee. The text read literally is a series of words — the text read metaphorically through the trope of narration becomes a narrative. Narration is, of course, not the only tropological operation that may be performed on a text, but it is the operation distinctive to narratological analysis. Narratological analysis is thus a performative discourse that makes the text it analyzes a narrative. This definition has the merit of including every example of what common sense and tradition would call narrative texts: every novel, short story, and narrative poem ever written. Surprisingly few of the definitions that have been proposed can make even this modest claim. This definition also brings in a large number of texts that common sense and tradition would not call narratives. One type of text that can be readily accommodated within this system is lyric poetry. A poem has a general narrator just as a novel or short story does. The absence of a narrator in drama would set it apart from the other two traditional generic categories of lyric and epic (narrative belonging to the latter).

Genette has already tentatively suggested a realignment of the genres for related reasons: "une fusion . . . entre lyrique et épique, laissant à part le seul dramatique, en tant que seule forme à enonciation rigoureusement 'objective'" (*Architexte* 70; "a fusion . . . between the lyrical and the epical that would leave the dramatic as the only form with a rigorously 'objective' enunciation" [*Architext* 65]). It would be possible, of course, to discuss the written text of a play, as opposed to the performance of one, under this model, since an implicit general narrator could readily be posited. Indeed, it is often difficult to distinguish between the text of a closet drama meant to be read and the text of a play intended for performance, and the extensive "stage directions" provided by a playwright like Eugene O'Neill (he precisely specifies the contents of the Tyrones' bookcases in *Long Day's Journey into Night*, for example) seem to function as purely textual (narrative) elements that would never be perceived by a theatrical audience. The application of this model could also extend across the traditional boundary between fiction and non-fiction (or, as Genette has proposed, "fiction and diction"). An autobiography, for example, can easily be read as if narrated and its historical author may be distinguished from its implied author and narrator.[9] Indeed, such reading of texts which traditionally had been considered non- or extra-literary has become one of the hallmarks of the new historicism. I would suggest that the reading of texts that traditionally have been considered non- or extra-narrative can readily be brought within the scope of narratology.

Take for the moment the following passage from *La jalousie*, a text that, as the numerous references given above suggest, remains one of the canonical examples of a work of fiction occupying a space somewhere near the border between the narrative and non-narrative:

> Elle est toujours habillée de la robe clair, à col droit, très collante, qu'elle portait au déjeuner. Christiane, une fois de plus, lui a rappelé que des vêtements moins ajustés permettent de mieux supporter la chaleur. Mais A . . . s'est contentée de sourire: elle ne souffrait pas de la chaleur, elle avait connu des climats beaucoup plus chauds — en Afrique par exemple — et s'y était toujours très bien portée. Elle ne craint pas le froid non plus, d'ailleurs. Elle conserve partout la même aisance. Les boucles noires de ses cheveux se déplacent d'un mouvement souple, sur les épaules et le dos, lorsqu'elle tourne la tête. (10–11)

> She still has on the light-colored, close-fitting dress with the high col-
> lar that she was wearing at lunch when Christiane reminded her again
> that loose-fitting clothes make the heat easier to bear. But A . . . merely
> smiled: she never suffered from the heat, she had known much worse
> climates than this — in Africa, for instance — and had always felt fine
> there. Besides, she doesn't feel the cold either. Wherever she is, she
> keeps quite comfortable. The black curls of her hair shift with a supple
> movement and brush her shoulders as she turns her head. (39)

I chose this passage more or less at random, having opened the only text I had at hand to this page. There are at least three text-types operating here: narration, inasmuch as the passage is narrated by the same narrator as the rest of the text, and exhibits the dual chronological perspective of the type; argumentation, since A . . . and Christine have a dispute about clothing; and description, primarily of A . . ., but implicitly of Christine as well and perhaps of the narrator. Indeed, the most controversial of these assignments may be calling this text a narration. Recall Prince's argument that the novel's events can not be reconstructed in chronological order and therefore lack the chain of events necessary to tell a story. This narrator, however, would not seem to be consciously telling a story at all, and it may be safer to say that telling a story is here a concern of the implied author but not of the narrator. As explained above, the narrator's inability to piece together the events in a complete sequence is itself part of that story.

But just as the definition of narration fails to provide criteria at the level of structure that can enable us to separate narrations from non-narrations, so do the usual definitions of argumentation and description. The sentences cited combine all three functions in the same words. A . . .'s reference to Africa's heat simultaneously tells of her past, offers evidence, and depicts the region. My point is that for narratology this makes no difference. Narratology is concerned exclusively with the passage as narration, or as what Lawrence Kramer has called *narratography*, "the practice of writing through which narrative and narrativity are actualized, the narrative performance through which stories actually get told" (144). One could, of course, study the text as an argument or as a description, but that would not be narrative analysis. It might be

argued that ideological critics do in fact study narratives as arguments rather than as narratives. Fredric Jameson praises Theo-
dore Dreiser as "our greatest writer" (161) and laments "the remarkable transformation of Henry James from a minor nineteenth-century man of letters into the greatest American novelist
of the 1950s" (222) precisely because he is reading a different
text-type than a narratologist, who would almost surely disagree
with those evaluations.

Take the chapter I am now writing as another example. We
would tend to study this as an argument and analyze it accordingly. We could, on the other hand, analyze it as narratography.
My narratee does not read French, requiring English translations,
though my implied reader is fluent (to a much higher degree than
the historical author) and my historical readers vary widely in
their command of the language. My narratee believes that I had
just now only a single literary text available (*La jalousie* — though
of course I had the French and English versions at hand), but my
implied reader knows that the implied author really chose that
text for several good reasons and will not be misled by my disclaimer. This last sentence featured analepsis and prolepsis.
Robbe-Grillet's novel is cited here as an embedded narrative at the
metadiegetic level. There have been characters (including the em-
blematically-named Prince!), events, existents, and all of the other
textual features susceptible of narratological analysis. When I cite
another text in a few minutes, after claiming to have had only one
available, my narrator may be called unreliable (especially if I now
[note the use of fictional deixis] fail to cite another text in a few
minutes).

To go through that last paragraph and substitute "arguer" or
"implied arguer" for every instance where I used "narrator" or
"implied author" would not be to produce a study of my text as
an argument, but simply to study it as narrative under different
rubrics, an unearned distinction without a difference. This is not a
matter of labels but of methodology, of frameworks. We could
similarly study this text as an argument without relabeling. This
would produce a different type of analysis whether we said ar-

guer or narrator, or X or Y. What changes is not the text, but the method of analysis. This is not to deny that there are text-types, but rather to argue that the point is of no consequence to narratology. As Barbara Herrnstein Smith has maintained, "it is questionable . . . if any absolute distinction can be drawn between narrative discourse and any other form of verbal behavior" ("Narrative" 228). The tools of narrative analysis can be applied to verbal discourse for any of the text-types with no adjustments or modifications whatsoever, and will yield the same kind of results.

Narratology has developed two main approaches to textual analysis, and we have not so much two definitions of narrative as two types of tools for studying narratives. One can use the tools for the study of story and discourse, the dual chronologic of narrative, with its concerns of order, duration, and frequency (though even here, of course, discourse is the foundational term from which the story is inferred), independently of the other set of tools for the analysis of voice and mood, with its concerns about point of view and narrative level, which are not dependent on the derivation of a story. Implicit here, it seems to me, is the notion of narratology as a sort of performative speech act. To use the tools of narratology on a text is to make that text into a narrative, almost as in the mathematical performative construction of "Let X be 7" or "Let angle A be 30°": "Let text Y be narrative." In other words, we can define narrative from the other direction: narratives are those texts that we use narratology to study.

5

NARRATIVE LEVELS AND EMBEDDED NARRATIVE

The model of narrating presented to this point postulates a minimal structure of three distinct agents for the production of every narrative: the historical author, the implied author, and the general narrator. Some narratives, like Samuel Beckett's *Le dépeupleur*, in which no characters within the diegetic world speak (or, in this case, have the ability to do so), are produced by these three agents only: the only discourse in the text is that of the general narrator. But the majority of narratives are structured in a more complicated manner. The general narrator usually attributes sections of the text to other speakers by the use of conventions like quotation marks, dashes, or indentation, producing a text composed of both narrator's discourse and characters' discourse. As Lubomír Dolozel has schematized this view, "T → DN + DC" (*Narrative* 4).[1] This attribution does not mean that the general narrator ceases to narrate. Textual production can, I think, be more economically and consistently accounted for by considering that the direct discourse of characters is cited or quoted within the discourse of the general narrator, who speaks in the character's person using a trope similar to the classical rhetorical device of dialogismus.

Beth Newman has aptly described such "word-for-word repetition of another speaker's discourse" as "an extended ventriloquism" (146).

The character who speaks addresses an audience, if only an audience consisting of itself. As argued in chapter four, any discourse can be seen as a narrative, since, given the proper context, any discourse can imply a story. Following this reasoning, the difference between a character addressing a speech to a listener and a narrator narrating a narrative to a narratee is not quantitatively determinable. One could thus label any character whose direct discourse is presented a narrator. One definition of "embedded narrative" would then be "character's discourse": all intradiegetic narrative is embedded narrative. Susan Lanser has foreseen this possibility and wishes to reject it: "Theoretically, any persona who utters discourse on his or her own behalf may be called a 'narrator,' though such a stretching of the term renders it rather useless" (*Narrative* 137). She proposes to make a distinction between characters who narrate and those who merely speak, but it proves to be one that she finds difficult to maintain. The distinction is offered in an introductory clause: "If I may set aside these momentary 'narrators' who are typical characters interacting with one another as actors rather than as storytellers . . ." (*Narrative* 137).

While her request is intended to be merely rhetorical, upon consideration it would seem to raise a genuine problem. The demonstrable impossibility of rigorously defining "story," and therefore "storyteller," would invalidate this distinction, and, obviously, rule out the possibility of defining "embedded narrative" as "a story within a story."[2] Lanser herself does not attempt to define "story" in this context, and, as noted in the previous chapter, now believes that theories of plot and story should "be reexamined to find alternatives to the notion of plot as active acquisition or solution and to incorporate the plot that may be generated by the relationship between narrator and narratee" ("Feminist" 357). Irene de Jong, pursuing the same problem, has suggested the possibility of distinguishing between actors who merely speak and those who narrate by examining the spatial and temporal content of their discourse. She considers that the actor can "refer to the 'hic et nunc' of the primary story and thereby remain in his position as actor" or can "tell a secondary story himself and thereby become a 'real' narrator" (9). In practice, however, these two types of speech may be combined, and de Jong notes that such overlapping is the norm in the text that she analyzes, the *Iliad*: "In the Homeric epics we never find an actor who tells a story without referring beforehand or afterwards to the actual situation in which he finds himself" (9). Even if these acts can be separated, the distinction does not seem useful. There would seem to be no advantage gained by labeling "I went to the store yesterday" a narrative and "I just returned from the store" non-narrative on the basis of the "hic et nunc" test.

Lanser's expressed reason for wishing such a distinction possible is that without it the term "narrator" would become "rather useless." While this concern appears quite reasonable at first view, in practice the problem does not arise. In fact it greatly facilitates narratological description if one abandons the attempt to distinguish between storytelling and nonstorytelling discourse. I would insist that the important question for narratological analysis is "who speaks?"; without the answer to this, the question "what is said?" can not even be addressed. And in Lanser's own analyses of embedded narratives she makes no attempt to apply the storytelling requirement. Her exemplary text begins in this way:

A   It was a dark and stormy night. We were standing on the deck.
      The ship was sinking. The Captain said, "Tell me a story, my
      son." And so I began:

B   "It was a dark and stormy night. We were standing on the
          deck. The ship was sinking. The Captain said, 'Tell me a
          story, my son.' And so I began:

C   "'It was a dark and stormy night. We were standing on the
              deck. The ship was sinking. The Captain said, "Tell me a
              story, my son." And so I began:'" (*Narrative* 134)

Lanser correctly notes that

> Each of these acts of narration occupies another diegetic level, with the
> preceding narrative act serving to make the next level of discourse pos-
> sible. The *primary* or 'first-degree' narrative, as Genette would call it,
> is in this case narrative A. Most texts do not, of course, repeat the
> same message again and again as this children's tale does. A more typi-
> cal example of the Chinese box narrative is Boccaccio's *Decameron*, in
> which level A would be occupied by the narrative about the ten story-
> tellers and the circumstances that lead them to tell their tales. Level B
> would be composed of the tales themselves; a level C would exist only
> if one of the tales contained a tale-within-a-tale. (*Narrative* 134)

She then observes that "Theoretically, in fact, 'Tell me a story, my
son' is also an inserted text and should be placed on the next level
from the sentences that precede it; like all direct discourse of
characters, it is part of a previous speech act that is only being
reported on the level where I have placed it" (*Narrative* 134 n. 33).
While it is true that she does not explicitly call each of the Cap-
tains a narrator, the fact that she assigns them to the next narrative level (B, C, and then D, by extension) even though they do not
appear to be unambiguously engaged in telling stories, argues that
the distinction, if she is making it here at all, is one without a real
difference. Further, the model of narrative levels and the distinction between narrators and speakers prove to be mutually incom-
patible theoretical positions.

Mieke Bal's position on this distinction is similar. Though she
also believes that a character may speak without narrating, she
finds herself obliged to discard the distinction when actually car-
rying out the analysis of embedded narratives, as in the following
passage:

> The character Ottiline thus becomes a speaker at the second level,
> which we shall indicate with CN2 [character-narrator at the second
> level]. Note, however, that the use of CN2 is not entirely correct.
> Though Ottiline, at least temporarily, speaks, she does not *narrate*:
> what she says is not a story. Nevertheless, we shall use this indication
> because it makes clear that the character is a speaker, just like the nar-
> rator. (*Narratology* 134–35)

But her position would seem to dictate that the character is a speaker *unlike* the narrator. To make the difference clear she might call her a CS2. This would, however, make the determination of narrative levels an entirely different problem, one never addressed by Bal, since she has not offered any examples of a CS2 or some similar category nor any discussion of such an agent's articulation into her scheme of narrative levels. What Bal's remark actually makes clear is that she, like Lanser, finds the distinction between narrating and nonnarrating speakers to be untenable in the analysis of narrative levels and embedded narrative. In fact, using the term "narrator" for all speakers is not a "rather useless" extension but a strategically necessary one. I would emphasize again, however, that my use of the term in this way is not dictated by this pragmatic consideration but by the conviction that an explicitly told "story" is not a necessary component of narrative and is not susceptible of clear definition, making it unusable as an element of other definitions. The practical obstacle encountered by Lanser and Bal does of course constitute an independent rationale for considering all direct discourse as narration. One effect of this approach is that even extremely short stretches of embedded discourse — we shall consider examples as brief as a single word — will be defined as narratives. Given that any embedded narrative is automatically encountered within a larger narrative context, however, the theoretical objections that would normally arise to this definition tend to evaporate in practice. As Philip Sturgess has noted, even the briefest segments usually come to exhibit considerable "narrativity" "once those mini-narratives are thought of as being contextualized in a completed work. . . . such passages could be seen to take a significant or signifying place in the narrativity of whatever might be their containing narratives" (17).

My approach to embedded narrative, then, resembles that of Bal and Lanser in assigning all direct discourse to a particular narrative level, though they do this in contradiction of their models and I do it in concord with mine. All three of us broadly follow Gérard Genette's theory of narrative levels to this end, but all depart from that theory to some extent. Lanser departs from

Genette for two reasons: "Because so many of my colleagues have found Genette's neologistic terminology counterproductive . . . and because my distinctions are not quite the same as Genette's . . ." (*Narrative* 133). Unfortunately, her system can not be correlated precisely with Genette's, and Lanser admits that this is a deficiency in her model because "his framework is more technically refined" in this regard than her own (*Narrative* 133). She attempts to adapt her system of public and private narrators to allow for the description of narrative levels, but she recognizes herself that the result is not entirely satisfactory: "In choosing to use these terms instead of Genette's I am risking the danger that they carry misleading connotations; Genette's language has the advantage of precision. Terms like 'public' and 'private' must be understood here as somewhat metaphoric terms . . ." (*Narrative* 137). I have argued elsewhere on other grounds that Lanser's categories are too imprecise for the description of narrative levels ("Problems" 209–11), but her own critique of her model will suffice here.

Genette's terminology is indeed somewhat disconcerting at first glance, but "counterproductive" may be an exaggeration.[3] His system is so technically refined and has such potential for descriptive precision, as Lanser points out, that it is well worth the inconvenience of learning a few new terms, especially since no one has been able to offer a simpler set of terms to describe the same relations. I will therefore follow Genette's model rather than Lanser's in this regard with the stipulation made in chapter two, that a narrative can have only one extradiegetic narrator, the general narrator. Bal has suggested a minor refinement of terminology, employing the prefix "hypo" rather than "meta" to mark narrative levels beyond the intradiegetic; I have elsewhere defended the utility of leaving "extra," "intra," and "meta" intact and designating subsequent levels by Greek prefixes marking the number of narrative levels represented in the text (Rev. of *Seuils*). Thus the level after the metadiegetic would be the tetradiegetic, followed by the pentadiegetic, the hexadiegetic, the heptadiegetic, octadiegetic, and so on. For general discussion, we might allow, with Gilberto Triviños, that "es posible hablar de 'relatos de tercer grado,' 'relatos de cuarto grado,' y 'relatos de quinto grado'" (145; "it is possible to speak of 'third-level narratives,' 'fourth-level narratives,' and 'fifth-level narratives'"). My own practice will generally be to use the simplest term sufficient to the context, recognizing that some distinctions may be blurred by the shorthand of "first-level."

Bal has argued that there are two different ways in which embedded narratives can be related to embedding narratives. She illustrates the two types of embedding by reference to The Thousand and One Nights and then to Balzac's *Le Lys dans la vallée*:

> C o mme l'on sait, dans le récit principal, qui englobe les autres et que j'indiquerai par R1, on raconte qu'un sultan qui a été trompé par sa f emme, tue désormais chacune de ses nouvelles f emmes après la nuit de noces. Pour l'empêcher de la tuer, Shéhérazade raconte au sultan des histoires captivantes. Les histoires racontées par Shéhérazade sont les récits enchâssés et seront indiqués par R2àX, formule qui veut rendre compte de leur nombre illimité. Les rapports entre R1 et R2àX sont ceux d'une double subordination, sur le plan des acteurs et sur le plan de l'action. Shéhérazade, acteur de R1, raconte R2àX: elle en est le narrateur. Narrés d'un acteur de R1, R2àX sont donc subordonnés à R1. En outre, R2àX ont une fonction à l'intérieur de l'action de R1: tant que Shéhérazade raconte des histoires, le sultan ne la tue pas. ...
>
> Bien que le terme d'*enchâssement* soit employé pour toute oeuvre où il y a *récit dans le récit*, je voudrais proposer, pour la clarté de l'analyse, de le réserver aux oeuvres où il y a une double subordination comparable à celle des *Mille et une nuits*. Si la subordination ne se réalise que sur l'un des deux plans, je propose d'utiliser le terme d'*encadrement*, employé par Balzac à propos de son *Lys dans la vallée*. Celui qui, dans ce roman, raconte le récit encadré R2 est le sujet du récit encadrant R1: il y a donc subordination des acteurs. Cependant la fonction de R2 par rapport à l'action de R1 se borne dans ce cas à fournir après coup une explication pour la conduite du sujet dans R1; cette conduite est déjà déterminée. Le fait même que R2 est raconté n'influence pas le déroulement de R1: il n'ouvre pas une alternative comme dans *Les mille et une nuits* (la mort ou la vie de Shéhérazade). Ici il s'agit donc d'une subordination simple. (*Narratologie* 61–62)

As everyone knows, in the principal narrative, which includes the others and which I will indicate by R1, we are told that a sultan, who has been deceived by his wife, subsequently kills each of his new wives after their wedding night. To prevent him from killing her, Sheherazade tells the sultan fascinating stories. The stories related by Sheherazade are embedded narratives and will be indicated by R2–X, a formula which takes into account their unlimited number. The connection between R1 and R2–X is that of a double subordination, on the level of the actors and on the level of the action. Sheherazade, an actor in R1, relates R2–X: she is their narrator. Narrated by an actor in R1, R2–X are thus subordinated to R1. Additionally, R2–X have a function within the action of R1: as long as Sheherazade tells the stories, the sultan will not kill her. . . .

Although the term *embedding* is employed for every work in which there is a *story within a story*, I would propose, for analytical clarity, to reserve it for works in which there is a double subordination comparable to that of the *Thousand and One Nights*. If the subordination takes place only on one of the two levels, I would propose the use of the term *framing*, employed by Balzac with respect to his *The Lily of the Valley*. In this novel, the one who relates the framed narrative R2 is the subject of the framing narrative R1: there is thus subordination of actors. Nevertheless the function of R2 with respect to R1 is limited in this case to providing after the fact an explanation of the conduct of the subject in R1; that conduct has already been determined. The mere fact that R2 is narrated has no effect on the unfolding of R1: it does not open up an alternative as in the *Thousand and One Nights* (the life or death of Sheherazade). This is thus a case of single subordination.

But examination of these two texts does not appear to support Bal's analysis. To consider her second example first, the embedded narrative does directly influence the conduct of its narratee and, as a result, the future of its narrator. The novel begins with a letter written by Félix de Vandenesse to Natalie de Manerville and ends with her letter in reply; framed between these letters is the narrative of Félix's life. Although Bal contends that the embedded narrative (the autobiography) does not affect the course of the embedding narrative (the story in the letters of Félix's wooing of and rejection by Natalie), the text contradicts her. Félix hopes that the effect will be to further his romance with Natalie: "Je voudrais que ma confidence redoublât ta tendresse" (*Lys* 771; "I should like my confidence to redouble your affection" [*Lily* 1]). In fact, the opposite result occurs: as Natalie's final letter unequivocally declares, it is as a direct result of having read his history, in which he inadvertently reveals his truly undesirable nature, that "Je renonce à la gloire laborieuse de vous aimer"; "Supprimons l'amour entre nous" (*Lys* 1029, 1030; "I give up the laborious privilege of loving you"; "Let us forgo love between us two" [*Lily* 253, 254]). She further informs him that his narrative will produce the same effect on any other woman he tells it to: "Si vous tenez à rester dans le monde à jouir du commerce des femmes, cachez-leur avec soin tout ce que vous m'avez dit: elles n'aiment ni à semer les fleurs de leur amour sur des rochers, ni à prodiguer leur caresses pour panser un cœur malade" (*Lys* 1032; "If you are anxious to remain in Society and to enjoy the company of women, take care to hide from them all that you have told me. They care neither to sow the blossoms of their love on rocks nor to waste their caresses in bandaging an ailing heart" [*Lily* 256]). Thus the functional aspect, which Bal denies the text, is explicitly present here.[4]

The subordination of actors, however, which she does find in the novel, presents an apparent complication. Both the opening letter and the autobiography it introduces are by and about Félix: he is both narrator and actor in both, and there is thus no subordination in Bal's sense. My own analysis would be that all three items (first letter, autobiography, second letter) are second-level narratives embedded within the first-level narrative of the effaced general narrator. The distinction can be made by genre and by narrative level: the general narrator narrates a *novel* to the general narratee, whereas the *letters* and *autobiography* are addressed only to intradiegetic narratees (the first letter to Natalie, the second letter to Félix). In this sense, then, there is a double rather than single subordination in *Le Lys dans la vallée*.

Instead it is in the story of Sheherazade that the dual subordination becomes problematic. Bal's contends that if Sheherazade ceases to tell the stories, the sultan will kill her. This argument is compromised by the fact that she does cease to tell stories and the sultan does not kill her. One might object that it is only the cumulative effect of the telling of 1001 stories that saves her life, but the sultan himself explicitly denies this interpretation. Sheherazade requests that her life be spared not on the basis of her storytelling but because of the three children she has had by the sultan:

"For their sake I implore you to spare my life. For if you destroy the mother of these infants, they will find none among women to love them as I would."

The King embraced his three sons, and his eyes filled with tears as he answered: "I swear by Allah, Shahrazade, that you were already pardoned before the coming of these children. I loved you because I found you chaste and tender, wise and eloquent." (Dawood 239)

If we take the sultan at his word, then, and allow for the terms of three pregnancies, she had been pardoned after the first few stories, and not exclusively or even primarily on the basis of her storytelling. The relation therefore is not that Sheherazade will be killed if she stops narrating but that Sheherazade believes that she will be killed if she stops narrating. But this is to say only that Sheherazade has a motive for narrating, and this holds true for all narrators.[5]

But my conclusion is not really that Bal's classification should be reversed, that *Le Lys dans la vallée* is an example of embedded narrative and the *Thousand and One Nights* is an example of framed narrative. Instead I would argue that Bal's distinction points to no significant structural features and is not a useful method of classification. Sheherazade's motivation contributes to the suspense of the story during a naive first reading and perhaps to an illusion of realism (though one would be hard pressed to find a reader so near the status of the zero degree narratee as to find this work realistic), but this motive has no structural component relevant to any objectively verifiable classificatory criterion. Sheherazade's earlier stories, which until some unspecified point would presumably exhibit this dual relation, differ in no discernible way from her later stories. One might as profitably try to guess which stories were told on Wednesdays and classify them on that basis. Similarly, while Natalie does suggest that certain particular aspects of Félix's tale were responsible for her decision, it would make no sense to separate these matters from the rest of the narrative and classify them differently.

No matter how often one rereads the book, Sheherazade will not stop narrating too soon and the sultan will not kill her; the mistaken belief that if she stops, then she will be killed is proper to Sheherazade, but not to the critical reader. Paul Valéry called these sorts of imaginings "superstitions littéraires," "Literary Superstitions": "J'appelle ainsi toutes croyances qui ont de commun l'oubli de la condition verbale de la littérature. Ainsi existence et psychologie des personnages, ces vivants sans entrailles" (*Oeuvres* 569; "I give this name to all beliefs having the common trait that they overlook the *verbal* condition of literature. This applies to the existence and the so-called psychology of 'characters' in books — living beings without entrails" [*Works* 14.124]).   Paul de Man made a related observation about such criticism of the debate conducted in *La nouvelle Heloïse*: "it would be naive to ask who wins the match since in this model Rousseau, as author, controls the moves of each of the antagonists . . . . All the interest focuses on how one fights (or seduces), on the how, the poetics of writing and of reading rather than the hermeneutics" (112–13).   Lucien Dällenbach has also criticized this type of reading: "le propre de la lecture n'est pas de fantasmer à partir d'un récit, mais, comme l'étymologie l'indique, d'en rélier, dans l'immanence, les éléments constitutifs" (166; "the appropriate goal of reading is not to develop fantasies from a narrative, but [his etymological point does not translate well] to connect together its immanently constitutive elements").

As noted above, the impossibility of discerning any differences between the early stories, which supposedly do help save Sheherazade's life, and the later stories, which do not, makes Bal's criterion inappropriate for narratological criticism.   That there is, however, a profound structural difference between the two works she uses as examples does provide the basis for distinguishing two types of embedding.   In Balzac's novel the opening letter and the autobiography are both written by Félix to Natalie; both are intrahomodiegetic narratives, as is Natalie's response. Bal dismisses this feature as irrelevant: "Que le sujet des deux récits soit le même acteur ou non n'a pas d'importance ici" (*Narratologie* 83, n. 4; "Whether the subject of the two stories is the same actor or not is of no importance here").   In doing so she ignores the most important distinction for narratological analysis.

As I have argued throughout this study, "who speaks?" is the fundamental question to be addressed by narratology. In the *Thousand and One Nights* the stories of Sheherazade are told as intradiegetic narratives within the general narrator's extradiegetic narrative. In this case there is a shift in narrator and narrative level between Bal's R1 and R2, but no shift in either between R2 and R3–X. In *Le Lys dans la vallée*, however, there is no shift in narrator or narrative level between R1 and R2 (I set aside here the point that there is an implicit extradiegetic level occupied by the effaced general narrator of *Le Lys dans la vallée*; the example is compromised in that I allow two levels here to Bal's one).

I would therefore postulate two structurally distinct types of narrative embedding: "horizontal" embedding, in which texts at the same diegetic level, but narrated by different narrators, follow one another; and "vertical" embedding, in which narratives at different diegetic levels are inserted within (Bal) or stacked on top of one another (Genette). The relation between Félix's and Natalie's discourses is horizontal, that between the general narrator's and Sheherazade's vertical. It should be noted that vertical embedding can be accomplished without a change of narrator: when the general narrator of *The Canterbury Tales* ("Chaucer the pilgrim") tells in his turn the second-level tales of *Sir Thopas* and *Melibee*, there is a shift in narrative level despite the apparent continuity of the narrating voice, most clearly signaled by a shift in narratee, from the general narratee to the Canterbury pilgrims ("following the narratee," by the way, often reveals the easiest path through these narrative mazes).

Bal has astutely pointed out that there is at least one type of narrative that common sense would call embedded that nevertheless would not be considered as such according to this model, that being the case of a narrative that contains a dream:

> Pour en rester à l'exemple de *La chatte*: le rêve d'Alain, au premier chapitre, est nettement senti par le lecteur comme un récit intercalé, un récit "métadiégétique." Il ne fait pas partie de la série d'événements qui constitue l'histoire du roman, et il contient lui-même une série indépendante d'événements. Où se situe la transition qui permet de caractériser le rêve comme "métadiégétique"? Il est absurde de lui dénier

cette qualité, puisque le consensus des lecteurs prouve, fût-il intuitive-
ment, qu'il est "méta-récit." (*Narratologie* 30)

> To go no further than the example of *The Cat*: Alan's dream in the first
> chapter is clearly felt by the reader to be an intercalated narrative, a
> "metadiegetic" narrative. It does not form part of the series of events
> which constitute the story of the novel, and contains itself an inde-
> pendent series of events. Where then is the transition found that per-
> mits us to characterize the dream as "metadiegetic"? It is absurd to
> deny it this status, since the consensus of readers proves, albeit intui-
> tively, that it is a "metanarrative."

One might object to certain details of this analysis. It is not clear
on what basis she claims that the dream is not one of the events of
the novel, and her valorizing of the intuitive consensus of readers
(a consensus of how many?) over the definitions of Genette is a
questionable methodology. She also fails to explain her contention
that a shift "d'un niveau à un autre" (*Narratologie* 30; "from one
level to another") takes place here. It could, of course, be argued
that since Alain dreams the dream to himself, he narrates the
dream to himself. In this reading there would indeed be a shift in
narrative level, with Alain becoming an intradiegetic narrator (and
narratee). But the general narrator does not necessarily yield the
narrating to an intradiegetic narrator in recounting a dream. A
clear example of a dream that is presented with no shift in narrative level is found in the case of a dream narrated subsequently
rather than as it is dreamed. In Chaucer's *Book of the Duchess* the
general narrator relates his own dream after it has occurred, at the
same narrative level as the rest of the text: "Loo, thus hyt was,
thys was my sweven" (270, line 290).

But granting for the sake of discussion that Bal is correct in
stating that there is no shift of level in Genette's sense, her conclusion does not necessarily follow. What Bal intuits here as a shift
in diegetic level is more economically explained as a shift in the
diégèse, "l'univers où advient cette histoire" (Genette, *Palimpsestes*
342; "the universe within which the story takes place"). In
Katharine Young's terminology, the shift takes place within the
"Taleworld," "the realm of the events the story is about," as opposed to the "Storyrealm," the "region of narrative discourse"

(177). The events of the dream are supposed to take place in an alternate universe created by a character's mind rather than being physically carried out in the spatial-temporal universe of the rest of the narrative, but they are none the less events narrated at the same level as other events of the novel.[6] We might characterize this type of structure by postulating a form of ontological shift that can be opposed to the epistemic shift of the other examples of embedding considered thus far. I use these terms not in any strict philosophical sense but in the rather metaphorical sense adopted by Brian McHale in his contrasting of Modernism and Postmodernism. Epistemic embedding by means of a shift in narrator is characterized by emphasis on the process of communicating knowledge: who imparts what to whom; ontological framing, as in dreams, hallucinations, or science-fiction stories of alternate dimensions, is characterized by emphasis on modes of being, by the shifting of levels of reality or existence. By way of simplifying this strikingly cumbersome pair of terms, I will offer "verbal" as a substitute for "epistemic" and "modal" in place of "ontological." Bal is certainly correct here in remarking that narratological models are more useful in describing verbal frames than modal frames, and my own emphasis will be on examples of verbal embedding. It should be recalled, however, that many of the structural and thematic relations we are about to examine in connection with verbal embedding may be set up by these modal shifts as well.

John Barth and Genette have proposed similar tripartite models for further classifying embedded narratives. The first version of Genette's system distinguished three principal types of relation between embedding and embedded narrative:

> Le premier type est une causalité directe entre les événements de la métadiégèse et ceux de la diégèse, qui confère au récit second une fonction *explicative*. . . . Le deuxième type consiste en une relation purement *thématique*, qui n'implique donc aucune continuité spatio-temporelle entre métadiégèse et diégèse: rélation de contraste . . . ou d'analogie . . . . Le troisième type ne comporte aucune rélation explicite entre les deux niveaux d'histoire: c'est l'acte de narration lui-même que remplit une fonction dans la diégèse, indépendamment du contenu métadiégétique:

fonction de distraction, par exemple, et/ou d'obstruction. (*Figures III* 242–43)

> The first type of relationship is direct causality between the events of the metadiegesis and those of the diegesis, conferring on the second narrative an *explanatory* function. . . . The second type consists of a purely *thematic* relationship, therefore implying no spatio-temporal continuity between metadiegesis and diegesis: a relationship of contrast . . . or of analogy . . . . The third type involves no explicit relationship between the two story levels: it is the act of narrating itself that fulfills a function in the diegesis, independently of the metadiegetic content — a function of distraction, for example, and/or obstruction. (*Narrative* 232–33)

The problem that arises here is that assignment of a narrative to one of these categories is a matter of literary interpretation, not a matter of the recognition of significant structural features. As a result, these categories are not mutually exclusive and hence are difficult to use for purposes of classification or description.[7] The same objections would apply to Barth's system of dramaturgical, thematic, and gratuitous relationships, which, though independently arrived at, are quite similar to Genette's categories ("Tales" 56–57). It is probably the case that any extensively studied embedded narrative could be found suitable by one or another reader for any or all of the three categories, depending on the literary judgment of the person doing the classification. As Genette himself has argued elsewhere, more in keeping with the spirit of his system as a whole, such a system of classification, "qui relève effectivement d'une 'interprétation,' n'est pas du ressort de la narratologie" (*Nouveau* 58; "which in reality has to do with 'interpretation,' does not lie within the province of narratology" [*Revisited* 87]). Narratology should rather provide a set of descriptive criteria that can precede interpretation and help direct it along profitable paths or even operate relatively independently of direct interpretation.

Genette's later critique of Barth's model and incorporation of it within his own, while not addressing these problems, does suggest in passing two additional criteria for the classification of embedded tales, one more useful than the other. The first is his distinction between analeptic and proleptic embeddings (*Nouveau* 62–63; *Revisited* 93). His restriction of the relevance of this temporal relation to his explicative and predictive functions seems unnecessarily limiting, since time-shifts could always serve a thematic function (as can any element of any narrative) but this temporal relation is generally objectively determinable and hence a readily verifiable basis for differentiation.

Genette's other suggestion seems less promising. Considering that narrative level has been accorded exaggerated importance by critics of his system, he argues that embedding narratives of very slight extent may be disregarded as insignificant:

> le caractère intra-diégétique d'une narration n'est bien souvent, comme on le voit clairement chez Maupassant, . . . qu'un artifice de présentation, un poncif à bien des égards négligeable. Et réciproquement, il suffirait d'une phrase de présentation . . . pour transformer, sans aucune autre modification nécessaire, une narration extradiégétique en narration enchâssée. (*Nouveau* 64)

> the intradiegetic character of a narrative is very often, as we see clearly in Maupassant . . . , only a stratagem of presentation, a conventionality that, in many respects, is insignificant. And reciprocally, all that is needed to convert an extradiegetic narration into an embedded narration is a sentence of presentation . . . without any other modification. (*Revisited* 95)

But the initial reason for using narrative level as a basis for classification is not that it is necessarily the most subjectively important criterion for the literary criticism of embedded narratives but that it is the most significant common structural feature for the description of embedded narratives. As Genette himself had argued some years earlier,

> il est évident qu'un récit second peut avoir une rélation de contenu diégétique plus ou moins étroite, plus ou moins lointaine avec le récit premier: toutes les gradations sont possibles. Ce que en revanche est absolu, c'est la différence de *statut narratif* entre l'histoire directement racontée par le narrateur . . . et l'histoire racontée dans cette histoire et par un de ses constituants (personnage ou autre): l'histoire au second degré. (*Figures II* 202)

It is evident that a second narrative can have a relationship of diegetic content more or less close, more or less distant with the first narrative: all gradations are possible. What is, on the other hand, absolute, is the difference in *narrative status* between the story related directly by the narrator . . . and the story related within that story by one of its constituents (one character or another): the story at the second degree.

Genette's choice of Maupassant as the epitome of the author whose embeddings are without critical interest underscores emphatically the relativity of such judgments and the need in narratological theory to avoid building a model on them. Almost before Genette's ink was dry, Angela Moger published two important articles devoted to close study of the ways in which Maupassant's seemingly gratuitous framing devices are in fact among the most significant elements to be considered in analysis of his stories. Despite this pitfall, Genette is not the only writer to have been attracted to the possibility of classifying embedded narratives by their relative length, and certainly the prospect of locating such a genuinely objective criterion merits thorough exploration. Sarah Kozloff, for example, has proposed an alternative means of classifying embedded narrations by their extent, labeling embedded narrators "micro-narrators" if their "story comprises less than 25 percent of the entire text" (49). Such stories would presumably be designated "micro-narratives." But Kozloff's assertion that in such cases this "quantitative difference becomes qualitative," which would be the clearest justification for the terminological distinction, is not developed.

Perhaps the most frequently-encountered version of this approach seeks to differentiate the "picture-frame" structure, with a single extended story framed within brief opening and closing passages at a different diegetic level, from the "multiple-story" or "episodic" or "linked" structure, with a narrator (or series of narrators) telling a series of tales surrounded by intercalated passages at a different diegetic level. According to Moger, "The framed story is then different from other story-within-a-story constructs (i.e., interpolated tales) — the very dimensions of the frame relative to the 'framed' make clear that the latter is the principal story and the former a kind of commentary about the con-

tained story's immediate and fundamental essence" ("Narrative"
325 n. 6).[8] This position seems undercut, however, by conflicting
characterizations: the framing story is "patently subordinate" to
the framed story ("Working" 7), but "the inner story is *not* valorized over the outer one"; there is instead "a mutually enhancing
and mutually compromising reciprocity between contained story
and containing story" (17–18 n. 12). These varying relations
would seem possible for any given picture-frame narrative, but
also possible for any intercalated or "Chinese-box" narrative as
well. David Ullrich similarly sets out distinctions between the
two forms that he quickly undercuts: "In the 'episodic' frame narrative, the distinction of primary and secondary story is not applicable, since each story constructs its own set of morals and
cause-and-effect relations independently" (216), yet "In addition,
some writers subvert the 'official' story and embedded moral instructions by contrasting the teller's story with the teller's actions
outside of the framed story. Chaucer's *Canterbury Tales* is such an
example . . ." (217). Most of Ullrich's distinctions are equally
easy to exemplify with either form: either may have stories interrupted, "continue for any length," or "achieve closure with or
without reference to the original enframing story" (214). Such approaches move too simply from description to interpretation;
whether a given second-level narrative is subordinate, valorized,
or reciprocal with respect to a first-level narrative can not be re-
duced to a function of relative length, and these attempts to graft
predetermined thematic or interpretative consequences onto the
structure seem to me inherently mistaken.[9]

My reluctance toward relying on the criterion of length or on
the dramatic and thematic and, especially, the gratuitous categories as bases for classification should in no way be interpreted as
meaning that these do not reflect important functions or effects of
the structures of narrative embedding. In fact, I would argue that
all embedded narrative has a dramatic impact, if only that of de-
ferring or interrupting the embedding narrative, and that all embedded narrative has a thematic function, if only one of relative
contrast or analogy. Even discontinuity or apparently gratuitous

relationships may be read as thematically significant. I insist on this irreducible minimum of potential dramatic and thematic weight only to cover unforeseen limit cases. In practice, a shift in narrator, as in horizontal embedding (*Le Lys dans la vallée*, the *Book of the Duchess*), or a shift in narrator and narrative level, as in vertical embedding (the *Thousand and One Nights*), always produces effects of some consequence.

One of the reasons for this was suggested by Boris Uspensky, who observed in his analyses of the psychological, spatial-temporal, phraseological, and ideological microtexts that may be found within every narrative that it is often the case that

> the frames of the microtexts on one level (on the plane of phraseology, let us say) do not concur with the frames which are manifested on another level (for example, on the plane of spatial-temporal characteristics). A text which is organized in this way cannot be broken down into its constituent microdescriptions, although the separations may be defined in terms of each level. (155)

The exception to this obscuring of the compositional elements of point of view is, precisely, the embedded narrative as marked by a shift in narrator:

> In literature the phenomenon of conjoining microdescriptions or particular texts in a more general text is represented by a composition employing a story within a story. The most obvious and simplest instance may be found in framed novellas and other clear-cut cases in which the change in narrator is presented explicitly, and the reader clearly perceives the borders between the separate stories. (154–55)

In such cases "the borders concur on all levels" (155); the shift of narrator is thus the most prominent marker of a range of other important shifts and the most obvious point to focus on in studying them. This shift creates a border with interpretative significance independent of the relative extent of the narratives it demarcates. This boundary should be most significant in cases of what I will call "deep" embedding, with both vertical and horizontal "movement," when the shift in narrator is accompanied by a shift in narrative level. This coincidence of differences at the boundary between embedded and embedding narratives is inevitably a site upon which to focus interpretation, automatically entailing additional structural and dramatic considerations that may provide sources of meaning.

As we have seen, a given author's manipulation of any structural component must be interpreted on a case-by-case basis; no rule of thumb proposed seems adequate to anticipate every spin a writer can put on a device. But we can seek to describe the places at which interpretative activity is typically activated, a set of narrative topoi associated with narrative embedding. Not every narrative will activate every topos, of course, and any topos may be propelled in multiple directions by a given context. Based on a survey of the interpretative strategies typically invoked by critics studying embedded narratives, and recognizing that other arrangements may be possible, I will suggest that three basic functional codes are likely to be implemented by the structures of narrative embedding: building freely on the terminology that Roland Barthes developed for *S/Z*, I will call these the hermeneutic, proairetic, and formal codes.

The invocation of the hermeneutic code, the code of interpretation, would seem to be an inherent function of all embedding. Barthes' version of the hermeneutic code includes "les différents termes (formels), au gré desquels une énigme se centre, se pose, se formule, puis se retarde et enfin se dévoile" (26; "the various [formal] terms by which an enigma can be distinguished, suggested, formulated, held in suspense, and finally disclosed" [19]). As Beth Newman has put it, working with the same sort of problem in mind, an embedded narrative "creates the same kinds of expectations as those set in motion by what Roland Barthes has called the 'hermeneutic code,' but instead of being encoded in words alone — in the 'lexia' — the presence of some enigma is signaled by the layering of stories, by the system of frames" (144). The enigma may either be resolved or disclosed within the text, or it may instead be left open or even gradually complicated, resulting in what Dittmar has called the "investigatory frame," which "presupposes that knowledge is subjective and ever-changing" (192). These two possibilities suggest two logical text-types, which Ullrich has usefully labeled "didactic" and "ironic": "The frame narrative is didactic and imparts a moral to the reader. This moral may be directly stated . . . , as occurs in 'The Rime of the Ancient Mariner,' many medieval ballads, and most fables and fairy tales. However, the moral commentary does not have to be accepted by the implied reader/audience . . ." (200). Obviously, the assignment of a text to either category remains a matter of interpretation rather than an objective property of any particular text.[10]

The hermeneutic semiosis of the embedding narrative can also function as a general cue to the reader that the world or genre of the embedded narrative will be mysterious or unusual rather than (or in addition to) posing any specific puzzle to be solved. Ullrich's contention, however, that the framing world or genre "will invariably be conventional" while the "extraordinary world will invariably be a part of the enframed world" (108) would seem to admit of frequent and wide-ranging exceptions: in John Barth's *Chimera* the exotic adventure of the outer narrative of Dunyazade (Sheherazade's sister) frames the inner narrative of a modern American writer leading rather ordinary romantic and professional lives; in *Frankenstein* the exotic setting of the arctic seas frames a tale set in familiar European cities; in the *Decameron* a frame set in refined aristocratic society encloses tales of contemporary middle- and lower-class life; and any number of epistolary novels embed letters within other (generically identical) letters. To note these variations, of course, is not to deny the acuity of Ullrich's observation of a general tendency that may be true for many, perhaps even the majority, of cases. The genres of the supernatural seem particularly apt to follow the pattern of proceeding from the familiar (through what Katharine Young calls an "orientation section" [295]) to the fantastic, and their virtually obligatory invocation of the hermeneutic code may in part explain the remarkable regularity with which such narratives rely on embedding. Newman has suggested that "the frames around Gothic and supernatural fictions signify at once something highly charged, even dangerous, and the barriers that protect us from it" (159).

Her observation that the frame is simultaneously a sign of danger and of safety is not a contradiction or paradox, but rather an instructive example of the general point that such structural cues are typically reversible or multivalent, with potential for activating a characteristic state or seme and also for distancing, ironizing, or familiarizing that state or seme.

In addition to functioning semiotically to foreground the hermeneutic code — the very introduction of an embedded narrative demands explanation — every embedded narrative functions to foreground what I will call a proairetic code, the Barthesian code of action: "on appelera *proaïrétique* ce code des actions et des comportements (mais dans le récit, ce que délibère l'action, ce n'est pas le personnage, c'est le discours)" (*S/Z* 25; "we shall name this code of actions and behavior *proairetic* [in narrative, however, the discourse, rather than the characters, determines the action]" [18]). The action here, of course, is the act of narrating itself, or, more properly, the presence of two such acts, and of two sets of characters engaged in them.[11] As Ross Chambers explains, narrational embedding places "narrative act within narrative act, narrative situation within narrative situation: it implies the representation, internally to the fictional framework, of a situation involving the major components of a communicational act (emitter-discourse-recipient) — and very frequently the mirroring within a story of the storytelling relationship itself: narrator-narration-narratee" (33). This structure constitutes one of Lucien Dällenbach's three elementary types of mise en abyme, which he has termed, following Roman Jakobson's model, *mise en abyme de l'énonciation* (61, 74). Moger has suggested that narrative embedding also produces what Dällenbach would call a *mise en abyme du code*: "Since, moreover, the framing of a narrative constitutes the explicitation of the self-referential quality of narrative (the frame compels the understanding that the story is about the telling of the story), we perceive the complexity of the paradigmatic axis engendered by the interplay of thematic element and structural element" ("Obscure" 136). To invoke another of Jakobson's formulations, "similarity is superinduced upon contiguity"

("Linguistics" 49); embedded narratives, in which formally similar units follow consecutively in the text, are not only metonymically but metaphorically related.

We might schematize these observations by suggesting that the doubling of the communication paradigm through embedding marks out three sites of latent or potential significance, any (or all) of which might be foregrounded by a given narrative context: the two stories, two narrators, and two narratees all offer topoi for comparative analyses. All three components enable the author to more closely direct interpretation (i.e., demonstrate intention). Moger has remarked that the structure of framing "signifies the basic cleft in the artistic imagination whereby the author both performs the conventional telling and judges it" ("Narrative" 323); I would extend her observation by suggesting that the (implied) reader is similarly required to cleave its own performance, not only hearing (observing) the narrator and narrative (narratee), but also judging them. Gilberto Triviños has offered a binary approach to classifying these potential judgments: "Los procesos narrativos que posibilitan la constitución del relato son narrativamente afirmados o negados en los relatos internamente duplicados" (149; "The narrative processes that enable the construction of the [outer] narrative are narratively affirmed or negated in the internally duplicated narratives").

At the locus of narrative, the reader is invited to determine the relation between the two stories: in Jakobson's terminology, to superimpose a paradigmatic relation onto the syntagmatic relation presented in the literal contiguity of the two stories. The second-level narrative may, as Triviños suggests, be *"no disyuntivos o disyuntivos," "non-disjunctive or disjunctive"*: "La relación entre elemento incluyente y elemento incluido, en el primer caso, expulsa de sí la contradicción" (158; "The relation between framing and framed elements, in the first case, eliminates all contradictions"). Here the embedded narrative confirms or amplifies the themes of the outer narrative. In disjunctive embeddings, on the other hand, "El relato de segundo grado critica o es criticado, niega o es negado, relativiza o es relativizado por el relato de primer grado"

(159; "The second-level story critiques or is critiqued by, negates or is negated by, relativizes or is relativized by, the first-level narrative"). The obvious parallels between Triviños's model, Ullrich's didactic and ironic modes, and the Barth/Genette relations of analogy and contrast work together here to confirm the utility of this binary approach. Theoretically two other possibilities should exist: irrelevance and identity. As I have argued above, the purely gratuitous relation would seem to be difficult to exemplify: any candidate would be susceptible to the next critic's interpretation, which would inevitably be targeted at bringing it into the fold, and of course a true lack of connection would itself provide profound thematic cues for a critic disposed to find them. Triviños has also discussed the type of the self-identical or self-reflexive embedded narrative, in which "El relato de segundo grado *repite, coincide con* o *duplica* el relato de primer grado" (159; "The second-level story *repeats, coincides with*, or *duplicates* the first-level story"). But in his examples the story is only alluded to, not performed, repeated at the level of story rather than discourse, and thus would not seem to constitute genuine parallels. Lanser's Captain's story, reproduced at the beginning of this chapter, would seem to be a truly reflexive embedding, in which the second-level literally repeats the first, but this subtype is probably rarely, if ever, found outside such hothouse varieties.

At the locus of the narrator's act, the doubling of embedding typically functions to provide, clarify, or complicate a narrator's motivation for telling a story, or to establish or undermine a narrator's credibility.[12] As Peter Brooks notes, "framed narration in general offers a way to make explicit and dramatize the motive for storytelling . . ." (259). Multiple narrators can confirm or disconfirm each other's stories, either reinforcing a single interpretation or forcing the reader to accommodate multiple viewpoints. To some extent these effects all draw upon the potential of embedding to create the illusion of verisimilitude through the depiction of a realistic chain of communication within the framing narrative. While the (often-effaced) general narrator only metaphorically "speaks" to the (almost entirely-effaced) general narratee, with whom the real reader can only partially, and quite artificially, identify, the intradiegetic agents producing and receiving an embedded narrative are typically dramatized characters in a realistic communicative circuit. As David Lodge has remarked,

> The Rise of the English novel in the eighteenth century began with the discovery of new possibilities of mimesis in prose narrative, through the use of characters as narrators — the pseudo-autobiographers of Defoe, the pseudo-correspondents of Richardson — thus making the narrative discourse a mimesis of an act of diegesis, diegesis at a second remove. These devices brought about a quantum leap in realistic illusion and immediacy . . . . (95)

Perhaps the doubling of the act of the narratee in embedded narratives has the most profound impact on interpretation, for the reason that every reader is called upon to fill that role (in addition to those of the implied and historical readers). The doubling of *our* (already multiple) function, which is precisely that of the interpreter, is inherently, indeed almost tautologically, fraught with interpretative consequences. Adapting Triviños's binary model, we may say that the text demands that we respond to — adopt or reject — the embedded audience's reading and reaction. This opposition between adopting and rejecting, refigured in a different pair of terms, seems parallel to Ullrich's didactic and ironic types of embedding (v). Most of the time, however, the interpretation is directed against the grain, or ironically, perhaps for the simple reasons that it is easier for an author to dramatize a partial or flawed reading than an exhaustive and ideal one, and that the depiction of an inadequate intradiegetic audience is a highly efficient means of reaching out to the (more adequate) extradiegetic audience. As Moger has explained, the technique of embedding narratees "creates several levels of awareness. Because we have to assess the ways in which the internal reader has misread, we must read more meticulously and self-consciously than we ordinarily do" ("Narrative" 316).

Prince has pointed out that the narratee also plays an especially important role in the creation of realism in embedded narratives:

Si le narrataire contribue à la thématique d'un récit, il fait aussi toujours partie du cadre de la narration. C'est souvent d'un cadre particulièrement concret qu'il s'agit, où narrateur(s) et narrataire(s) sont tous des personnages . . . . La plupart du temps, il s'agit de naturaliser le récit. Le narrataire joue alors, comme le narrateur, un role "vraisemblabilisant" undéniable. Parfois, ce cadre concret fournit le modèle organisateur en fonction duquel se développe un ouvrage, une narration. Dans le *Décaméron* ou dans l'*Heptaméron*, chacun des narrataires est censé devenir un narrateur à son tour et le devient. Plus qu'un simple signe de réalisme, plus qu'un indice de vraisemblance, le narrataire représente dans ces circonstances un élément indispensable à l'articulation du récit. ("Narrataire" 195)

If the narratee contributes to the thematic of a narrative, he is also always part of the narrative framework, often of a particularly concrete framework in which the narrator(s) and narratee(s) are all characters . . . . The effect is to make the narrative seem more natural. The narratee like the narrator plays an undeniable *verisimilating* role. Sometimes this concrete framework provides the model by which a work or narration develops. In *The Decameron* or in *L'Heptameron*, it is expected that each of the narratees will in turn become a narrator. More than a mere sign of realism or an index of verisimilitude, the narratee represents in these circumstances an indispensable element for the development of the narrative. ("Narratee" 22–23)

Like the narrator, the narratee also may have motives underlying its responses, which may become identified with or seen as opposed to those of the reader. Todorov has analyzed this interaction, which he finds especially significant in the case of vertically embedded tales like those of the *Decameron*, which have dramatized intra- and meta-diegetic narratees: "Boccace a le souci de toujours introduire un personnage, souvent secondaire, qui sert de témoin, et avec lequel le lecteur peut s'identifier. Le lecteur n'est pas le seul à connaître tous les secrets (si fréquents dans le *Décameron*), ce qui lui aurait donné une conscience de voyeur" (*Grammaire* 13; "Boccaccio is careful to always introduce a character, often a secondary one, who serves as a witness, and with whom the reader can identify. The reader is thus not the only one to know all the secrets [so frequent in the *Decameron*], which would have made him conscious of his being a voyeur").

Finally, the presence of embedded narrative activates a formal code, setting for our consideration boundaries *within* the text that require us to more closely examine those *around* the text. The characteristic interpretative consequences of such formal analysis cluster around such properties as unity/fragmentation, closure/openness, and symmetry/asymmetry, overlapping pairs which are not easy to keep separate from each other in practice, but are mentioned under one rubric or another by almost all students of the genre. Katharine Gittes has suggested that a frame narrative can produce the illusion that it has a "natural" (*Framing* 147) structure, even in the absence of unifying events or themes. As Linda Dittmar has observed, "There is something comforting — even pleasurable! — about symmetrical brackets" (195). Moger has suggested that the presence of an embedding narrative functions as the setting does for a jewel: "The frame story lends the symmetry and weight that, through a kind of trompe l'oeil, make the central story seem properly proportioned, formally complete" ("Narrative" 321). Barbara Herrnstein Smith has suggested some of the reasons that "symmetrical" embedding, in which the first-level narrative both opens and closes a work, often has a structuring effect of unity and closure; the fact that a narrator yields to an embedded narrator means that the resumption of the narrative by the first narrator will affect the reading of the whole:

> any terminal element that has been in some way predetermined will strengthen closure by fulfilling the reader's expectation of it. One may observe, however, that the occurrence of predetermined elements also increases the reader's experience of validity: that is, by conforming to his expectations, such an element becomes both stable and self-validating and extends these effects to the whole utterance of which it is a part. It would seem then, that any device that predetermines the occurrence or form of terminal elements will tend to strengthen both closure and the sense of validity. (*Poetic* 154–55)

Goffman has suggested, however, that in many cases structural effects like those predicted by Smith will still be produced even if the text ends after an asymmetrically-embedded discourse without an explicit return to the embedding frame:

> Consider now the possibility that the bracket initiating a particular kind of activity may carry more significance than the bracket terminating it. For — as already suggested in regard to the notational system of

mathematics — it is reasonable to assume that the beginning bracket
not only will establish an episode but also will establish a slot for
signals which will inform and define what sort of transformation is to
be made of the materials within the episode. . . . Closing brackets
would seem to perform less work, perhaps reflecting the fact that it is
probably much easier on the whole to terminate the influence of a frame
than to establish it. However, epilogues do try to summarize what has
occurred and ensure the proper framing of it. (255–56)

This might explain why writers so often leave off the final explicit return to the embedding frame: the opening frame has provided all of the context necessary for presenting the embedded
narrative and the structure is felt as complete even though open-
ended. In the case of *The Turn of the Screw*, Henry James's introductory frame accounts completely for the existence and transmission of the governess's embedded narrative, producing a sense
of formal completeness, even though the lack of a final frame produces a radical incompleteness for interpretation; as Bernard
Duyfhuizen has explained, "The extradiegetic narrative introduction stages the reading and listening, but the aftermath, the
'effect,' is missing. The extradiegetic narrator never returns to tell
us how the 'hushed little circle' broke its silence and responded to
the reading of the governess' text. Response is transferred, instead, to the reader of the novel" (169). It should be added that
James does give us the reaction of one reader, Douglas, which enables him to preserve the sense of communicative closure while
still withholding the key reactions of the extradiegetic narrator
and "hushed circle." The other logical type of asymmetrical narrative, which leaves off the initiating part of the embedding narrative and reveals only at the end that the story has been embedded
("it had all been a dream") runs a greater risk of being perceived
as poorly structured. That is not to say that such a surprise ending may not be effectively handled in other cases, of course. In
Ambrose Bierce's "An Occurrence at Owl Creek Bridge," for example, the sudden intrusion of the terminal frame has been carefully prepared to challenge rather than frustrate readers, making
"them re-adjust their understanding of that depiction in relation
to a frame that re-interprets it" (Dittmar 195).[13]

While embedding is frequently a latent source of unity and closure, it also has the potential to produce fragmentation and open-endedness. Moger's analyses more often lead to the thematic interpretation that "The function of the frame, then, would be to undercut the framed, to make clear that the central narrative's appearance of substantiality is an optical illusion, and to mock the pretensions of the conventional reading of such a story" ("Obscure" 134). John Matthews has suggested a structural explanation for this function as well: "the existence of the frame narrative signals that the central story lacks self-sufficiency" (29). While Matthews' comment is specifically aimed at *Wuthering Heights*, his conclusion would seem relevant for any embedded narrative; the embedding and embedded narratives can always be viewed in terms of supplement and lack. Thus narrative embedding often has the paradoxical effect not only of producing the illusion of a more profound realism or aesthetic unity, as the analyses of Smith, Lodge, and Prince explain, but also of undercutting that illusion at the same time.

This survey is intended to be representative rather than exhaustive, and if it leads to any simple conclusion, it would be that of Gregory Bateson, that "a frame is metacommunicative. Any message, which either explicitly or implicitly defines a frame, ipso facto gives the receiver instructions or aids in his attempt to understand the messages included within the frame" (188). Or, in Dittmar's thrifty formulation, "framing narratives function semiotically" (196). Every embedded narrative, however brief or simple, must be considered to have strong potential for structural/formal, dramatic/proairetic, and thematic/hermeneutic significance by virtue of the sole fact of its being embedded.

Barth's "Menelaiad" offers a striking limit case both of the depth to which a story can be embedded and also of the degree to which context can lend significance to the slenderest embedded narrative. The narrative comprises fourteen chapters, numbered I–VII [let us suffix the first seven "a"] and then VII–I ["b"], in the approximate center of which (VIIa) the tale climaxes with Helen's famous reply to Menelaus's question "Why?": """""""Love!"""""""

(*Lost* 150; in an effort to limit the possibility of confusion, I omit "my own" quotation marks and reproduce Barth's text as printed, with seven quotation marks on either side). The question "Why?" and the response "Love" are at this point octadiegetic narratives, at the eighth level of embedding: Helen's reply to Menelaus on their bridal bed (8th level) is quoted by Menelaus to Helen years later in Troy (7th level) within Menelaus's subsequent narration to Eidothea (6th level) which makes up part of Menelaus's narration to Proteus (5th level) which is set within Menelaus's narration to Helen on a ship after leaving Troy (4th level) as part of a story Menelaus narrates to Telemachus and Peisistratus in Sparta (3rd level) as part of a monologue between Menelaus and his own alter-ego (2nd level), the entirety of which is embedded within the discourse of the voice of Menelaus-as-text narrating extradiegetically the entire story to the extradiegetic narratee.[14]

As this outline shows, Menelaus, though only one of several narrators to speak at most of these levels (by definition, of course, he is the only narrator at the outermost, extradiegetic, level), narrates at all eight different narrative levels (he even says "Love" together with Helen the second time she says it [151]). His multiple narrating roles embody structurally the theme of his (perhaps overly) intricate self-analysis and his search for the "unrefracted fact" (145), for a stable identity among his own multiple selves and voices ("husband, father, lord, and host he played" [151]). Despite the one-word length of this tortuously embedded narrative, there is no doubt of its significance for interpretation for the story; indeed, one obvious "ironic" or "disjunctive" thematic reading places the brevity and simplicity of this message against the indirection, complication, and endless deferral of meaning formally signaled by the exaggeratedly circuitous means of transmission through eight narrative levels. Menelaus's intricately mediated and self-conscious search for answers is finally brought to closure through the plainest of messages. As critics have noticed, of course, the intertextual freight, especially biblical, carried by this word makes it rather less plain for the implied reader than for most of these various narratees.

Characteristically, Barth takes this convoluted structure one more step, to what would seem to be the furthest edge of the narratological envelope. When Menelaus, initially unable to comprehend Helen's word, seeks illumination at Delphi, the oracle responds *""""""*   *""""""* (*Lost* 153; as above, I omit "my" quotes). The quotation at the octadiegetic level of a *silence* now offers itself as the interpretative key at the center of the narrative. The thematic implications here would include, for example, an existentialist reading, foregrounding the role played by humans in providing (verbally) a concept — Love — to fill the gap left by a silent (or nonexistent) divinity.

Numerous other interpretations are possible, of course, and the narrators and narratees at each of these levels might profitably be analyzed in far more detail and depth than I have devoted to a single word at a single one of the eight levels. Indeed, many of them have been. Zack Bowen, for example, notes that Menelaus's "fictive listener, Peisistratus," in his role as metadiegetic (third level) narratee, functions as "our critical surrogate in the frame tale of 'Menelaiad,'" and in his role as metadiegetic narrator "speaks for the reader when he admonishes Menelaus," providing interpretative hints or parameters for the reader (62, 63). Proteus, at the pentadiegetic level, "represents the epitome of that which you can't catch hold of and keep, the slippery ambiguity which makes great fiction both a challenge and a pleasure" (Bowen 63). Helen, second only to Menelaus in the range of roles she plays in this narrative structure, has also drawn considerable attention. Patricia Tobin finds that "For Menelaus, the splendid metaphor that was Helen has been shattered into the reality of two Helens, one in Egypt and another in Troy, and with the fracturing of his beloved, his own self has split and lost its materiality" (96). I would add that both characters' fragmentation is figured by their telling their stories at multiple narrative levels (indeed, more than two Helens would seem to be necessary here). William J. Krier, commenting on the narrative functions of Menelaus, takes a different tack in aligning the narratee with Helen (herself, I would note, a narratee at multiple levels and thus structurally positioned to invite such analysis): "Love between a storylistener and Menelaus, metaphorically comparable to the love which exists between 'Menelaus' and 'Helen,' will make Menelaus real" (110). Not to be outdone by his critics, Barth has his characters show their own awareness within the narrative that these multiple levels provide the basis for diverse interpretations; Menelaus finds himself trying "to hold fast to layered sense by listening as it were to Helen hearing Proteus hearing Eidothea hearing me; critic within critic, nestled in my slipping grip . . ." (145; Barth's ellipsis).

To this somewhat dizzying range of effects produced by embedded narrative — potentially activated, as noted above, by a single embedded silence — we must add one more, derived from the most complex class of embedded narratives: those in which the most emphatically structured frame, deep embedding, is violated by use of the trope of the metalepsis. This function of narrative embedding results from what Newman has called "framing's double logic, the tendency of the frame simultaneously to establish boundaries and to announce, even to invite, their violation" (154). Since most narrative texts contain more than one narrative level, they have at least the potential for narrative metalepsis, the move by means of which a character, frequently a narrator, moves from one diegetic level to another. The term, at least as used with this sense, is another Genettian coinage, defined by him as "toute intrusion du narrateur ou du narrataire extradiégétique dans l'univers diégétique (ou de personnages diégétiques dans un univers métadiégétique, etc.), ou inversement . . ." (*Figures III* 244; "any intrusion by the extradiegetic narrator or narratee into the diegetic universe [or by diegetic characters into a metadiegetic universe, etc.], or the inverse . . ." [*Narrative* 234–35]). While his definition does not follow directly from that of the classical trope of metalepsis, a brief look at the earlier usage will lead to a refinement of Genette's model.

The standard analysis of the classical sense of metalepsis is presented by Quintilian in the eighth book of the *Institutio Oratoria* in his discussion of tropes: "Superest ex his, quae aliter significant, metalepsis, id est transumptio, quae ex alio tropo in alium

velut viam praestat . . . . Est enim haec in metalepsi natura, ut
inter id quod transfertur et in quod transfertur sit medius quidam
gradus, nihil ipse significans sed praebens transitum . . ." (vi. 37–
38; "There is but one of the *tropes* involving change of meaning
which remains to be discussed, namely, *metalepsis* or *transumption*,
which provides a transition from one *trope* to another. . . . It is the
nature of *metalepsis* to form a kind of intermediate step between
the term transferred and the thing to which it is transferred, having no meaning in itself, but merely providing a transition"). He
goes on to provide an example of the trope: "Nam id eius frequen-
tissimum exemplum est *cano canto, canto dico*; ita *cano, dico*. Interest medium illud *canto*" (vi. 38–39; "The commonest example is
the following: *cano* [sing] is a synonym for *canto* [meaning "sing"]
and *canto* [meaning "repeat"] for *dico* [relate], therefore *cano* is a
synonym for *dico*, the intermediate step being provided by *canto*").
Richard Lanham has argued from this admittedly cryptic example
that "The main element would thus seem to be omission of a central term in an extended metaphor" (66).

For my purposes, however, Quintilian's definition highlights
two important features for the use of the term in describing narrative levels: the role played by the metalepsis in providing a transition ("praebens transitum") between two otherwise separated
elements, the elements being narrative levels rather than terms
(emphasized by the meaning of "sharing" carried by the prefix
"meta"); and the idea that the metalepsis has no independent
meaning as "content" but produces significance by purely structural means, making it particularly amenable to structural description. This definition also leads to an initial characterization of
what I will define as the basic "unmarked" case of metalepsis.
Genette provides an example of this with an illustration drawn
from Balzac's *Illusions perdues*: "'Pendant que le vénérable ecclési-
astique monte les rampes d'Angoulême, il n'est pas inutile
d'expliquer . . .' comme si la narration était contemporaine de
l'histoire et devait meubler ses temps morts" (*Figures III* 244;
"'While the venerable churchman climbs the ramps of Angoulême,
it is not useless to explain . . . ,' as if the narrating were contempo-

raneous with the story and had to fill up the latter's dead spaces"
[*Narrative* 235]). In this case the metalepsis is not precisely either
a movement by the extradiegetic narrator into the intradiegetic fiction nor a movement by the intradiegetic character to the extradiegetic level. There is rather a temporary sharing of a common
level. Granting this as the unmarked case, then, two other possibilities that are distinctly marked may be identified.

The first may be illustrated by the incident in chapter 55 of
John Fowles's *The French Lieutenant's Woman* in which the twenti-
eth-century extradiegetic narrator enters a nineteenth-century
railway coach and observes (and is observed by) one of his intradiegetic characters (318). This movement from an "outer" embedding level to an "inner" embedded level might be termed in-
trametaleptic. The opposite movement may be seen in Virgil's
Aeneid at the point where Aeneas exclaims "crudelis tu quoque"
(line 407). This is a quotation of his own creator's *Eclogue* 8, in
which the phrase is repeated as a refrain through lines 48–50.
Later in the *Aeneid* (lines 603–05), Virgil has Aeneas allude to Catullus 76, lines 17–26, elaborating the device by giving his ancient
character knowledge of another contemporary poet (Fordyce 368).
This movement, which gives a character in the diegesis knowledge
of the other works of his historical author, in a movement
"outward" as opposed to the movement "inward" of Fowles's
narrator, might, in the interest of symmetry, be termed ex-
trametaleptic.

These examples suggest two other means by which metalepses may be classified. The first takes into account the temporal
relation: Fowles's narrator goes back in time a hundred years,
while the prehistorical Aeneas exhibits familiarity with the works
of poets centuries before their births. The first possibility would
thus constitute, by analogy with Genette's other definitions of
temporal relations, an analeptic intrametalepsis. The second, extending his terminology by the same logic, would be a proleptic
extrametalepsis. The two examples also differ in another way:
Fowles's narrator moves physically to a different diegetic world,
where Aeneas only displays knowledge of the other world. Here

my distinction between modal and verbal emphases in embedding may be reinvoked to characterize these metalepses as, respectively, ontological (or modal) and epistemological (or verbal). Aeneas engages therefore in an verbal proleptic extrametalepsis, Fowles's narrator in a modal analeptic intrametalepsis. I am painfully conscious of the unwieldy nature of these terms, but their awkwardness may be compensated for in some degree by their precision. There are, mercifully, no further categories to specify, and it is possible to turn to the less tortuous activity of suggesting in broad outline the major implications of metalepsis for interpretation.

Genette has observed that the use of metalepsis most often produces "un effet de bizarrerie soit bouffonne (quand on la présente . . . sur le ton de la plaisanterie) soit fantastique" (*Figures III* 244; "an effect of strangeness that is either comical (when . . . it is presented in a joking tone) or fantastic" [*Narrative* 235]). Robyn Warhol has used her model of the distancing and engaging narrator to explain how the metalepsis functions not only to produce comedy but also to emphasize the effect of realism, which, as noted above, is frequently produced by narrative embedding: "A distancing narrator uses metalepsis humorously, as Genette has pointed out . . . . An engaging narrator, though, uses the device to suggest that the characters are possibly as 'real' as the narrator and narratee, who are, in these cases, to be identified with the actual author and actual reader" (814). But these generally comic or realistic effects are also accompanied by an intensified hermeneutic demand for a more complex model of reading. The interpenetration or overlapping of levels forces the reader to make other connections between the characters and worlds of the different levels. The metalepsis leads the reader to cross narrative levels along with the discourse, to read the two connected levels in terms of each other. As Dällenbach has noted, such slippage between narrative levels has the function "de provoquer des collusions spéctaculaires entre les . . . niveaux narratifs" (44 "of giving rise to spectacular collusions among narrative levels"). Genette has argued that these interactions, by foregrounding the codes of narrative, finally may produce effects that are rather unsettling than comic:

> Tous ces jeux manifestent par l'intensité de leurs effets l'importance de la limite qu'ils s'ingenient à franchir au mépris de la vraisemblance, *et qui est precisément la narration (ou la représentation) elle-même*, frontière mouvante mais sacrée entre deux mondes: celui où l'on raconte, celui que l'on raconte.... Le plus troublant de la métalepse est bien dans cette hypothèse inacceptable et insistante, que l'extradiégétique est peut-être toujours déjà diégétique, et que le narrateur et ses narrataires, c'est-à-dire vous et moi, appartenons peut-être encore à quelque récit. (*Figures III* 245)

> All these games, by the intensity of their effects, demonstrate the importance of the boundary they tax their ingenuity to overstep, in defiance of verisimilitude — a boundary *that is precisely the narrating (or the performance) itself*: a shifting but sacred frontier between two worlds, the world in which one tells, the world of which one tells.... The most troubling thing about metalepsis indeed lies in this unacceptable and insistent hypothesis, that the extradiegetic is perhaps always diegetic, and that the narrator and his narratees — you and I — perhaps belong to some narrative. (*Narrative* 236)

Genette is drawn to this last remark about the metaleptic effect by Borges' well-known analysis of the mise en abyme effect produced by certain metalepses: "¿Por qué nos inquieta que Don Quijote sea lector del *Quijote* y Hamlet espectador de *Hamlet*? Creo haber dado con la causa: tales inversiones sugieren que si los caracteres de una ficción pueden ser lectores o espectadores, nosotros, sus lectores o espectadores, podemos ser ficticios" (*Otras* 55: "Why does it disturb us that Don Quixote is a reader of the *Quixote* and Hamlet a spectator at *Hamlet*? I think I have put my finger on the cause: such inversions suggest that if the characters in a fiction can be readers or spectators, then we, their readers or spectators, can be fictitious"). What neither Genette nor Borges considers here is that their conclusions apply not only to metalepsis but to all embedded narrative. Hamlet views not *Hamlet*, after all, but "The Murther of Gonzago" (2.2.537–38) or "The Mouse-trap" (3.2.237). Properly speaking, there is no metalepsis involved in the play within a play. That thematic and dramatic parallels exist between the embedding and embedded plays is not a function of an explicit metalepsis but rather of the structure of embedding and its potential for yielding interpretative prompts by stressing — in both senses of the word — the hermeneutic, proairetic, and formal codes I have been sketching.

My conclusion is therefore that any narrative context within which a character reads or writes, hears or tells a narrative can produce these same relations between embedding and embedded narratives. The trope of metalepsis, especially as implemented by deep embedding with a shift of narrator and narrative level, more directly foregrounds this interplay of narrative levels, but such interplay is implicitly active in all embedded narratives, and it may be said that all embedded narratives elicit, in some degree, the effects of metalepsis.

CONCLUSION

The theoretical focus of this study has been structuralist and more specifically narratological. The golden age of structuralist theories of narrative had its beginnings in the mid–1960s, as Harold F. Mosher has noted (88), and this three-decade span of more or less continuous interest has put narratology in an interesting relation to both older and more recent schools of critical theory. Adherents to the earlier humanistic and New Critical approaches, still active in large numbers at most universities in the United States, tend to see in narratology a new and sometimes intimidating discipline, part of that "critical theory" business, while poststructuralists and deconstructionists generally find it hopelessly old-fashioned. Shlomith Rimmon-Kenan offered a similar analysis over a decade ago: "In many circles, including some universities, the poetics of narrative fiction is either ignored or treated with suspicion. . . . In other circles, this discipline is already considered dead or at least superseded by deconstruction" (130).

The objection of humanistic critics to narratology has usually been that it slights interpretation with its attempts to reduce texts to diagrams or formulas. Early narratological writings seemed to support this idea that there is a distinct boundary between literary interpretation and structuralist poetics, the former being more of an art and the latter a science. Roger Seamon has traced the history of this "program of scientific poetics" and concluded that its "enabling distinction, . . . the distinction between readings and objective commentary, is utterly obliterated and the project of

modern poetics comes undone" (303). I would gladly accept
Seamon's arguments and insist that the application of a model
such that offered in this book does not at all eliminate the need for
interpretive "readings" but rather presupposes and in fact underscores it. The precision of our definitions of the unreliable narrator and the ironic narrator will not tell us mechanically which is
present in Jonathan Swift's "A Modest Proposal." The assignment of narrative levels in *Les liaisons dangereuses* depends upon a
series of literary judgments. No definition will tell us whether
Chaucer's *Retraction* is an element of the text or the paratext.
These and the other illustrations I have touched upon throughout
are meant to affirm implicitly the interdependence of narrative
theory and interpretation, and the necessity of combining theoretical discussion with practical application. One of the seldom-
appreciated strengths of structuralist criticism has been its readi-
ness to modify theories to accommodate exceptional cases; the
"rules" of any structuralist model are always provisional, however confidently presented, and any given narrative instance can
"disprove" them and demand their rethinking. Many of the limitations of other approaches, it might be argued, stem from their
inability to modify or question their own "rules": no new text
could conceivably put into question any of the important tenets of
deconstruction or many other poststructuralist approaches, and
certainly deconstruction's tendency to produce identical and inevitable readings of the most disparate texts fueled the impatience
of its critics and bored its journals' referees.

Seamon locates a further "deep theoretical weakness" in
structuralist criticism as a result of the impossibility of distinguishing poetic language from language generally: "If there is no
way to distinguish poetic utterances from any others, the entire
project collapses" (303). As I have argued in chapter four, I agree
that the field of application of these methodologies seems impossible to define. But granting, as I do, that we can not define terms
like "poetic utterance" or "narrative," it seems to me that Seamon
might more properly conclude not that structuralist critiques are
thus incapable of analyzing any texts at all, but rather that they

can be called into play for the analysis of any and all verbal discourses. Our inability to distinguish poetic from non-poetic texts does not limit but instead extends the range of application of the model. And given a set of shared definitions and clear structural principles, critics can better isolate and describe the textual elements upon which these analyses are made and better arrive, if not always at a consensus, more often at a productive dialogue.

At the other end of the critical spectrum, theorists committed to the cutting edge of the various poststructuralisms have had very different but equally grave reservations about structuralist poetics. For them, this very effort to develop a systematic critical apparatus, the narratological project of providing a model for the use of what J. Hillis Miller has characterized as "an international community of researchers sharing the same goals, the same norms and procedures, and speaking the same language of analysis" (189), however reassuring it may be to humanistic critics, is a central source of poststructuralist dissatisfaction with "scientific" structuralist models. As Miller explains, "The system of assumptions defining the collective enterprise of scientific mastery is one of the things [deconstruction] wants to put in question by disarticulating it or by showing that it disarticulates itself. This means showing that it contains contradictions and aporias making its enterprise impossible" (190). My own model is certainly liable to such a questioning. While I have tried to keep it internally consistent, the premises upon which the model rests are no more than strategic moves that are not grounded in either concrete reality or transcendent truth. Narrators do not literally speak and no one will ever know how the implied reader would interpret a given text.

This line of analysis does not, however, forcibly lead to the conclusion that it is impossible to continue to work with such models. The deconstructive critique serves rather the more positive function of requiring that proponents of theories about narrative discourse exhibit a higher degree of self-consciousness, that they do not uncritically believe in the premises they rest on but recognize that their hypotheses are made for certain purposes and are only valid in certain contexts. This awareness that one's premises are provisional and strategic is not at all the same as the naive assumption-making that is the source of Miller's concern. Indeed, it might be argued that poststructuralists have become the school most guilty of blind acceptance of their premises, with scores of young critics taking Foucault or Lacan on faith the way older critics accepted now largely-superseded figures like Marx and Freud. We may still read discourses "as if" they were narrated by narrators to narratees and make what use we can of theories built up from that foundation without forgetting that there are other ways to read and that such theories may obscure some properties of texts at the same time that they highlight others.

Rimmon-Kenan speculated in 1983 that for deconstructionists her own book on narrative poetics "would be an obituary" (130). I would hope that deconstruction's fondness for *bricolage* would have precluded even a corpse from being entirely useless. But in any event it did not follow that deconstruction had to be an obituary for narratologists. My own view, as this study presumably makes clear, is that the structuralist project was never completed. Indeed, a rapidly growing number of obituaries have been written for deconstruction, which now appears to have been something of a flash in the pan by comparison to narratology, which seems to be in the midst of a renaissance: *Narrative*, devoted to mainstream narrative theory, won the 1993 CELJ prize for best new journal, and the field seems to be thriving, with new ground being broken since Rimmon-Kenan's obituary in such fields as musical narratology.[1] I suspect that many poststructuralists will follow the lead of Miller himself, much of whose recent work hardly breathes the word "deconstruction," concentrating rather on (highly perspicuous) analyses of narrative voice and point of view. Perhaps the era of deconstruction will come to be viewed with hindsight as a transitional phase of structuralism rather than as its successor, a period of experimentation and reevaluation that sparked a more sophisticated and self-conscious version of structuralist thought.

NOTES

INTRODUCTION

1   As Gittes notes, most of the stories in the *Panchatantra* exist in earlier versions, and their exact origins are unknown (9). Some idea of
just how ambitious — and fascinating — a full-blown history of embedded narrative would have to be may be inferred from Stuart H.
Blackburn's detailed analysis of just one of the embedded tales from
the *Panchatantra* "through four major variants and their frame
texts: a Vedic ritual manual, c. 1000 B.C.; the *Mahabhrata* epic, c.
400 B.C.–A.D. 400; a collection of stories, *Kathasaritsagara*, c. A.D.
1100; and a modern Tamil oral tradition" (527). Barring some as-
tounding scholarly coup, the task seems possible only if undertaken a
piece at a time in a series of studies circumscribed by period and na-
tion (e.g., Claudine Chadeyras' dissertation on the evolution of
framed narratives in sixteenth-century French literature) or perhaps by clusters of authors (e.g., Judith Neville's dissertation on
embedded narratives in Hawthorne, Poe, and Melville).

2   Gittes, for example, is led by her notion of what constitutes framing
to a particular view of its history: "The Greeks and Romans did not
develop the frame narrative, although some of their longer narratives frame short, complete tales: the tales Odysseus tells at Alci-

nous' court (*Odyssey* 7–12) . . ." ("*Canterbury*" 238). Operating from slightly different premises (rigorous definitions of the form are seldom offered and almost never explicitly justified), one might maintain instead that the *Odyssey* is one of the most highly developed examples of narrative framing in literature: Henry Barrett Hinckley, in one of the earliest surveys of "The Framing-Tale," lists seven examples (besides the stories to Alcinous) of significant "tale-boxing" in the poem (74), and by my count the work features a total of fifty-nine separate dramatized narrators, several of whom relate multiply-embedded narratives.

3   As Genette explains,

> le souci de vraisemblance ou de simplicité détourne généralement le récit factuel d'un recours trop massif aux narrations du second degré: on imagine mal un historien ou un mémorialiste laissant à l'un de ses "personnages" le soin d'assumer une part importante de son récit, et l'on sait depuis Thucydide quels problèmes pose au premier la simple transmission d'un discours un peu étendu. La présence du récit métadiégétique est donc un indice assez plausible de fictionalité — même si son absence n'indique rien. (*Fiction* 79)

> the concern with verisimilitude or with simplicity generally orients factual narrative away from excessive reliance on second-degree narrations. It is hard to imagine a historian or a memoirist letting one of his "characters" take responsibility for a major part of his narrative, and we have known since Thucydides what problems the historian faces in simply transmitting a speech of any length. The presence of the metadiegetic narrative is thus a fairly plausible index of fictionality — even if its absence indicates nothing at all. (*Fiction* 69; translation slightly modified)

4   Numerous literary and extra-literary approaches taken to the "frame" are enumerated in chapters two and three (pp. 28–180) of David W. Ullrich's dissertation and in chapter one (pp. 7–77) of Dianne Owens Armstrong's dissertation.

CHAPTER 1 | HISTORICAL AND IMPLIED AUTHORS AND READERS

¹ Compare Patrick O'Neill's comment that "in an important sense narratological theory requires us to read *every* narrative in terms of its embeddedness. The situation of embeddedness, . . . far from being just some incidental structural luxury to be employed occasionally for special effect, is the central structural characteristic of all narrative" (65–66). O'Neill's fine book, which appeared not long after the journal publication of an earlier version of this chapter, arrives quite independently and perspicuously at many of the same conclusions reached here about the implied author.

² The determination of what counts as "extratextual" as opposed to "intratextual" has proven problematic, to put it mildly. The definitive study of the vast gray area of the "paratextual" is Gérard Genette's *Seuils*, but not all of his conclusions have been accepted. Patrick O'Neill, for example, would assign titles to the implied author (166 n. 9), while claiming that Genette would assign them to the narrator. Rather than impose either rule, we might consider that some narrators are aware of and claim responsibility for the titles of the works they narrate and that titles are also assignable to the historical author (though not always to the writer — much of Chaucer's poetry, for example, has been titled by editors). In the case of John Barth's *LETTERS* (discussed later in this chapter) the narrator explicitly demonstrates his knowledge of the title (664), which we must therefore assign to all three agents. Susan Lanser goes rather further than O'Neill in extending the implied author's paratextual range, arguing that "to label [a book] 'Penguin Classic' rather than 'Harlequin Romance'" (124) is a function of the implied author (her "extratextual voice"). I would limit the production of such publisher's blurbs to the historical author.

³ I should stipulate that in describing this model of levels I do not pretend to be describing the variable practice of historical readers.

The serious historical reader will naturally have recourse to as wide a range of data as possible in attempting to understand a literary work; I assume, for instance, that almost any critic would be sure to read a reliable biography of any author that he or she was working on. The implied reader is the agent that restricts itself entirely to the text proper; but even for historical readers, the text is usually privileged above extratextual sources of information as evidence in support of interpretative readings.

4   O'Neill has suggested (I'm not sure how seriously) that certain postmodernist texts call for the concept of the

> unreliable implied author. The implied author of Robbe-Grillet's *La Maison de Rendez-vous* would be an example of this, in that the structure of the narration in that text undermines the very notion of authority.... Such an entity is in effect an *implied implied author*, since his or her unreliability can in turn be assessed only by recourse to the reliability of a "real" implied author. But this latter could be unreliable — and so on. (70)

But surely the only unreliability to be accounted for is that of the narrator, who makes all of the contradictory and confusing statements that disorient the narratee and the historical (but not implied) reader. The narrative's structure and undermining of authority are the effect of the implied author's (entirely reliable) intention to produce a novel with these features.

5   The importance of this narrative technique for literary history is emphasized by Elaine Showalter, who uses the appropriation of male voices by female writers as the *terminus a quo* for *A Literature of Their Own*: "Like Eve's fig leaf, the male pseudonym signals the loss of innocence" and marks the beginning of the feminine novel (19).

6   In response to a paper I delivered at the 1995 meeting of the Modern Language Association, in which I discussed this issue, Donna Burrell made the excellent point that gender is not necessarily a simple binary opposition. Upon reflection, I would argue that the Victorians appear to have been acutely aware of this, and that many of the early reviews of the Brontës may be read as informed by an assumption that there are several degrees of femininity (often marked by

accompanying class distinctions). Viewing the matter in this way does not seem to compromise the analysis offered in this chapter, but does provide an opportunity for further refinement.

[7] There are, of course, nearly as many permutations to the nineteenth-century games of anonymity and pseudonymity as there were writers, and men as well as women were caught up in them whether they wanted to be or not. In the case of Nathaniel Hawthorne, G. R. Thompson notes, "Both the editor of the gift annual *The Token* and the editor of the *New-England Magazine* filled their pages with Hawthorne's works but kept the author's name obscure via nonattribution and pseudonyms, possibly so that readers would not know that there were so many pages by one author in a single issue" (23). On the other hand, *The Token* would usually credit the works of an established female author like Catherine Sedgwick by name, an indication that economic pressure and gender discrimination were factors not always operating in the same direction.

[8] Miriam Allott lists sixty-two early British reviews, all unsigned. She assigns seventeen to men, and three to women, leaving forty-two unidentified. We might increase the number of women to four or five: Tom Winnifrith believes that the *Sharpe's London Magazine* reviewer (Allott # 76) "may well have been a woman" (125), and I suspect that Anne Mozley may have contributed the 1848 *Christian Remembrancer* review (Allott # 16). This tentative figure of about 20% women reviewers, by the way, is the same percentage Richard Altick arrives at for the ratio of women to men novelists throughout the period ("Sociology" 392), a correspondence that offers at least indirect confirmation.

[9] By way of symmetry, we might note a final Brontëan example addressing the separation of the writer and author in Anne's second novel, *Wildfell Hall*. Charlotte went so far as to argue in a letter to her publisher, William Smith Williams, that the novel did not merit reprinting because of the disparity between the historical and implied authors: "The choice of subject in the work is a mistake — it was too little consonant with the character — tastes and ideas of the gentle, retiring, inexperienced writer" (Barker 654). Many later

critics and biographers would argue in turn, of course, that Charlotte's assessment of both writer and author was mistaken.

[10] Wilson's own discussion of the implied reader is generally very solid, especially in his treatment of seldom-discussed German theorists such as Erwin Wolff and Hannelore Link, but unluckily limited, as he notes himself, by the publication, just as his own essay was coming out, of a number of articles on fictional readers and narratees (863 n. 50). Booth's second edition (incorporating Rabinowitz's model) and Genette's *Nouveau discours* have, of course, dated Wilson's survey as well. His terminology is somewhat unfamiliar (he rejects as "jargonistic neologisms" such now-standard coinages as Prince's "narratee" [856]), but clear and consistent, and his article remains one of the best on this topic.

[11] Readers wishing to read Prince's seminal essay in English should be warned that the translation is incomplete, and that the editorial omissions are not clearly marked. Despite these problems, the translation has been reprinted in Hoffman and Murphy.

[12] Walter Slatoff, one of the earliest critics to note the multiple nature of historical readers reading, deplored

> the tendency of most aestheticians and critics to speak as though there were only two sorts of readers: the absolutely particular, individual human being with all his prejudices, idiosyncrasies, personal history, knowledge, needs, and anxieties, who experiences the work of art in solely "personal" terms, and the ideal or universal reader whose response is impersonal and aesthetic. Most actual readers, except for the most naive, I think, transform themselves as they read into beings somewhere between these extremes. They learn, that is, to set aside many of the particular conditions, concerns, and idiosyncrasies which help to define them in everyday affairs. (54)

[13] See Rabinowitz 126–27 for his presentation of these types.

[14] Mieke Bal and Lanser are two other important theorists of narrative with reservations about the implied author, but neither really questions the utility or definition of the concept, at least as it is presented here. Bal objects that the concept is not unique to narrative texts, but applies to all texts, and therefore is not one of the concerns

of narratology proper (*Narratology* 119–20). My own definition of narrative, offered in chapter four, views all texts as potentially narrative and thus defuses this objection (though it might raise some new ones). Lanser's opposition "has more to do with the history of the term than with abstract meaning" (*Narrative* 120), and she has offered "extratextual voice" as a substitute label for much the same concept. As this chapter demonstrates, I agree entirely with Lanser about the term's unsatisfactory connotative baggage and history of inconsistent definitions, but feel more optimistic than she does about the chances for its rehabilitation (or perhaps simply less sanguine about the chances that any new term will finally prove immune from the vicissitudes of critical treatment).

[15] Martin Esslin's analysis of Bertolt Brecht provides the neatly symmetrical converse case of a professedly Marxist historical author who creates a much different implied author in his plays, which "based as they are on his intuitive perception of reality rather than his consciously held beliefs, constantly belie the pedantic concepts of Marxism" (210):

> . . . to Brecht himself, who could not suffer the idea that he was not wholly in control of his own activity, the obvious divergence between his intentions and the effect of his work on the public must have been truly tragic. . . . Yet such is the paradox of the creative process, that, had he succeeded in his objectives, he would merely have been a flat and boring party hack. He failed — and became one of the most puzzling, one of the most hotly debated, but also one of the most important writers of his age. (236)

[16] Genette specifically applies this remark to instances involving "dramatized" homodiegetic narrators, but the logic here seems to me quite independent of the circumstances of the narrator; my argument for the distinction between the historical and implied authors obtains (or does not) for the same reasons in every instance he cites.

[17] Genette does consider two other "peripheral" cases in the course of his discussion: "ghostwritten" texts, in which (historical, though of course not implied) readers are misled about the *identity* of the writer, and those (pseudonymous) collaborative texts in which

readers are misled about the *number* of the writers. My model, which allows for a variety of multiple historical authors, would readily accommodate these exceptions.

18 For an alternative line of argument for the utility of the implied reader model see Franc Schuerewegen, whose analysis of a much-discussed passage from Balzac leads him to the conclusion that "la différence entre lecteur et narrataire . . . nous oblige, dans certains cas au moins, à conserver le concept de lecteur implicite . . ." (254; "the difference between the [historical] reader and the narratee . . . forces us, at least in certain cases, to retain the concept of the implied reader . . .").

19 Another example here might be Pope's *An Epistle to Dr. Arbuthnot*, in which David B. Morris finds that three distinct voices intertwine: "the historical Alexander Pope . . . the dramatic speaker of the poem . . . and the author of the poem" (28). That my two examples are both eighteenth-century British authors may be only coincidental.

CHAPTER 2 | THE GENERAL NARRATOR

1 A more detailed discussion of Fowles's novel, in the context of a critique of the theories of Genette and Lanser, is offered in my essay in *Style* 18.2 (1984).

2 Roger Fowler (48–54) and Susan Lanser (*Narrative* 269 ff.) meticulously trace a range of subtle cues in the story that suggest somewhat greater sympathy even on the narrator's part for the members of the local community than for the outsiders Al and Max. The gap between the disinterested role of the narrator and the judgmental role

of the implied author would thus be a matter of degree rather than absolute; it seems likely that any limit case of objective narration would yield similar traces of what Chatman would call "implicitly-expressed slant" under sufficiently close scrutiny.

3   Lanser argues that "It is especially safe to refer to the narrator of this story as 'he,' not only because of the rules for equivalence between author and narrative voice, but because the story is taken from a collection entitled *Men Without Women*" (*Narrative* 267 n. 11). But there seems to be no compelling reason to connect the story with that collection title or even to give priority to the version in *Men Without Women* in the first place: the story was originally published in *Scribner's Magazine* (Smith 141), which would seem to eliminate her second argument at least for those who read the original (perhaps the implied reader?). I cite the story from *The Complete Short Stories*, and most historical readers doubtless encounter the work in anthologies. In the absence of other support, the bare argument from "rules" is unpersuasive.

4   Richard Shryock proposes the complementary notion of "receiver-absent" narrative (87), what we might call "nonnarrateed narrative." I offer no detailed analysis here of the concept, as his suggestion has not proven influential to this point, but my objections to this category may be readily inferred from those I make against nonnarrated narrative. I would note that Shryock's qualifications of his category closely resemble those offered by Chatman. For example, he covers a list of exceptions with the concession that "perhaps 'minimally-present receiver' would be more precise" (87) and, as Chatman does, stipulates that "my reader should keep in mind that this absence is usually not absolute" (88).

5   This is not to concede that paragraph breaks are purely conventional and without interpretative importance. In the two Hemingway examples discussed above, the significance of the character's turning to the wall is emphasized by the formatting of the description into a single-sentence paragraph, a meaningful use of the conventions of typography which may be attributed to the implied author instead of the narrator.

6 Lanser also finds here evidence of what I would call the implied author: "The repetition of a reference to the 'arc-light' constitutes the only overt use of symbol in the text . . ." (*Narrative* 268). Lanser, however, appears to attribute this symbolic intent to the narrator rather than the implied author. If the arc-light is "overt," then it might be stipulated that Ole Andreson's turn to the wall is also overtly symbolic, as are many other aspects of the story.

7 This and all other unattributed translations are mine. I have attempted throughout to provide published translations, partly because of my own inaptitude for that (criminally undervalued) work and partly to avoid the pitfall of unconsciously slanting translations to suit my own readings. The handful of cases in which I have supplied my own translations is merely evidence that no good translation has come into my hands, not that none exists — I have occasionally had interlibrary loans fail to materialize and doubtless left many a stone unturned in my searches. In the case of Borges, of course, the frustration with published translations is widespread. As Emir Rodriguez Monegal and Alastair Reid have remarked, "Borges has something of a patchwork existence in English" (xi). Yu Tsun's reading over and signing his confession, by the way, appears to offer an example of the unusual device of having an intradiegetic narrator contribute to an extradiegetic textualization of its narrative; Bernard Duyfhuizen cites Frankenstein's contribution to Walton's narrative as the only example he has encountered (215).

8 The failure of editors to reproduce Swift's use of italics to signal this shift is especially egregious and, unfortunately, widespread in modern anthologies, whose readers so often need all the cues they can get. This use of repetition to set off or "frame" a section of narrative is one of several types of framing devices ably studied by Mary Ann Caws, but would not, as will become apparent, fit my definition of embedded narrative, a label I would reserve for a particular subtype of framed narrative — which Caws refers to, incidentally, as "the garden variety of narrative frames" (86).

9 Monika Fludernik has edited a special number of *Style* (28.3) devoted to the study of second-person narrative. In her introductory es-

say, she claims to "have noted a great number of second-person texts that have neither a narrator or narratee (i.e., current addressee of the discourse)" (287). These are examples in which there is no "I" but only "you," which evidently refers to the protagonist whose consciousness and impressions are being given. As her parenthetical remark suggests, the non-narrated status of these examples depends upon the definitions being used. On the basis of the examples she gives, I would call this intradiegetic narration, with the narrator and narratee both being the protagonist (the character "thinks to herself"), transmitted at the extradiegetic level by another narrator. Fludernik provides a useful bibliography of second-person narrative, covering primary and secondary materials, in *Style* 28.4 (1994).

10 The term "monstrator" has been suggested by André Gaudreault, whose hierarchy of coinages for film analysis also includes "filmographic narrator," "profilmic monstrator," "filmographic monstrator," "filmic mega-monstrator," and "filmic mega-narrator" (279). The more conservative approach to terminology is well-represented by Chatman, who offers "cinematic narrator" in his *Coming to Terms*. Both approaches have their drawbacks — Gaudreault's terminology is genuinely forbidding, while Chatman's single agent appears to overlap considerably with the implied author at one end and voice-over narration at the other — and it may be that some middle level of complexity will eventually be found workable.

11 For my purposes, it seems economical to group the occasional footnotes with the "Avertissement" and the concluding "Note de l'Editeur" (386; "Publisher's Note" [352]); although I can imagine a reading in which the notes are attributed elsewhere, the matter seems complicated enough as is.

12 Richard Aldington, whose dated but readily-accessible translation I have been providing, claims that the "Publisher's Note" is "An ironic comment by Laclos himself" (1), but seems to be generally alerting the unwary reader rather than dictating a particular interpretative strategy.

[13] Nancy K. Miller sees the two prefaces as playing a similar thematic role in her reading of the novel as an "allégorie de l'acte même de l a lecture" (48; "allegory of the very act of reading").

[14] Bernard Duyfhuizen also considers the additional layer of transmission involved in treating the publisher as a fictional construct: "his or her response to the text, when printed before the editor's preface, usurps the editorial convention of authority and subverts the extradiegetic reader's expectations . . . . The ironic stances of both note and preface enfold one another as the shifting contact between the publisher and editor creates an interpretive aporia for the reader" (147–48). Duyfuizen's insightful reading of the novel finds aporia where I find only bifurcation, an example of the different routes like-minded critics can be steered down by a difference in their theoretical models.

[15] This is not the same thing as a narrator's actually lying about the events it narrates, and a lying narrator is not the same thing as an unreliable narrator, who usually tells the truth as it sees it, but whose moral or ethical standards diverge from those of the implied author. While examples of narrators who lie intradiegetically to other characters are common, extradiegetic narrators who lie to the extradiegetic narratee appear to be quite rare. Susan Amper summarizes the obvious obstacle: "It will be asked, however, and it must be considered, how we are to judge the truth of the various assertions the [extradiegetic] narrator makes. Since we rely on him for all our information, it may seem hopeless for us to determine with any assurance when he is speaking the truth and when he is lying" (478). Amper goes on to note that "This problem, however, proves more difficult in theory than in practice," and presents a persuasive case for viewing the extradiegetic narrator of Poe's "The Black Cat" as a liar.

[16] Patrick O'Neill discusses the parallel convention of representing in English speeches supposedly "really" delivered in foreign languages in films made for English-speaking audiences (132–34).

CHAPTER 3 | FOCALIZATION

[1] José Antonio Alvarez Amorós offers an illuminating discussion of the origins of this confusion, which he traces back to Percy Lubbock's attempts to systematize the narrative practices and critical reflections of Henry James.

[2] In an earlier version of this chapter, published in *Poetics Today* in 1990, I claimed credit for the coinage "free focalization," but upon recently rereading *The Narrative Act*, Susan Lanser's classic discussion of the poetics of point of view, I was surprised to discover that she refers to "unfocalized or freely focalized narrative" (214) as well as to "free focalization" (213–14, 224). I had of course read Lanser before publishing that article — indeed, I discussed her book in some detail in a 1984 essay in *Style* — and have no doubt that I must have unconsciously lifted the term from her usage (although our much different views of focalization result in our assigning a different meaning to the term). Doubtless there are many other such unacknowledged borrowings in my work, and I hope that the writers who recognize them will take a charitable view of my good intent to give credit (however belatedly) where it is due.

[3] Lanser's own analysis of these three sentences is somewhat different, as she considers all three cases similarly ambiguous: "the three 'extra' sentences providing objective information about Nick may or may not constitute subjective information as well; it is not clear whether these are Nick's or the narrator's thoughts" (*Narrative* 271). As Lanser also notes (although her different approach to point of view lends the matter a different emphasis), the mere fact that "the narrator knows the names of Nick and George" constitutes another "subtle departure from the convention" (*Narrative* 162, 163) of external narration.

[4] O'Neill, who largely agrees with Bal's analysis otherwise, also argues for "situating the ultimate locus of focalization on the level of the *implied author* rather than the narrator" (96). Shlomith

Rimmon-Kenan, another critic who accepts Bal's model, seems to be favorably disposed toward this modification as well (85).

5   For a detailed argument for the logical necessity of the narrator for any unified account of narrative, however, see Marie-Laure Ryan, "Pragmatics."

6   A further example of mixed fruit results from Bal's decision to use "external" to mean "heterodiegetic" and "internal" to mean "homodiegetic," producing a system in which *all* focalization is internal. While Bal's own analyses do not always foreground this difficulty, its consequences are clear in Patrick O'Neill's application of her model. According to this theory "external focalization" thus indicates internal focalization between an extradiegetic narrator and an intradiegetic character (Genette's $N = C$) and his "internal focalization" indicates internal focalization between an intradiegetic (but non-narrating) character and another character as filter (i.e., the distinctly non-Genettian $C = C$). This move leads to a series of unnecessarily convoluted analyses of point of view situations: O'Neill's "$F = (EF (CF1_{Lynley} (CF2_{Dougal})))$" (103), for example, represents an example of internal focalization ($N = C$) in which the narrator tells us what a character is thinking (the subtle presentation of what that character thinks is quite interesting, and O'Neill's sensitive readings of his well-chosen illustrations are consistently enlightening; as with many of the examples I cite, the critic works much better than the theory he uses). More fundamentally, however, the change in terminology would seem to eliminate the free/internal/external division that is the prerequisite for the analyses of point of view that the theory was developed for in the first place, effectively undoing Genette's work and returning us to square one.

7   One might also analyze the passage (admittedly taken here out of context) as an instance of free focalization, considering that Camille herself is unaware of the precise cause of her perturbation, and that therefore $N > C$. As always, these difficult judgments about point of view highlight the inextricable interdependence of theory and interpretation.

⁸ Magny implies much the same idea about this difference between
the modes: "In a movie, every scene is of necessity photographed
from a certain point of view, and this point of view is part of it, in-
separable from its essence" (88).

⁹ Bal herself has extended her model of focalization to cover the
viewing of visual art, with the terms "external focalizer" and
"internal focalizer" designating the viewer of a painting and the
viewer depicted (painted) within a painting (*Reading* 159). It remains to be seen whether art critics will be persuaded of the need for
these terms.

¹⁰ For a survey of the psychological research relevant to visual imaging in reading, see Ellen J. Esrock's *The Reader's Eye*. As Esrock recognizes, the frequently-observed lack of consistency among individual visualizations produced by a given textual stimulus has made
most literary critics skeptical about the interpretative profit to be
gained by such studies. Esrock's call for further research is, I think,
phrased with sufficient caution to satisfy most critics: " . . . the af-
fective power of imaging does not manifest itself in ways that are so
entirely idiosyncratic as to preclude study within a literary context"
(149–50).

¹¹ Ruth Ronen presents several interesting examples of the relation of
fictional space to characters' perceptions, but her analyses are compromised by her adoption of Bal's model of focalization, which produces much the same kind of interpretative non sequiturs for her as it
does for Bal, Vitoux, O'Neill, and the other critics to have applied
it.

¹² Aromarama and Smell-o-Vision (also known as Scentovision), two
experiments in filmmaking that emerged briefly during the early
wars with television, relied on air-conditioning systems or strategi-
cally-positioned atomizers to transmit the odors perceived by the
characters in the films; according to David A. Cook, "when working
properly, both could create an impressive olfactory illusion." Cook
also notes the less technologically ambitious revival of the technique for John Waters' *Polyester* (1981), which provided "theater

patrons with 'Odorama' scratch-and-sniff cards keyed to numbers flashed on-screen" (532).

CHAPTER 4 | STORIES WITHOUT STORIES: NARRATIVE AS A TEXT-TYPE

[1]   The Russian Formalists, though even they on occasion spoke of themselves collectively, were of course a heterogeneous group, and have probably been subjected to too much of this sort of blanket generalization. Peter Steiner has nimbly walked the line between collective and individual characterization of the movement's views with the apt term "polyphonic unity" (17). The most useful tools in English for surveying the Formalist critics' writings are David Gorman's comprehensive "Bibliography of Russian Formalism in English" and subsequent "Supplement."

[2]   See Carolyn Abbate for a good example of a study of the narrative effects available to opera.

[3]   Still shorter is Anderson Imbert's "The Prince," which seems to me at least equally eligible for candidacy as a potential "limit case" story (the ellipsis is authorial):

> When the prince was born there was a great national celebration. Dancing, fireworks, pealing of bells, shooting of cannons . . . .
> With so much noise, the newborn baby died. (222)

[4]   Bremond's initial stipulation about human interest would seem to be too subjective to be useful; surely any number of readers are persuaded that certain highly popular (or extremely scholarly) books are of no genuine human interest. One of the most thoroughly devel-

oped of these "sociopoetic" models defining story in terms of human interest is that of Denis Jonnes, who argues that "When we speak of a 'story' we are referring neither to a particular order of sentence, nor to some system of rhetorical or poetic devices, but to a class of signifier denominative of a restricted order of relation and event — specifically, those constitutive or disruptive of the 'familial'" (253). It may be generally true that most narratives are of human interest and deal with families, but either the exceptions will be numerous or the definitions so sweepingly inclusive as to evaporate. After all, how many human beings have never been (at least biologically or genetically) part of a family? And would such an unusual situation, if it arose (Adam and Eve?), not allow the critic to claim justifiably that the subject of familial relations has been raised precisely by its striking absence?

5   Philip Sturgess has made the related general point that "Every sequence in a narrative will tell a story, *namely the story of its narrativity,* but the ways in which this story is discussible in terms of the story being told will be many and various" (22). Sturgess's extended and tightly-argued definition of "narrativity" resists brief summary, but I recommend his book to those interested in pursuing this complex issue further.

6   Another subtype of fiction marginalized by the privileging of story is that of present-tense narrative, which Suzanne Fleischman, for example, finds "inherently unstable" (127). See James Phelan for a summary of this position and a refutation of it on the grounds that "it privileges *fabula* as the defining element of narrative" ("Present" 225). For a temperate deconstructive reading of the story and discourse opposition, see Jonathan Culler (169–87).

7   Patrick O'Neill provides a convenient comparative chart of several of these binary and tripartite systems (21). O'Neill himself decides, as he puts it, to "stretch Ockham's patience and operate with a *four*-term model, involving the four narrative levels of *story, text, narration,* and *textuality*" (23), the latter designating "the interactive process of the text's production by an author and its reception by readers" (25). As O'Neill sensibly concedes, "Whether we *need* so

elaborate a scheme, of course, is determined by what we need it *for"* (25), and my own decision to treat this extratextual level of communication three chapters ago renders his fourth level more or less dispensable for my present discussion.

[8] One of these limit cases, that of musical narrative, would seem to be approachable only by a discourse-based model of the type argued for here. As Lawrence Kramer has noted, "the very premise of musical narratology is the recognition that music cannot tell stories." He goes on to observe, however, that "This defect — or virtue — is not affected by the ability of music to deploy narratographic strategies or to perform narrativistic rituals; both the strategies and the rituals are migratory, easily displaced from the avenues of storytelling" (154). The metaphor of "migration" offers a useful way to account for the ease with which narrative analysis seems applicable to texts and genres traditionally considered nonnarrative.

[9] Dorrit Cohn, in an insightful discussion of the sometimes porous lines between factual and fictional biographies and autobiographies, claims that, for autobiography, "the principal criterium for differentiating between real and fictional self-narration . . . hinges quite simply on the ontological status of its speaker — by which I mean his identity or non-identity with the author under whose name the narration has been published" ("Fictional" 13). I would object that these agents may be differentiated in any number of ways (including ontological status), and that the author's name is not really a formal property of the text being analyzed. Even that marker, however, is not always a sure indicator of what orientation to take toward a text. *Walden,* for example, has probably been read just as often (and just as profitably) for its narrative structure as for its biographical content, despite the fact that the narrator and author have the same name. In fact, Thoreau's decision to compress the two years-plus of his stay into a one-year narrative would put it on the fictional side of at least one of Cohn's criteria, through its failure to follow "the chronotope of biographical time. Indeed one of the distinctions of fictional as compared to historical narrative is that the former is able to make an entire life come to life as a unified whole

in a short span of story time . . ." (3). Cohn herself notes a number of indeterminate cases for classification, and her remark that "we cannot conceive of any one given text as more or less fictional, more or less factual, but . . . we read it in one key or another" (16) may well be compatible with my notion of narrative analysis as contingent upon a reader's decision to read in a certain way rather than on any formal textual features.

CHAPTER 5 | NARRATIVE LEVELS AND EMBEDDED NARRATIVE

1   Dolozel's formulation, while perfectly accurate for most narrative texts, would actually deny narrative status to Beckett's work (and many others) because there is no characters' discourse: "*Every* narrative text T is a concatenation and alternation of DN [narrator's discourse] and DC [characters' discourse]: T → DN + DC" (*Narrative* 4; my emphasis). Works in which only the narrator speaks would belong to the genre of the lyric, and works in which only the characters speak would belong to the genre of the drama (3). There is no denying the theoretical appeal of Dolozel's elegant untying of this Gordian knot, but in practice there seems to be nothing in Beckett's text that causes any problems for narrative analysis. As suggested in the previous chapter, it may be more efficient to view the lyric as a type or branch of narrative in a dualistic model than to artificially prohibit the application of narrative theory to the lyric.

2   The same logic would eliminate such definitions of "frame story" as Harry Shaw's "A story within a narrative setting, or frame."

3　G. R. Thompson has also faulted Genette's model on this basis: "the hyperstructuated models of Genette . . . in my opinion are too complicated to be useful in practical critical discourse, and I do not employ his terminology" (249 n. 10). Not surprisingly, a tradeoff ensues, with a gain in readability for Thompson's extremely perceptive readings of Hawthorne's early experiments in narrative framing, but a loss in the wider applicability of his approach to other texts and writers. The ends properly dictate the means here, of course. Despite what would seem to be considerable overlap in our interests, I have been unable to adapt much from Thompson in piecing together a model for describing narrative embedding, though his book taught me a great deal about Hawthorne — which was, after all, his purpose.

4　As often happens in the *romans-fleuves* of writers like Balzac and Faulkner, intertextual connections can provide interpretative dilemmas. In this case, Henri de Marsay, in *Le Contrat de Mariage*, tells Paul de Manerville that Félix and Natalie are lovers (and perhaps parents). As Anthony Pugh points out, "From *Le contrat* we presume that Félix is the successful lover of Natalie; from the end of *Le Lys* we know that Natalie repelled him in the early stages of his attempted wooing" (119). For readers who conclude that the discrepancy was inadvertent, the historical author alone is to blame, and no interpretative consequences are forthcoming. For Herbert J. Hunt, on the other hand, the apparent contradiction is intentional, and therefore the product not only of the writer but the (career) implied author: "this objection [Balzac's negligence] can hardly apply to the almost simultaneous *Lys* and *Contrat de mariage*. So one must pay tribute to Balzac's ability to confirm the illusion of reality by deliberately leaving these uncertainties, and thereby inveigling his readers into trying to remove them" (121). Pugh, who evidently leans toward the "simpler explanation" that Balzac just forgot, summarizes the question even-handedly: "Whatever the motives, the discrepancy . . . is real, and the effect exasperating or poetic according to taste" (119).

5   The detailed analysis of such motivations for embedded narrators, and of the effects of their narratives on embedded narratees, is the focus of Richard Shryock's work, though his definition of embedded narrative differs importantly from mine in including those not actually reproduced within the embedding text.

6   For a comprehensive classification of these "alternate universes" see Marie-Laure Ryan's "The Modal Structure of Narrative Universes," especially pages 720–32.

7   For an alternative critique of Genette's typology of embedded narratives, see Shryock, who finds logical inconsistency in his combining of categories drawn from both narratology and speech-act theory (6–8).

8   Moger cites Tzvetan Todorov in support of this point: "L'importance de l'enchâssement se trouve indiquée par les dimensions des histoires enchâssées. Peut-on parler de digressions lorsque celles-ci sont plus longes que l'histoire dont elles s'écartent?" (*Poétique de la prose* 84; "The importance of embedding is indicated by the dimensions of the embedded stories. Can we even call them digressions when they are longer than the story from which they digress?" [*Poetics* 72]). But as Todorov's discussion makes clear, he is arguing for the independent importance of "interpolated tales" rather than discussing a "picture-frame" structure; in other words, he contradicts rather than supports her argument.

9   Moger further proposes an "evolution" (21) in the framing device, according to which this picture-frame structure is "the descendant of" (6) but "different from the more common and relatively more primitive story within a story" (7) a position which is also taken by Katharine Gittes and David Ullrich, despite the fact that, as Ullrich admits, "the exact historical relationship between these two forms has not been determined conclusively" (210). Certainly it seems risky to build a model on the presupposition that the *Canterbury Tales* represents a more primitive form than Maupassant's short stories. The logic behind these evolutionary paradigms is often dubious: Gittes claims that the fact that the number of Chaucer's

Canterbury pilgrims is given as both twenty-nine and thirty-one is a "striking Arabic feature" ("*Canterbury*" 246) of the work, since "Arabic elements are open-ended and unfinished" (238). But surely the inconsistency can be more economically accounted for (incomplete revision seems a plausible hypothesis), and the notions that open-endedness is somehow "Arabic" while closure is "Indian" seems to court a naive Orientalism. Further, Gittes's account rests on debatable definitions of framed narrative which rule out, for example, all Greek and Roman literature, including such standard touchstones as Plato's *Symposium* and Ovid's *Metamorphoses*, which virtually all commentators cite as clear-cut cases of framed narrative.

[10] Again, Ullrich's invariable pairing of "didactic" with "earlier" and "ironic" with "later" (108) admits of any number of exceptions; as he later notes, "if one substitutes . . . a 'sophisticated' but 'early' text such as the *Canterbury Tales* or the *Decameron* in place of the so-called 'didactic' frame narratives, then the cultural sophistication of the author is reflected in the literary apparatus the author employs . . ." (144–45). I would argue further that the sophistication of the author is *inferred from* the literary work rather than simply reflected by it, which would seem to make interpretation logically prior to any historical or biographical rules of thumb.

[11] A partial exception is offered by those cases in which the narrator of the inner and outer narratives remains the same, as in the *Canterbury Tales* when the general narrator ("Chaucer the pilgrim") of the outer level tells the tales of Thopas and Melibee as an intradiegetic narrator to the Canterbury pilgrims, a shift only of narratee and not narrator. The narrator does, however, shift rhetorically or verbally as he shifts narrative levels — the reader is no longer addressed directly by the narrator of the tales and is called upon to contrast the two performances and performers — and the function of multiple agency persists as a trope or figure despite the "literal" — though hardly "real" — identity of the two speakers.

[12] For detailed analyses of the effects of narrative embedding on narrators' motives, see Shryock; for examples of close readings of the

implications of embedding for narrative authority and credibility, see Moger, Newman, and Shryock's third chapter.

[13] Such terminal asymmetrical frames would, obviously, constitute exceptions to the rule proposed by John Matthews: "Whatever specific effects any individual frame has for its core story or stories, we may generalize about its status by observing that the frame is always that which is first to be passed through or beyond" (26).

[14] Duyfhuizen, with understandable caution, affirms only that the "Menelaiad" "contains embeddings to at least the seventh degree" (255 n. 21). The number seven may be derived from what appears to be an allusion to that story in Barth's *Chimera*; the Genie (who represents John Barth to some extent) and Scheherazade speculate that a writer might "conceive a series of, say, *seven* concentric stories-within-stories, so arranged that the climax of the innermost would precipitate that of the next tale out . . ." (24). Genette arrives at a count of seven levels exactly, which he describes as "*Narrateur 1 (Ménélas (Ménélas (Ménélas (Ménélas (Ménélas (Ménélas — Hélène de Troie) Idothée) Protée) Hélène de Sparte et de Pharos) Télémaque) Narrataire 2) Narrataire 1)*, chaque narration étant nécessairement postérieure à celle qu'elle englobe (qu'elle narre)" (*Palimpsestes* 391–92; "Narrator 1 (Menelaus (Menelaus (Menelaus (Menelaus (Menelaus (Menelaus —Helen of Troy) Eidothea) Proteus) Helen of Sparta and Pharos) Telemachus) Narratee 2) Narratee 1), each narration being necessarily posterior to that which it englobes [which it narrates]"). Genette omits in this summary the crucial eighth level, which takes place on the bridal bed of Menelaus and Helen years before the Trojan encounter and is thus embedded within Genette's seventh level narrative: " " " " " " " "Speak!" Menelaus cried to Helen on the bridal bed,' I reminded Helen in her Trojan bedroom," . . . (*Lost* 150, again omitting "my" quotation marks in this citation; as Genette correctly suggests, reconstructing the temporal sequence can be a helpful rule of thumb for sorting out these levels).

CONCLUSION

[1]   There seems to be a loose consensus that the most convenient terminus
a quo for musical narratology may be Anthony Newcomb's 1987 essay, "the critical text that has done more than any other to stimu-
late the discussion of music and narrative" (Kramer 146).   Newcomb's study, by the way, focuses on the ways in which "A series of
musical fragments is held together by framing narrative devices . . ."
(170), one more suggestion of the centrality of the structures of embedding for narrative analysis. Lawrence Kramer has taken the interesting step of applying the concepts of "speaker" and "voice" to
musical passages, which are susceptible to acts of "quotation" by
(hence embedding within the speeches of) other speakers (159).

BIBLIOGRAPHY

Abbate, Carolyn. "Erik's Dream and Tannhauser's Journey." *Reading Opera*. Ed. Arthur Groos and Roger Parker. Princeton: Princeton UP, 1990. 129–67.

Adams, Hazard. "Titles." School of Criticism and Theory at Dartmouth College. Hanover, NH, 17 July 1986.

Allott, Miriam, ed. *The Brontës: The Critical Heritage*. London: Routledge and Kegan Paul, 1974.

Altick, Richard. *The English Common Reader: A Social History of the Mass Reading Public, 1800–1900*. London: Chatto and Windus, 1932.

——. "The Sociology of Authorship." *Bulletin of the New York Public Library* 66 (1962): 389–404.

Amorós, José Antonio Alvarez. "Henry James, Percy Lubbock, and Beyond: A Critique of the Anglo-American Conception of Narrative Point of View." *Studia Neophilologica* 66 (1994): 47–57.

Amper, Susan. "Untold Story: The Lying Narrator in "The Black Cat." *Studies in Short Fiction* 29.4 (1992): 475–85.

Anderson Imbert, Enrique. *The Other Side of the Mirror: El grimorio*. Trans. Isabel Reade. Carbondale: Southern Illinois UP, 1966.

Aristotle. *Aristotle's Poetics: A Translation and Commentary for Students of Literature*. Trans. Leon Golden. Englewood Cliffs, NJ: Prentice, 1968.

Armstrong, Dianne. "Framing the Text: Metadiscourse and the Dialogy of Otherness." Diss. University of Southern California, 1992.

Aronne-Amestoy, Lida. "El Mito contra el mito: Narración e ideografía en *El otoño del patriarca.*" *Revista iberoamericana* 52 (1986): 521–30.

Baker, John Ross. "From Imitation to Rhetoric: The Chicago Critics, Wayne C. Booth, and *Tom Jones.*" *Novel* 6.3 (1973): 197–217.

Bal, Mieke. *La Complexité d'un roman populaire (ambigüité dans "La Chatte").* Paris: La Pensée Universelle, [1974].

_____. "The Laughing Mice or: On Focalization." *Poetics Today* 2.2 (1981): 202–10.

_____. "The Narrating and the Focalizing: A Theory of the Agents in Narrative." *Style* 17.2 (1983): 234–69. Trans. Jane E. Lewin. Trans. of "Narration et focalisation," Chapter 1 of *Narratologie.*

_____. *Narratologie: Essais sur la signification narrative dans quatre romans modernes.* 1977. Utrecht: HES, 1984.

_____. *Narratology: Introduction to the Theory of Narrative.* Toronto: U of Toronto P, 1985.

_____. "Notes on Narrative Embedding." *Poetics Today* 2.2 (1981): 41–59.

_____. *Reading "Rembrandt": Beyond the Word-Image Opposition.* Cambridge: Cambridge UP, 1991.

Balzac, Honoré de. *The Lily in the Valley.* Trans. Lucienne Hill. London: Elek, 1957.

_____. *Le Lys dans la vallée. La Comédie Humaine. VIII. Etudes de mœurs: Scènes de la vie en campagne.* Paris: Librarie Gallimard, 1949.

Banfield, Ann. "Narrative Style and the Grammar of Direct and Indirect Speech." *Foundations of Language* 10 (1973): 1–39.

Barker, Juliet. *The Brontës.* New York: St. Martin's, 1994.

Barth, John. *Chimera.* New York: Random, 1972.

_____. *LETTERS: A Novel.* New York: Putnam's, 1979.

_____. *Lost in the Funhouse: Fiction for Print, Tape, Live Voice.* 1968. New York: Bantam, 1969.

_____. *Sabbatical: A Romance.* New York: Putnam's, 1982.

_____. "Tales Within Tales Within Tales." *Antaeus* 43 (1981): 45–63.

Barthes, Roland. "Introduction à l'analyse structurale des récits." *Communications* 8 (1966): 1–27.

_____. "Introduction to the Structural Analysis of Narratives." *Image — Music — Text*. Ed. and trans. Stephen Heath. New York: Hill and Wang, 1977. 79–124.

_____. *S/Z*. Paris: Seuil, 1970.

_____. *S/Z*. Trans. Richard Miller. New York: Hill and Wang, 1974.

Bateson, Gregory. *Steps to an Ecology of Mind*. San Francisco: Chandler, 1972.

Beckett, Samuel. *Le dépeupleur*. Paris: Minuit, 1970.

_____. *Imagination morte imaginez*. Paris: Minuit, 1965.

_____. *Malone Dies*. New York: Grove, 1956.

Birge-Vitz, Evelyne. "Narrative Analysis of Medieval Texts." *Modern Language Notes* 92 (1977): 645–75.

Black, David Alan. "Genette and Film: Narrative Level in the Fiction Cinema." *Wide Angle* 8.3/4 (1986): 19–26.

Blackburn, Stuart H. "Domesticating the Cosmos: History and Structure in a Folktale from India." *Journal of Asian Studies* 45.3 (1986): 527–43.

Boccaccio, Giovanni. *The Decameron*. Trans. Mark Musa and Peter Bondanella. New York: Norton, 1982.

Booth, Wayne C. *Critical Understanding: The Powers and Limits of Pluralism*. Chicago: U of Chicago P, 1979.

_____. *The Rhetoric of Fiction*. 2nd ed. Chicago: U of Chicago P, 1983.

Bordwell, David. *Narration in the Fiction Film*. Madison: U Wisconsin P, 1985.

Borges, Jorge Luis. *Obras completas*. Buenos Aires: Emecé Editores, 1974.

Bowen, Zack. *A Reader's Guide to John Barth*. Westport: Greenwood, 1994.

Bremond, Claude. "La Logique des possibles narratifs." *Communications* 8 (1966): 60–76.

Briosi, Sandro. "La narratologie et la question de l'auteur." *Poétique* 68 (1986): 507–19.

Brontë, Charlotte. *Jane Eyre*. 1847. New York: Bigelow, 1899.

Brontë, Emily. *Wuthering Heights: An Authoritative Text with Essays in Criticism*. Ed. William M. Sale, Jr. 1847. New York: Norton, 1963.

Bronzwaer, W. "Mieke Bal's Concept of Focalization: A Critical Note." *Poetics Today* 2.2 (1981): 193–201.

Brooks, Peter. *Reading for the Plot*. New York: Knopf, 1984.

Burney, Fanny. *Evelina*. 1778. Oxford: Oxford UP, 1982.

Butor, Michel. *La Modification*. Paris: Minuit, 1957.

Camus, Albert. *La chute*. Paris: Gallimard, 1956.

Caplan, Jay. *Framed Narratives: Diderot's Genealogy of the Beholder*. Minneapolis: U of Minnesota P, 1985.

Carroll, David, ed. *George Eliot: The Critical Heritage*. New York: Barnes, 1971.

Caws, Mary Ann. *Reading Frames in Modern Fiction*. Princeton: Princeton UP, 1985.

Chadeyras, Claudine. "Étude du cadre dans les recueils narratifs au seizième siècle en France." Diss. University of Iowa, 1991.

Chambers, Ross. *Story and Situation*. Minneapolis: U of Minnesota P, 1984.

Chatman, Seymour. "Characters and Narrators: Filter, Center, Slant and Interest-Focus." *Poetics Today* 7.2 (1986): 189–204.

——. *Coming to Terms*. Ithaca: Cornell UP, 1990.

——. "Degrees of Narratorhood." Unpublished paper.

——. "Discourse: Nonnarrated Stories." *Essentials of the Theory of Fiction*. Ed. Michael J. Hoffman and Patrick D. Murphy. Durham, NC: Duke UP, 1988. 366–79.

——. *Story and Discourse: Narrative Structure in Fiction and Film*. Ithaca, NY: Cornell UP, 1978.

——. "The Structure of Narrative Transmission." *Style and Structure in Literature: Essays in the New Stylistics*. Ed. Roger Fowler. Oxford: Basil Blackwell, 1975. 213–57.

——. "What Novels Can Do That Films Can't (and Vice Versa)." Mitchell 117–36.

Chaucer, Geoffrey. *The Complete Works of Geoffrey Chaucer*. Ed. F. N. Robinson. 2nd ed. Oxford: Oxford UP, 1957.

Chickering, Howell D., ed. *Beowulf: A Dual-Language Edition*. New York: Anchor, 1977.

Clements, Robert J., and Joseph Gibaldi. *The European Tale Collection from Boccaccio and Chaucer to Cervantes*. New York: New York UP, 1977.

Cohen, Ralph. *The Art of Discrimination*. Berkeley: U of California P, 1964.

Cohn, Dorrit. "The Encirclement of Narrative." *Poetics Today* 2.2 (1981): 157–82.

_____. "Fictional *versus* Historical Lives: Borderlines and Borderline Cases." *Journal of Narrative Technique* 19 (1989): 3–24.

_____. *Transparent Minds*. Princeton: Princeton UP, 1978.

Colette, Sidonie-Gabrielle. "The Cat." 1933. Trans. Antonia White. In *7 by Colette*. New York: Farrar, 1955. 71–193.

_____. *La Chatte*. 1933. Paris: Hachette, 1960.

Conrad, Joseph. "Preface to *The Nigger of the Narcissus*." 1897. In *The Nigger of the Narcissus*. Ed. Robert Kimbrough. New York: Norton, 1979.

Cook, David A. *A History of Narrative Film*. 2nd ed. New York: Norton, 1990.

Crane, R. S. *The Languages of Criticism and the Structure of Poetry*. Toronto: U of Toronto P, 1953.

Culler, Jonathan. *The Pursuit of Signs: Semiotics, Literature, Deconstruction*. Ithaca: Cornell UP, 1981.

Dällenbach, Lucien. *Le Récit speculaire*. Paris: Seuil, 1977.

Dawood, N. J., trans. *The Thousand and One Nights*. Edinburgh: Penguin, 1961.

de Jong, Irene J. F. "*Iliad* 1.366–392: A Mirror Story." *Arethusa* 18.1 (1985): 5–22.

de Man, Paul. *The Resistance to Theory*. Minneapolis: U of Minnesota P, 1986.

Dickens, Charles. *David Copperfield*. 1850. London: Oxford UP, 1949.

Dittmar, Linda. "Fashioning and Re-fashioning: Framing Narratives in the Novel and Film." *Mosaic* 16 (1983): 189–203.

Dolozel, Lubomír. *Narrative Modes in Czech Literature*. Toronto: U of Toronto P, 1973.

_____. "Truth and Authenticity in Narrative." *Poetics Today* 1.3 (1980): 7–25.

Donovan, Josephine. "Sarah Orne Jewett's Critical Theory: Notes toward a Feminine Literary Mode." *Critical Essays on Sarah Orne Jewett*. Ed. Gwen L. Nagel. Boston: G. K. Hall, 1984. 212–25.

Duyfhuizen, Bernard. *Narratives of Transmission*. Rutherford: Farleigh Dickinson UP, 1992.

Eberwein, Jane Donahue, ed. *Early American Poetry*. Madison: U of Wisconsin P, 1978.

Edmiston, William. "Focalization and the First-Person Narrator: A Revision of the Theory." *Poetics Today* 10.4 (1989): 729–44.

Erickson, Susan. "Musil's 'Der Vorstadtgasthof': A Narrative Analysis." *Neophilologus* 69 (1985): 101–14.

Esrock, Ellen J. *The Reader's Eye: Visual Imaging as Reader Response*. Baltimore: Johns Hopkins UP, 1994.

Esslin, Martin. *Brecht: A Choice of Evils*. 1959. London: Eyre & Spottiswoode, 1971.

Faulkner, William. *As I Lay Dying*. Novels 1930–1935. New York: Library of America, 1985.

———. *These 13*. Jonathan Cape and Harrison Smith, 1931.

Fleischman, Suzanne. *Tense and Narrativity: From Medieval Performance to Modern Fiction*. Austin: U of Texas P, 1990.

Flint, M. "Kipling's Mowgli and Human Focalization." *Studia Neophilologica* 65 (1993): 73–79.

Flora, Joseph M. *Hemingway's Nick Adams*. Baton Rouge: Louisiana State UP, 1982.

Fludernik, Monika. "Second-Person Narrative: A Bibliography." *Style* 28.4 (1994): 525–48.

———, ed. *Second-Person Narrative*. *Style* 28.3 (1994).

Fordyce, C. J. *Catullus*. Oxford: Clarendon, 1961.

Fowler, Roger. *Linguistics and the Novel*. London: Methuen, 1977.

Fowles, John. *The French Lieutenant's Woman*. 1969. New York: Signet, 1970.

Gates, Barbara Timm. "Introduction." *Critical Essays on Charlotte Brontë*. Boston: G. K. Hall, 1990. 1–14.

Gaudreault, André. "Showing and Telling: Image and Word in Early Cinema." *Early Cinema: Space, Frame, Narrative*. Ed. Thomas Elsaesser and Adam Barker. London: British Film Institute, 1990. 274–81.

Genette, Gérard. *The Architext: An Introduction*. Trans. Jane E. Lewin. Berkeley: U California P, 1992. Trans. of *Introduction à l'architexte*.

_____. *Fiction and Diction*. Trans. Catherine Porter. Ithaca: Cornell UP, 1993.

_____. *Fiction et diction*. Paris: Seuil, 1991.

_____. *Figures II*. Paris: Seuil, 1969.

_____. *Figures III*. Paris: Seuil, 1972.

_____. *Figures of Literary Discourse*. Trans. Alan Sheridan. New York: Columbia UP, 1982 Trans. of eleven essays selected from *Figures I-III*.

_____. *Introduction à l'architexte*. Paris: Seuil, 1979.

_____. *Narrative Discourse*. Trans. Jane E. Lewin. Ithaca: Cornell UP, 1980. Trans. of "Discours du récit," a portion of *Figures III*.

_____. *Narrative Discourse Revisited*. Trans. Jane E. Lewin. Ithaca: Cornell UP, 1988. Trans. of *Nouveau discours du récit*.

_____. *Nouveau discours du récit*. Paris: Seuil, 1983.

_____. *Palimpsestes: la littérature au second degré*. Paris: Seuil, 1982.

_____. *Seuils*. Paris: Seuil, 1987.

Gerlach, John. "The Margins of Narrative: The Very Short Story, the Prose Poem, and the Lyric." *Short Story Theory at a Crossroads*. Ed. Susan Lohafer and Jo Ellyn Clarey. Baton Rouge: Louisiana State UP, 1989, 74–84.

Gibson, Walker. "Authors, Speakers, Readers, and Mock Readers." *College English* 11 (1950): 265–69.

Gide, André. "The Journal of *The Counterfeiters*." 1926. Trans. Justin O'Brien. In *The Counterfeiters*. New York: Modern Library, 1951, 367–417.

Gittes, Katharine. "The *Canterbury Tales* and the Arabic Frame Tradition." *PMLA* 98.2 (1983): 237-51.

_____. *Framing the Canterbury Tales: Chaucer and the Medieval Frame Narrative Tradition*. New York: Greenwood, 1991.

Goffman, Erving. *Frame Analysis*. Cambridge: Harvard UP, 1974.

Gomez-Arcos, Agustin. *L'agneau carnivore*. Paris: Stock, 1975.

Gordon, Jan B. "Gossip, Diary, Letter, Text: Anne Brontë's Narrative *Tenant* and the Problematic of the Gothic Sequel." *ELH* 51.4 (1984): 719–45.

Gorman, David. "Bibliography of Russian Formalism in English." *Style* 26.4 (1992): 554–76.

_____. "Supplement to a Bibliography of Russian Formalism in English." *Style* 29.4 (1995): 562–67.

Greimas, A. J. *Du Sens II*. Paris: Seuil, 1983.

Gutiérrez, Raquel. "La Focalización: Génesis y desarollo de un concepto." *Semiosis* 17 (1986): 113–35.

Hamburger, Käte. *The Logic of Literature*. 1968. Trans. Marilynn J. Rose. Bloomington: Indiana UP, 1973.

Hammett, Dashiell. *The Glass Key*. 1931. *The Novels of Dashiell Hammett*. New York: Knopf, 1965.

_____. *The Maltese Falcon*. 1930. *The Novels of Dashiell Hammett*.

_____. *Red Harvest*. 1929. *The Novels of Dashiell Hammett*.

Hemingway, Ernest. *Across the River and Into the Trees*. New York: Scribner's, 1950.

_____. *The Complete Short Stories of Ernest Hemingway: The Finca Vigía Edition*. New York: Scribner's, 1987.

Henault, Anne. *Narratologie, Sémiotique générale: Les enjeux de l a sémiotique: 2*. Paris: Presses Universitaires de France, 1983.

Henderson, Brian. "Tense, Mood, and Voice in Film." *Film Quarterly* 36.4 (1983): 4–17.

Hinckley, Henry Barrett. "The Framing-Tale." *Modern Language Notes* 49.2 (1934): 69–80.

Hitchcock, Alfred. *Dial M for Murder*. Warner, 1954.

Hoffman, Michael, and Patrick Murphy, eds. *Essentials of the Theory of Narrative*. Durham: Duke UP, 1988.

Holland, Norman N. *5 Readers Reading*. New Haven: Yale UP, 1975.

Homer. *The Odyssey*. Trans. Robert Fitzgerald. Garden City: Doubleday, 1961.

Honan, Park. *Jane Austen: Her Life*. New York: St. Martin's, 1987.

Horace. *Ars Poetica*. c. 20 B.C. *Horace: Satires, Epistles, Ars Poetica*. Trans. H. Rushton Fairclough. Cambridge: Harvard UP, 1947. 450–89.

Hunt, Herbert J. *Balzac's Comédie Humaine*. London: Athlone, 1959.

Huston, John. *The Maltese Falcon*. Warner Brothers, 1941.

Ifri, Pascal A. "Focalisation et récits autobiographiques: L'exemple de Gide." *Poétique* 72 (1987): 483–95.

Iser, Wolfgang. *The Act of Reading: A Theory of Aesthetic Response*. Baltimore: Johns Hopkins UP, 1978.

_____. *The Implied Reader: Patterns of Communication in Prose Fiction from Bunyan to Beckett.* Baltimore: Johns Hopkins UP, 1974.

Jakobson, Roman. "The Dominant." 1935. *Readings in Russian Poetics: Formalist and Structuralist Views.* Ed. Ladislav Matejka and Krystyna Pomorska. Cambridge: MIT Press, 1971. 82–87.

_____. "Linguistics and Poetics." 1960. *Modern Criticism and Theory: A Reader.* Ed. David Lodge. Singapore: Longman, 1988. 32–57.

Jameson, Fredric. *The Political Unconscious: Narrative as a Socially Symbolic Act.* Ithaca: Cornell UP, 1981.

Jauss, Hans Robert. "The Alterity and Modernity of Medieval Literature." *New Literary History* 10 (1979): 181–229.

Jonnes, Denis. *The Matrix of Narrative: Family Systems and the Semiotics of Story.* Berlin: Mouton de Gruyter, 1990.

Jost, François. "Narration(s): en deçà et au-delà." *Communications* 38 (1983): 192–212.

Joyce, James. *Ulysses.* 1922. Ed. Hans Walter Gabler. New York: Vintage, 1986.

Kant, Immanuel. *Critique of Pure Reason.* Trans. J. M. D. Meiklejohn. New York: Willey, 1943.

_____. *Critique de la raison pure.* Trad. A. Tremesaygues et B. Pacaud. Paris: Presses Universitaires de France, 1967.

Kiernan, Kevin S. *Beowulf and the Beowulf Manuscript.* New Brunswick: Rutgers UP, 1981.

Kolve, V. A. *Chaucer and the Imagery of Narrative.* Stanford: Stanford UP, 1984.

Kozloff, Sarah. *Invisible Storytellers: Voice-Over Narration in the American Fiction Film.* Berkeley: U of California P, 1988.

Kramer, Lawrence. "Musical Narratology: A Theoretical Outline." *Indiana Theory Review* 12 (1991): 141–62.

Krier, William J. "*Lost in the Funhouse*: 'A Continuing, Strange Love Letter.'" *Boundary* 2 5 (1976): 103–16.

Labov, William, and Joshua Waletzky. "Narrative Analysis: Oral Versions of Personal Experience." *Essays on the Verbal and Visual Arts.* Ed. June Helm. Seattle: U of Washington P, 1967. 12–44.

Laclos, Choderlos de. *Les Liaisons dangereuses. Oeuvres complètes.* Ed. Laurent Versini. Paris: Gallimard, 1979.

Lanham, Richard A. *A Handlist of Rhetorical Terms: A Guide for Students of English Literature.* Berkeley: U of California P, 1968.

Lanser, Susan S. *The Narrative Act: Point of View in Prose Fiction.* Princeton: Princeton UP, 1981.

———. "Toward a Feminist Narratology." *Style* 20.3 (1987): 341–63.

Lawrence, D. H. "The Blind Man." 1922. *The Complete Short Stories.* Vol. 2. New York: Viking, 1961. 3 vols. 347–65.

Leonardi, Susan J. "Recipes for Reading: Summer Pasta, Lobster à l a Riseholme, and Key Lime Pie." *PMLA* 104 (1989): 340–47.

Lodge, David. "Mimesis and Diegesis in Modern Fiction." *SPELL* 1 (1984): 89–108.

MacShane, Frank. *The Life of Raymond Chandler.* New York: E. P. Dutton, 1976.

Magny, Claude-Edmonde. 1948. *The Age of the American Novel: The Film Aesthetic of Fiction Between the Two Wars.* Trans. Eleanor Hochman. New York: Ungar, 1972.

Martínez-Bonati, Félix. *Fictive Discourse and the Structures of Literature.* Trans. Philip W. Silver. Ithaca: Cornell UP, 1981.

Mathieu-Colas, Michel. "Frontières de la narratologie." *Poétique* 65 (1986): 91–110.

Matthews, John T. "Framing in *Wuthering Heights.*" *Texas Studies in Language and Literature* 27.1 (1985): 25–61.

Matthiessen, F. O. *American Renaissance: Art and Expression in the Age of Emerson and Whitman.* London: Oxford UP, 1941.

McCarthy, Patrick A. "Joyce's Unreliable Catechist: Mathematics and the Narration of 'Ithaca.'" *ELH* 51.3 (1984): 605–18.

McConkey, James. "The Voice of the Writer." *The University of Kansas City Review* 25.2 (1958): 83–90.

McGann, Jerome J. *A Critique of Modern Textual Criticism.* Chicago: U of Chicago P, 1983.

McHale, Brian. "Change of Dominant from Modernist to Postmodernist Writing." *Approaching Postmodernism.* Ed. Douwe Fokkema and Hans Bertens. Amsterdam: John Benjamins, 1986. 53–79.

McKenzie, Gordon. "Swift: Reason and Some of Its Consequences." *Five Studies in Literature.* Ed. J. S. P. Tatlock, et al. Berkeley: U of California P, 1940. 101–29.

Miller, J. Hillis. "A Guest in the House: Reply to Shlomith Rimmon-Kenan's Reply." *Poetics Today* 2.1b (1980/1981): 189–91.

Miller, Nancy K. "*Les Liaisons Dangereuses* pas à pas." *Modern Language Studies* 12.4 (1982): 44–50.

Mitchell, W. J. T., ed. *On Narrative*. Chicago: U Chicago P, 1981.

_____. *Picture Theory: Essays on Verbal and Visual Representation*. Chicago: U of Chicago P, 1994.

Moger, Angela S. "Narrative Structure in Maupassant: Frames of Desire." *PMLA* 100.3 (1985): 315–27.

_____. "That Obscure Object of Narrative." *Yale French Studies* 63 (1983): 129–38.

_____. "Working Out (of) Frame(ed) Works: A Study of the Structural Frame in Stories by Maupassant, Balzac, Barbey, and Conrad." Diss. Yale U, 1980.

Monegal, Emir Rodriguez, and Alastair Reid, eds. *Borges: A Reader*. New York: E. P. Dutton, 1981.

Morris, David B. *Alexander Pope: The Sense of Genius*. Cambridge: Harvard UP, 1984.

Mosher, Harold F., Jr. "Recent Studies in Narratology." *Papers in Language and Literature* 17.1 (1981): 88–110.

Mosher, Harold F., Jr, and William Nelles. "Guides to Narratology." *Poetics Today* 11.2 (1990): 419–27.

Nelles, William. "Getting Focalization into Focus." *Poetics Today* 11.2 (1990): 365–82.

_____. "Historical and Implied Authors and Readers." *Comparative Literature* 45.1 (1993): 22–46.

_____. "Medieval Textuality: Two Structures of Embedding in Chaucer's Poetry." *Semiotics 1987*. Ed. John Deely. Lanham: University Press of America, 1988. 211–18.

_____. "The Narrating of Chaucer's *Merchant's Tale*." *Semiotics 1986*. Ed. John Deely and Jonathan Evans. Lanham: University Press of America, 1987. 15–22.

_____. "Problems for Narrative Theory: *The French Lieutenant's Woman*." *Style* 18.2 (1984): 207–17.

_____. Rev. of *Seuils*, by Gérard Genette. *Style* 23.1 (1989): 141–47.

_____. "'Thise bin the cokkes wordes, and nat mine': Narrative Levels in the *Nun's Priest's Tale*." *Semiotics 1985*. Ed. John Deely. Lanham: University Press of America, 1986. 751–58.

Neville, Judith Malone. "Interpolated Narratives in Selected Works of Hawthorne, Poe, and Melville." Diss. Brandeis U, 1984.

Newcomb, Anthony. "Schumann and Late Eighteenth-Century Narrative Strategies." *Nineteenth-Century Music* 11 (1987): 164–74.

Newman, Beth. "Narratives of Seduction and the Seductions of Narrative: The Frame Structure of *Frankenstein*." *ELH* 53.1 (1986): 141–63.

Nichol, John W. "Melville's '"Soiled" Fish of the Sea.'" *American Literature* 21 (1949): 338–39.

O'Neill, Patrick. *Fictions of Discourse: Reading Narrative Theory*. Toronto: U of Toronto P, 1994.

Oxford English Dictionary. 2nd ed. Oxford: Clarendon, 1987.

Pascal, Roy. *The Dual Voice: Free Indirect Speech and Its Functioning in the Nineteenth-Century European Novel*. Manchester: Manchester UP, 1977.

Phelan, James. "Present Tense Narration, Mimesis, the Narrative Norm, and the Positioning of the Reader in *Waiting for the Barbarians*." Phelan and Rabinowitz 222–45.

Phelan, James, and Peter J. Rabinowitz, eds. *Understanding Narrative*. Columbus: Ohio State UP, 1994.

Pinget, Robert. *Baga*. 1958. Trans. John Stevenson. London: Calder & Boyars, 1967.

Plato. *The Republic*. Trans. Paul Shorey. 2 vols.. Cambridge: Harvard UP, 1963. Vol. 1.

———. *The Symposium*. Trans. W. Hamilton. Baltimore: Penguin, 1951.

Prince, Gerald. *A Grammar of Stories*. The Hague: Mouton, 1973.

———. "Introduction à l'étude du narrataire." *Poétique* 14 (1973): 178–96.

———. "Introduction to the Study of the Narratee." Trans. Frances Mariner. *Reader-Response Criticism: From Formalism to Post-Structuralism*. Ed. Jane P. Tompkins. Baltimore: Johns Hopkins UP, 1980. 7–25.

———. "Narratology and the Double Logic of Narrative." Northern Illinois University. DeKalb, IL, 23 April 1987.

Pugh, Anthony R. *Balzac's Recurring Characters*. Toronto: U of Toronto P, 1974.

Quintilian. *The Institutio Oratoria of Quintilian*. 4 vols. Trans. H. E. Butler. London: William Heinemann, 1966. Vol. 3.

Rabinowitz, Peter J. "Truth in Fiction." *Critical Inquiry* 4 (1977): 121–41.

Richards, I. A. *Practical Criticism: A Study of Literary Judgement.* New York: Harcourt, 1935.

Riffaterre, Michael. "Describing Poetic Structures: Two Approaches to Baudelaire's 'Les Chats'." *Yale French Studies* 36–37 (1966): 200–42.

_____. *Fictional Truth.* Baltimore: Johns Hopkins UP, 1990.

Rigby, Elizabeth. Rev. of *Vanity Fair, Jane Eyre,* and *Governesses' Benevolent Institution Report for 1847. Quarterly Review* 84 (1848): 153–85.

Rimmon-Kenan, Shlomith. *Narrative Fiction: Contemporary Poetics.* London: Methuen, 1983.

Robbe-Grillet, Alain. *The Immortal One.* 1958. Trans. A. M. Sheridan Smith. London: Calder & Boyars, 1971.

_____. *L'Immortelle.* Paris: Minuit, 1958.

_____. *La Jalousie.* Paris: Minuit, 1957.

_____. *Jealousy.* 1957. *Two Novels by Robbe-Grillet: Jealousy & In the Labyrinth.* Trans. Richard Howard. New York: Grove, 1965.

Ronen, Ruth. "La focalisation dans les mondes fictionnels." *Poétique* 83 (1990): 305–22.

Ross, Harris. *Film as Literature, Literature as Film.* New York: Greenwood, 1987.

Ryan, Marie-Laure. "The Modal Structure of Narrative Universes." *Poetics Today* 6.4 (1985): 717–55.

_____. "The Pragmatics of Personal and Impersonal Fiction." *Poetics* 10 (1981): 517–39.

Schoeck, Richard J. "Chaucer's Prioress: Mercy and Tender Heart." *Chaucer Criticism, Vol. 1: The Canterbury Tales.* Ed. Richard J. Schoeck and Jerome Taylor. Notre Dame: U of Notre Dame P, 245–58.

Schuerewegen, Franc. "Réflexions sur le narrataire: Quidam et Quilibet." *Poétique* 70 (1987): 247–54.

Seamon, Roger. "Poetics against Itself: On the Self-Destruction of Modern Scientific Criticism." *PMLA* 104 (1989): 294–305.

Shakespeare, William. *The Riverside Shakespeare.* Boston: Houghton, 1974.

Shaw, Harry. *Concise Dictionary of Literary Terms.* New York: McGraw-Hill, 1972.

Showalter, Elaine. *A Literature of Their Own: British Women Novelists from Brontë to Lessing.* Princeton: Princeton UP, 1977.

Shryock, Richard. *Tales of Storytelling: Embedded Narrative in Modern French Fiction.* New York: Peter Lang, 1993.

Sidney, Philip. *An Apology for Poetry.* 1595. *Critical Theory Since Plato.* Ed. Hazard Adams. New York: Harcourt, 1971. 155–77.

Slatoff, Walter J. *With Respect to Readers.* Ithaca, NY: Cornell UP, 1970.

Smith, Barbara Herrnstein. *The Margins of Discourse: The Relation of Literature to Language.* Chicago, U of Chicago P, 1978.

_____. "Narrative Versions, Narrative Theories." Mitchell, *On Narrative* 209–32.

_____. *Poetic Closure.* Chicago: U of Chicago P, 1968.

Smith, Paul. *A Reader's Guide to the Short Stories of Ernest Hemingway.* Boston: G. K. Hall, 1989.

Stanzel, F. K. *A Theory of Narrative.* Trans. Charlotte Goedsche. Cambridge: Cambridge UP, 1984.

Stein, Gertrude. *Narration.* New York: Greenwood, 1935.

Steiner, Peter. "Russian Formalism." *The Cambridge History of Literary Criticism. Volume 8. From Formalism to Poststructuralism.* Ed. Raman Selden. Cambridge: Cambridge UP, 1995. 11–29.

Sternberg, Meir. "Polylingualism as Reality and Translation as Mimesis." *Poetics Today* 2.4 (1981): 221–39.

Sterne, Laurence. *The Life and Opinions of Tristram Shandy.* 1759–1767. London: Penguin, 1967.

Stewart, Philip. *Rereadings: Eight Early French Novels.* Birmingham: Summa, 1984.

Sturgess, Philip J. M. *Narrativity: Theory and Practice.* (Oxford: Clarendon, 1992.

Swift, Jonathan. *Gulliver's Travels.* 1726. Ed. Robert A. Greenberg. New York: Norton, 1970.

_____. "A Modest Proposal." 1729. *Gulliver's Travels and Selected Writings in Prose and Verse.* Ed John Hayward. London: Nonesuch, 1990.

_____. *Irish Tracts 1728–1733.* Ed. Herbert Davis. Oxford: Basil Blackwell, 1955.

Thomas, D. M. *Arafat.* New York: Viking, 1983.

Thompson, G. R. *The Art of Authorial Presence: Hawthorne's Provincial Tales.* Durham: Duke UP, 1993.

Thompson, Kristin. *Breaking the Glass Armor: Neoformalist Film Analysis.* Princeton: Princeton UP, 1988.

Tobin, Patricia. *John Barth and the Anxiety of Continuance.* Philadelphia: U Pennsylvania P, 1992.

Todorov, Tzvetan. *Grammaire du Décameron.* The Hague: Mouton, 1969.

———. *Introduction to Poetics.* Trans. Richard Howard. Minneapolis: U of Minnesota P, 1981. Trans. of *Qu'est-ce que le structuralisme: Poétique.*

———. *Littérature et signification.* Paris: Larousse, 1967.

———. *The Poetics of Prose.* Trans. Richard Howard. Ithaca: Cornell UP, 1977. Trans. of *La Poétique de la prose.*

———. *La Poétique de la prose.* Paris: Seuil, 1971.

———. *Qu'est-ce que le structuralisme: Poétique.* Paris: Seuil, 1968.

Tomashevsky, Boris. "Thematics." Trans. Lee T. Lemon and Marion J. Reis. *Russian Formalist Criticism: Four Essays.* Lincoln: U of Nebraska P, 1965, 62–95.

Toth, Emily. "Comment on Barbara Bellow Watson's 'On Power and the Literary Text.'" *Signs* 1 (1976): 1005.

Triviños, Gilberto. "Los relatos de relatos." *Estudios Filológicos* 15 (1980): 145–78.

Ullrich, David William. "'Organic Harps Diversely Fram'd': A Theory of the Frame and the Frame Narrative, Including a taxonomy and Its Application to Nineteenth-Century British Literature." Diss. U of Wisconsin–Madison, 1986.

Uspensky, Boris. *A Poetics of Composition.* Trans. Valentina Zavarin and Susan Wittig. Berkeley: U of California P, 1973.

Valéry, Paul. *Collected Works.* 15 vols. Princeton: Princeton UP, 1970. Vol. 14.

———. *Oeuvres.* 2 vols. Paris: Gallimard, 1960. Vol. 2.

Verne, Jules. *Vingt mille lieues sous les mers.* 2 vols. Paris: Gallimard, 1983.

Virgil. *The Aeneid of Virgil, Books 1-6.* Ed. R. D. Williams. New York: St. Martin's, 1972.

———. *The Eclogues and Georgics.* Ed. R. D. Williams. New York: St. Martin's, 1979.

Viswanathan, Jacqueline. *"Echanger sa vie por une autre*: Focalisation multiple dans *Mrs. Dalloway* et *Le Sourd dans la ville*." *Arcadia* 20 (1985): 179–94.

Vitoux, Pierre. "Le jeu de la focalisation." *Poétique* 51 (1982): 359–68.

Warhol, Robyn R. "Toward a Theory of the Engaging Narrator." *PMLA* 101 (1986): 811–18.

Watt, Ian. *The Rise of the Novel: Studies in Defoe, Richardson, and Fielding*. Berkeley: U of California P, 1957.

White, Hayden. *Tropics of Discourse: Essays in Cultural Criticism*. Baltimore: Johns Hopkins UP, 1978.

Williams, Kathleen, ed. *Swift: The Critical Heritage*. New York: Barnes & Noble, 1970.

Wilson, W. Daniel. "Readers in Texts." *PMLA* 96 (1981): 848–63.

Winnifrith, Tom. *The Brontës and Their Background: Romance and Reality*. London: Macmillan, 1973.

Young, Katharine. "Edgework: Frame and Boundary in the Phenomenology of Narrative Communication." *Semiotica* 41.1/4 (1982): 277–315.

INDEX

WILLIAM NELLES is an assistant professor of English at the University of Massachusetts Dartmouth. He received his Ph.D. in English from Northern Illinois University. In addition to publishing numerous articles in scholarly journals and books, he has served since 1991 as Bibliography Editor of the journal of literary theory *Style*.

www.ingramcontent.com/pod-product-compliance
Lightning Source LLC
Chambersburg PA
CBHW060337100426
42812CB00003B/1023